THE GREAT EXHIBITION

JOHN R. DAVIS

SUTTON PUBLISHING

First published in 1999 by
Sutton Publishing Limited · Phoenix Mill
Thrupp · Stroud · Gloucestershire · GL5 2BU

British Library Cataloguing in Publication Data
A catalogue record for this book is available from the British Library

ISBN 0-7509-1614-1

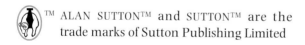 ^{TM} ALAN SUTTON™ and SUTTON™ are the
trade marks of Sutton Publishing Limited

Typeset in 10/12.5pt Photina.
Typesetting and origination by
Sutton Publishing Limited.
Printed in Great Britain by
Redwood Books, Trowbridge, Wiltshire.

For Carsten

CONTENTS

ACKNOWLEDGEMENTS

In acknowledgement of their invaluable help, I would like to thank Lady de Bellaigue, Registrar of the Royal Archives, Windsor Castle; Susan Bennett, Curator at the Royal Society of Arts, London; Valerie Phillips, Archivist at the Royal Commission for the Exhibition of 1851; and Helen Pye-Smith at the National Art Library, Victoria and Albert Museum, London.

I would like to acknowledge the gracious permission of Her Majesty the Queen to make use of the Royal Archives, Windsor Castle. For access to their collections, I would also like to acknowledge the kindness of the Royal Commission for the Exhibition of 1851, the National Art Library at the Victoria and Albert Museum, London, the Public Record Office, Kew, London, and the Royal Society of Arts, London.

Acknowledgements are due to the Royal Society of Arts, London, for illustrations on pages 13, 65, 80, 85, 118, 128, 130, 132, 133, 136, 137, 139, 142, 144, 149, 151, 153, 154, 156, 158, 160, 163, 165, 169, 170, 173. I also thank the National Art Library for allowing me to reproduce the illustration on page 35.

I dreamt I was
Within a temple made of glass,
In which there were more images
Of gold, standing in sundry stages,
In more rich tabernacles
And with jewels, more pinnacles,
And more curious portraitures,
And quaint manner of figures
Of gold-work than I saw ever.

Then saw I stand on either side,
Straight down to the doors wide
From the dais many a pillar
Of metal that shone out full clear.

Then gan I look about and see
That there came ent'ring in the hall
A right great company withal,
And that of sundry regions,
Of all kinds of conditions
That dwell on earth beneath the moon,
Poor and rich.

Such a great congregation
Of folks as I saw roam about,
Some within and some without,
Was never seen nor shall be more.

Chaucer, *House of Fame*, quoted in Maré, 1972

INTRODUCTION

The Great Exhibition of 1851 captured the enthusiasm and imagination of observers from the moment its doors opened. Between 1 May and 15 October 1851, an event took place in the Crystal Palace – in its original position in Hyde Park – that has remained fascinating to academics, the press and public alike. In part this fascination stems from the photogenic nature of the Exhibition. Surrounded by the terminology of mystery, magic and awe, connected for many with a time of glory and grandeur, offering a unique show-case of mid-nineteenth century life and a wealth of symbols to understand it, and filled with objects significant in aesthetic, scientific, economic and cultural spheres, we are tempted again and again to look at the Crystal Palace. We also cannot decide whether the glass through which we are looking is indeed a lens to inspect Victorian life or a mirror in which we view ourselves at an early stage of our modern existence.

On the face of it, the first problem facing anyone researching the Great Exhibition appears to be the overwhelming volume of literature on the subject. One of the aims of the Exhibition was self-promotion and, even at the time, an enormous number of works were printed relating to it. The critic, and later statesman, Sir Charles Wentworth Dilke, member of the Executive Committee of the Royal Commission of 1851 – the body that organised the Exhibition – began cataloguing such material into a collection which today is housed at the National Art Library in the Victoria and Albert Museum and totals over 1,700 items. Since Dilke's time, the volume of works dealing with the Exhibition – books, chapters in books, articles, conference papers, newspapers – has swollen to proportions that inevitably daunt any historian of the subject.[1]

In terms of scope, too, material relating to the Great Exhibition covers a great variety of subjects and disciplines – from aesthetics to medicine, from horology to the history of science, from architecture to ship-building. Anyone intending to write about the Great Exhibition is faced not just with an enormous volume of material, but also with the prospect of immersing themselves in a multitude of disciplines in order to unravel this tangle of interconnections. And this is before they face the prospect of learning the countless languages that are needed in order to follow up the records and literature on the subject in other countries: after all, this was officially 'The Great Exhibition of the Industry of All Nations', and in some important respects it was perhaps more significant abroad than at home. The records of the Great Exhibition are scattered throughout the world and together constitute an enormous, possibly incomprehensible, mass.

Therefore, rather than confronting the subject head-on, in broad but detailed studies, the tendency has been to treat the Exhibition superficially – there have been few

The Grand Entrance to the Great Exhibition. The transept of the Crystal Palace from the south side (Kensington Road).

thorough attempts to answer objective and fundamental questions about its aims, significance and results, for example, and more pick-and-mix selections from the vast storehouse it provides. In more traditional British political histories, where the aim has frequently been to map out the progress of British society, the Great Exhibition has been a much-visited and easily regognised landmark, representing industrial strength, commercial liberalism and enlightened cosmopolitanism. This has fed through into more popular realms: in speeches, newspaper articles and in the public discourse, the Great Exhibition has become part of the national furniture, a fixed point of reference for anyone interested in promoting the British sense of identity and self-worth.

Centenaries and anniversaries of the Exhibition have prompted the expenditure of many words – and the Millennium, as well as the 150th anniversary of the Exhibition which follows, is no exception to this trend. The British Millennium Dome project has been promoted by, among other things, comparisons with the Exhibition of 1851. Perhaps for the sake of investors and marketing, it is hoped that some of the Great Exhibition's renowned success will rub off on Greenwich. Present celebrations are also fitted into some kind of historical perspective, creating an impression of long-held tradition and, by definition, importance. As a public discourse develops about the Millennium celebrations and the 150th anniversary of the Exhibition, academic attention is attracted to the subject and, perhaps at a more mercenary level, books are commissioned. Much the same thing happened during the Festival of Britain celebrations of 1951, when several books were published[2] of a celebratory tone rather than an objective one.

A vast array of interests connected with the Exhibition have felt compelled since 1851 to reassert its importance as a way of strengthening themselves. Free trade and liberalism are two political forces that remained dominant in Britain into the twentieth century and became global, and for those supporting the 'Victorian cult of progress', the Great Exhibition was talismanic.[3] Pro-liberal historical writing, meanwhile, reflected this in its uncritical and frequent references to the Exhibition.[4] Ironically, British nationalists and imperialists have also sought solace in the era of superiority and grandeur represented by Crystal Palace.[5] Monarchist writers have been keen to refer to the Great Exhibition as a demonstration of the harmony that existed between the British public and Victoria and Albert.[6] Meanwhile organisations connected with the Great Exhibition and still in existence – like the Royal Society of Arts – have bathed in the glory of the Exhibition as a way of reiterating their own importance.[7]

Others have also chosen to tackle the problem selectively. The subject has proved of immense interest, for example, to antiquarians – that is, those who are interested in the physical objects of Victoriana, often abstracted from their context.[8] This has at times degenerated into a rather depressing tendency to treat the Crystal Palace as a kind of peep-show, revelling in objects and details which to the present-day observer appear perhaps impossible, absurd, horrendous, comic or ludicrous.[9] As in 1851, it has been difficult to stop bored visitors to the subject wandering away from educative works to gawp at the dramatic or the vast. Economic historians, meanwhile, have dealt with the Exhibition superficially at best – either swallowing the rhetoric of its promoters and asserting its importance in economic terms without any kind of substantial evidence, or else tentatively seeking proof of the Exhibition's significance in the realms of technology transfer only to give up at the first hurdle and without considering other areas of economic significance.[10] Political historians, though they may mention the Exhibition's significance as symbolising the pinnacle of British commercial liberalism and sense of confidence in the 1850s, do not look beyond this into, for example, its relevance to the continental revolutions of 1848, the social question at home or the government's contemporary difficulties in Parliament.

On the one hand, therefore, there has been a tendency to glorify the Exhibition. Nasty details and complicated issues are dropped: one hears little about the intricate structure of local committees in Britain that organised subscriptions of money to the Great Exhibition and therefore determined its size, or about the local committees' role in choosing the artefacts which went into the Exhibition and thus the degree of democratic control they exercised over the contents of the Crystal Palace. The international side of the Exhibition is also played down. The fact that the whole eastern half of the Crystal Palace was given over to foreign countries and a large part of even the western half was occupied by British colonies, together with the Exhibition's impact abroad, are placed in the background. Moreover, there has been a tendency to view the Great Exhibition as a British project and there has been all too little on the continuities that existed with continental expositions prior to 1851.

Instead, the myths that surrounded the Exhibition at the time, many of them created by the Royal Commission of 1851 and the Exhibition's supporters, are frequently repeated unchallenged. The complex organic growth of an exhibition movement and the pragmatic and often contradictory decisions taken by the Royal Commission are ignored, and instead the Commission's own propaganda of a highly efficient, well-planned undertaking is put forward. Rather than being explored through the nitty-gritty of an issue which at the time degenerated into an embarrassing spat between its progenitors, all too often the Exhibition is seen simply as Prince Albert's project. Heroes – like Joseph Paxton, the architect of the Crystal Palace, or Henry Cole, one of the Executive Committee of the Royal Commission of 1851 and a main instigator of the project – are worshipped uncritically, while the work of others of perhaps equal importance to the success of the Exhibition – Robert Peel, Conservative Prime Minister until 1846, Colonel Reid, head of the Executive Committee, or Lyon Playfair, commissioned to arrange the juries of the Exhibition – is insufficiently appreciated. Too little is written about the opposition that existed towards the Exhibition and the important reasons that lay behind this, and too much about the venture's success. Rather than hear about the embarrassing and almost calamitous financial arrangements of the Exhibition and the vexed relations between all concerned, one learns only of the profit generated at the end and of sweetness and light. The Exhibition's results are assessed all too often along the lines of the laudatory *Lectures on the Results of the Great Exhibition*[11] commissioned by Prince Albert himself in the wake of the event, and with little appreciation of the complexity of the question.

These are not insignificant issues: leaving out the detail, the boring, the negative, the complex, might serve any number of purposes, but it risks underrating the Victorians' achievements and the Great Exhibition as much as overrating them. There is a danger, once the Great Exhibition is separated from its complex background, that it and the Victorians themselves become caricatures rather than real people faced with real issues. Take, for example, Nikolaus Pevsner's *High Victorian Design. A Study of the Exhibits of 1851*, a book that was as misleading as it was, perhaps, harmful.[12] Pevsner failed to acknowledge adequately the Exhibition's aim of raising the artistic design of industrial produce by enlightening producers through the comparison of their own goods with those of others, and through a system of prizes. He also overlooked the complicated structure by which exhibits were chosen. Instead, based on an unrepresentative selection of the so-called 'lions' of the Exhibition (those things which were popular rather than those which received awards and official praise), on the specimens illustrated in the populist *Art Journal*,[13] and on curios titillating for twentieth-century readers, Pevsner produced a work on Victorian aesthetics that was simplistic and damning in tone. He spoke of the 'confusions' of Victorian design, borrowing heavily, as it did, from the past. Further characteristics of Victorian design revealed by the Exhibition were, for Pevsner, 'bulkiness' and 'bulges', 'all curves' were 'eminently generous, all outlines broken or blurred', and a 'general tendency to top-heaviness is essential to the authentic effect'.[14] Overlooking the complexities of the Exhibition, but also the economic issue, Pevsner explained:

> The patrons of 1850 were no longer the patrons of 1800. A new class had come to the top and settled down smugly. The years between 1840 and 1860 or 1870 are a phase of assured possession between two phases of restlessness and revolt, in the economic life of the nation as well as the intellectual. Shelley and Byron had gone, Engels and Marx not yet gathered a following . . . It was all enormously impressive,

though much of it was not edifying to the eye. For the new masters had no time to bother about civilized appearances nor had they had a youth to make them demand what would look good. No education and no leisure, these two deficiencies explain nearly all that is aesthetically distressing about 1851. The appreciation of aesthetic values in architecture and design, of proportions, textures, harmonies of colours, requires training and time. The appreciation of the emotional values in painting and sculpture also requires a readiness to listen, to follow a lead and be captured, and this cannot be expected in one whose mind is occupied with machine and counting-house . . . Thus effects were bound to become louder and more obvious. A bulgy curve will be taken in more easily than a delicate one, richly glowing colours than subtle shades, and stories carved in relievo than sheer satisfying proportions. We can say that what appeals to the child, appealed to the big men with the heavy purses in 1851.[15]

In the quieter, more detailed, recesses of his book Pevsner admitted that the people promoting the Exhibition were well aware of the exhibits' defects in aesthetic terms and expressed their thoughts, for example, in the contemporary *Journal of Design*, edited by the above-mentioned Henry Cole. Pevsner also recognised that this was a 'most welcome corrective of the impressions transmitted to us by the catalogues and publications of 1851'.[16] In general, however, the Exhibition revealed for Pevsner only the lack of taste of Victorian designers and the Victorians themselves as materialistic boors. Their 'voluptuousness', 'self-abandon' and 'self-indulgence' in design, meanwhile, emanated from a physicality, even a sexuality, missing from other areas of repressed Victorian life.

The mid-Victorian world, with all its talk of 'progress' and its idealism and naivety, has been more easily lampooned and derided than other historical periods. Yet perhaps Pevsner's stance can be best understood as just one part of a general attack by one generation on the way of thinking and achievements of its immediate forebears: as the historian Roy Porter has commented, 'ever since Lytton Strachey's debunking of "eminent Victorians", our great-grandparents have been fair game for criticism exposing earnestness and high-mindedness as, at bottom, humbug'.[17] Pevsner's rebellion against the Victorian began in the pre-war period; his *Pioneers of Modern Design*, published in 1935, set the tone by stating that 'the low standards of 1851 inspired an arduous struggle, gaining impetus with time, towards the light, clarity, and rationality of the Bauhaus style'.[18] But just as many of the ideals and values of the Victorian era remained widely held into the early twentieth century, and their rejection became a protracted affair. The onslaught continued as social structures came under scrutiny and, for example, as modernism hit home in the art world. Other authors seemed often to outbid even Pevsner in their attacks – for example Elizabeth Burton in her book *The Early Victorians at Home* commented on Victorian design that 'by mid-century the muddle of styles had reached its height and furniture was as costly as it was dark and elaborate. What seems evident is that an almost total adherence to what were believed to be historical styles, improved by self-congratulatory wealth of ornamentation, is indicative of poverty of invention . . . It seems almost axiomatic that new money has a lamentable facility for driving out good taste, and probably at no other time in our history were there quite so many newly rich people'.[19] Simon Jervis notes that in terms of Pevsner's selective methodology, moreover, 'a number of recent books and exhibitions on Aesthetic, Arts and Crafts, and Art Nouveau themes is evidence of a continued

Some examples of Pevsner's Victoriana.
(Clockwise from top) the Albert Vase, the
Dorothea Lily Bracket 'fitted for gas', a
'voluptuous' fireplace, and a piece of
carved furniture from Dublin.

penchant for Pevsnerian pioneers of modern design'.[20] Pevsner's attitude towards Victoriana was thus passed on to a later generation; his standards became the new aesthetic orthodoxy, possibly with disastrous results for the treatment of Victorian heritage. How often do we hear, for example, of 'tasteless' Victorian frescoes being ripped unceremoniously off walls to reveal more highly prized works of an earlier period?

The way of looking at the Great Exhibition and Victorian design embodied by Pevsner has spread far and wide, but this was an approach based on unrepresentative and possibly prejudiced selection, and without due regard for the complexity of the Victorian world. It was also simply part of, as well as a cause of, a general diminution of things Victorian.[21] This can also be seen in the tendency to view the Great Exhibition from a viewpoint of moral righteousness, objecting to it, for example, as a piece of imperialistic propaganda or else as a project of the monied bourgeoisie at the expense of the poorly-paid which exacerbated the social question, or even simply as a capitalist project. Tom Corfe, for example, stated that throughout Victoria's reign 'Englishmen looked back with pride to the days of the Great Exhibition . . . It had shown them that they were the cleverest and richest people in the world. It made them feel that they could do anything they wanted. It made them think that they were always right, and their way of doing things was always best for everyone. He then asked a leading question: 'is it good for men to be so proud and so sure of their own cleverness?'[22] Paul Greenhalgh, meanwhile, berated the Great Exhibition's 'abject racism' in having lent a hand to imperialism and in a postscript he regretted that 'such magnificent conceptions' as exhibitions 'could be designed with such negative aims in mind'.[23] Though awareness of the hypocrisy and contradictions involved in the Great Exhibition is perhaps one important result of this type of writing, it is only of value when placed against the full backdrop of Victorian life. The Open University has done just this in its Arts Foundation course by asking students to compare the Great Exhibition with a reading of Charles Dickens' *Hard Times* in the hope that they 'will discover that they complement rather than contradict each other and that they both shed valuable light on a society which was undergoing rapid social, economic and political changes'.[24] Where balance and broadness of scope is not maintained, however, the Great Exhibition in particular, and Victorian society in general, are in danger of becoming subject to caricature, moralising historicism and rejection.

Fortunately, it is becoming easier to appreciate the complexity of the background to the Exhibition and the problems faced by its promoters. Historical literature has recently become far more conscious of previously unappreciated dimensions of Victorian life, and many of the assumptions and conclusions about it passed to us by intermediate generations are now being questioned and, in many cases, discarded. Imperialism, for example, is no longer viewed as something the Victorians simply decided to undertake, with all the moral condemnation this implied. Recent writers on the subject have highlighted that a variety of factors contributed to it and that expansion often appeared to come through a 'fit of absence of mind'[25] as much as through blatant disregard of others' rights. Without losing sight of the hardships endured by many, more recent writing on the social question has painted the Victorian holders of power less as the vindictive profiteering from the poverty of the masses, and more as individuals with an understanding of the moral and practical issues involved.[26] More sense of a quite different Victorian state of mind or ideology has emerged, in particular with regards to the dominance of free trade and liberalism across a broad band of British society in the mid-nineteenth century.[27] Writers like Asa Briggs, meanwhile, have begun rescuing the artefacts of Victorian domestic life from the destructive scalpels of Pevsner's disciples by highlighting the significance and complexity of the considerations that they expressed.

Perhaps this new three-dimensionality in our appreciation of the Victorian period has much to do with the fact that we are not now quite so emotionally involved with the Victorians and their values, but are able to stand back – at least to an extent – to evaluate the time more objectively, and often with more appreciation of the similarities between the Victorians and ourselves. This has also been helped by a growing awareness of the extent to which modernism has shaped our lives and an attempt to view this shaping process more disinterestedly. The result has been recognition of the importance of the Victorian period in terms of setting the tone of modernism or, in other words, in defining the economic patterns, aspirations and values of the present. Nineteenth-century Britain, it is now more clearly recognised, was a crucial period: society underwent enormous adjustments to accommodate industrialisation and many of the social groups, interests and concerns of industrial society that still affect us today were formed.

One result of this is that writers have focused on the bourgeoisie – that is, the educated élite, industrialists and persons of property – as the most influential and effective class in terms of setting the trend of modernism in the nineteenth century, impregnating other classes with their values, and exporting them to like-minded groups internationally. As a consequence, nineteenth-century exhibitions have been reassessed as highly important in terms of unifying and integrating the bourgeois class, defining the terms upon which it communicated internally and with other classes, and also advertising the bourgeois way of life and transferring it to other classes.[28] More attention has been given to the tradition of exhibitions that began in continental Europe before 1851, to post-1851 international exhibitions, and to what this says about changing bourgeois concerns. Post-modernist investigations, meanwhile, have delved further in order to explain how exhibitions came into being in the first place and what economic forces lay behind them, and to describe the process by which a united bourgeois idiom was formed. Much has been uncovered about the role of exhibitions in the development of markets and fashion. All of this has suggested that nineteenth-century exhibitions were particularly important in terms of facilitating a transition of ideas about industrialisation and modernity.

This type of research has encouraged a reawakened interest in exhibitions' economic value. Until recently economic historians had only suspected that exhibitions contributed to industrialisation, pointing to the spreading of information about technical innovations as the most likely area for this. Though evidence does exist of exhibitions being important channels of technology transfer, most economic historians have judged this process too complex to be worthy of deep investigation. Any other line of research appears to have been barred by a prevailing understanding of economic history that set store by numbers and case histories. Perhaps partly as a result of recent studies, which have recognised more clearly the force of modernisation in history, or perhaps as a result of a relaxing of economic historical writing in general, there appears now to be more willingness to consider 'the people' as part of the equation: for one thing, research has increasingly come to the conclusion that 'social overhead capital' – that is, the state of education, training and the general attitude to technological progress – is crucial to the success of technology transfer. As modernist/post-modernist writing has shown, exhibitions were indeed important in 'fetishising the machine', making industry fashionable, contributing to permanent institutions devoted to technological progress and education. In general there appears now to be much more awareness among economic historians of the importance of sociological factors to the process of industrialisation. This focuses attention once more on exhibitions.

In the last two decades of the twentieth century, therefore, interest in the Victorian period has been reawakened and there is more willingness to treat Victorians on their own terms – faced as they were with complex and important issues – rather than on the basis of present preoccupations. It is clear there has also been a renewed sense of the importance of exhibitions and their centrality to the process of modernisation and industrialisation. Until now, however, the history of the Great Exhibition has not been rewritten with all this in mind: no substantial work on the subject has been produced that embodies the new three-dimensionality of writing on the period, and much of the work of modernist/post-modernist writing on exhibitions has yet to be applied to the Great Exhibition itself. The most substantial book to have done the latter – Utz Haltern's work of 1971 – restricted itself to a modernist agenda and missed as a consequence some of the colour of the Exhibition. The aim of this book, therefore, is to present an account of the Great Exhibition that is free of the generalisation, partisanship and moral censure of past writing, and that incorporates and summarises the findings of more recent works. In this way, perhaps, the Great Exhibition's true importance and the secret of its real success may become apparent.

THE DESIGN

His Highness Prince Albert woke up one day;
'Twas four in the morning,
The gray light just dawning;
So he said to himself, as he sleepless lay,
'Here's a desperate bore,
I can't doze any more . . .
And as he lay he thought to himsel'
Many more things than I can tell.
But when of such thoughts he had had a satiety,
It occurred to his mind that the Fine Arts' Society
Had sent to invite
Him to meet them that night;
So he thought it would be but becoming his station
To go and accept this kind invitation,
And make a fine speech
Which some moral might teach . . .
He pondered, and pondered, and turned in the bed,
'Till at last an idea came into his head,
And these were the words that his Highness said:–
'We'll get up a fair
Of things costly and rare,
Every class of British art
In this show shall have its part;
To the meeting I will go,
And my plans I there will show,
This idea I will moot,
Every member it will suit,
It will please every person, I'm sure.'
etc

Anon, *The History of the Great Exhibition in Rhyme*, Evans and Abbott, Bristol, EX.1851.147, NAL

1

❦

THE ROOTS OF THE EXHIBITION

Though at the time many people spoke of the Great Exhibition as a stroke of genius on the part of Prince Albert, and though afterwards historians have stressed its importance as the beginning of a new tradition, the event was in fact the result of a long evolutionary process and on-going discussion about important problems. The Exhibition only begins to make sense when one takes account of the way in which it came about. Like many important events in history, the idea of holding an exhibition emerged gradually and was modified and added to as it went through various stages of gestation. By the time it opened, the Exhibition was an amalgam of many different traditions and aims. Contemporary observers, as well as later historians, were perplexed by the contradictions and imperfections of the Exhibition. However, these were perfectly explicable given the background.

The key to understanding the Great Exhibition is perhaps to recognise that it was both the product of a changing dialogue that had existed prior to 1851 and a means of communication itself. The economic consequences of the French Revolution and subsequent industrialisation of the European continent kept exhibitions on the agenda for industrialists, artisans, and civil servants, and a tradition was maintained that itself drew on previous models from medieval times and the scientific shows of the enlightenment period in the eighteenth century. It was recognised soon that exhibitions relieved not only economic demands but also political ones because they underpinned consumption. Therefore, the propertied classes and other groups – the educated classes, the politically engaged and the industrially minded aristocracy – were drawn to them. In the face of industrialisation and the threats it posed to political and social order, as well as in the aftermath of domination by aristocratic governments, exhibitions became exercises of integration between these groups and celebrations of their values, and the outcome reflected this.

Yet because of the economic and political function they began to serve, exhibitions also became a means of communication. Through them the bourgeois classes aimed to reconfigure society using self-affirmation, persuasion and education to make the world more conducive to themselves. Exhibitions were therefore part of a dialogue with a wider audience, a communication soliciting a response. As a result, the Great Exhibition was a compromise not just between the views of its promoters, but also between those of its promoters and the wider audience. The former anticipated, aimed to attract, sell to and educate the latter. Therefore it would be wrong to view the Great Exhibition as offering a true image of the Victorians. It was rather a compromise between the reality of 1851 and the way a small group of activists thought this reality should look.

I

Depending on the criteria used, the genealogy of exhibitions can be traced back as far as the Middle Ages to the trades fairs and markets held throughout Europe. Though primarily about selling goods and really only distant relations of exhibitions, which were to be far more educative in purpose, these fairs often involved the art of display; markets were turned into local festivals, and trades fairs became great civic events.[1] In addition to local markets, Britain had its Sturbridge Fair in Cambridge, its St Giles's Fair in Oxford and a 'Mop' Fair in Stratford upon Avon.[2] On the continent there was a system of trades fairs, which often sold goods from more than one country, in Amsterdam, Champagne, Frankfurt, Leipzig and Brunswick, as well as further east in Poland and Russia. As transport and production methods improved, such fairs held to sell commodities became restricted to a few, larger events more about providing an overview of samples. In fact, sample fairs were a result of new technology of production and a revolution in transport in a similar fashion to the Great Exhibition. By the first half of the nineteenth century the world of commerce was already familiar with events which involved comparing and contrasting goods on a large scale.

From the late seventeenth century the Enlightenment suggested that education was good in itself – a way of moving society on from the religious and political battles of the past. New scientific and technical developments were exhibited for the public good. New organisations were founded to spread education, such as the Royal Society in London, the Dublin Society for Improving Husbandry, Manufactures and other Useful Arts (or Royal Society of Dublin), and the Welsh Society of Cymmrodorion. Through such organisations, a section of society conversed with itself: societies took in members of the intelligentsia, inventors and artists, as well as aristocrats, who were often involved in the main industry of the day – agriculture. In 1754 the economic value of such organisations and the public good generated by increased production became more pronounced with the foundation of the Society for the Encouragement of Arts, Manufactures and Commerce in London. Much production at this point was still done by artisans, so it was natural that the society should include artistic techniques in its remit.

Emerging from informal meetings at coffee houses in London, the Society of Arts, as it rather misleadingly became known, attracted a large membership as its benefits – in terms of social connections, the dissemination of information and increased profitability – were recognised. It was soon based in the Strand and then moved to its current accommodation in the Adelphi (an area between the Strand and the Thames). It promoted advances in production techniques through a system of prizes and exhibitions of entries. As early as 1756, the Society put on an exhibition with prizes for improvements in machine-production of wallpaper, carpet and porcelain.[3] Apparently drawn from the experiences of the Society's founding father, William Shipley, at the Northampton Horse Fair, the prize system soon encompassed some 380 classes and handed out over £16,000 in its first twenty-two years, amounting to a substantial stimulus to the Industrial Revolution that was now beginning in Britain. The criteria for awards and the proceedings of the Society were published in a variety of journals and volumes.[4]

As such journals were sent abroad, and since the aristocracy and intelligentsia in any case amounted to an international community of sorts, the Society of Arts inspired a series of sister institutions in continental Europe. These organisations promoted similar aims to a greater or lesser extent depending on the cultural traditions of their home countries. The economic incentive was accompanied by a patriotic one as the value of increased profits from production to state governments was recognised. The new institutions included the Societé d'Encouragement de l'Industrie National, founded in Paris in 1764, the Gesellschaft zur Beförderung der Künste und nützlichen Gewerbe, founded in Hamburg in the same year, and the k.k. patriotisch-ökonomische Gesellschaft, founded in Prague in 1767.[5] Apart from introducing a new variation on the tradition of exhibitions – this time with an educational spin as well as the objective of promoting industrial development – these societies attracted to themselves a mixture of artisans and producers, aristocrats and intellectuals united in their desire to see the improvement of production methods but also tending to support political liberalisation and democratisation. (The Society of Arts had a democratic structure of sorts at a time when such a system was still seen as highly progressive and societies, due to their primarily educational and economic aims, were generally able to avoid attracting the opposition of the state.)[6] Thus these institutions resembled in embryonic form the group of interlinked interests that were to be so influential in bringing about the Great Exhibition.

Another important antecedent was the tradition of art exhibitions that developed in the eighteenth century. Since time immemorial, the possession and promotion of artwork had been one of the most important ways to demonstrate power and wealth. This meant that while the viewing of art was a privilege accorded to a small minority and public access to artwork prior to the eighteenth century was extremely restricted, there was also a temptation to demonstrate or exhibit wealth and nowhere, perhaps, was this temptation stronger than in pre-revolutionary France. The Enlightenment's impulse to give higher social standing and more institutional recognition to artists vindicated this and lent weight to the annual exhibitions of art of the French Académie des Beaux Arts in the Louvre, Paris, begun in 1667.[7] The revelation of objects previously accessible only to the few proved a great success, and later exhibitions elsewhere would continue to emphasise the theme of privilege to ensure their success. In 1763 the economic direction that Enlightenment ideas were taking played itself out at these exhibitions with the introduction of *arts industriels* – that is artistic production as applied to industry, in this case the designs of silk and porcelain products.[8] Not only had a tradition of exhibitions for the purpose of demonstrating power begun but so too had the promotion of artistic production. The benefits of associating themselves with artistic exhibitions now became clear to a select group of manufacturers.

The same lesson was being learned in Britain. The democratic turn taken by government and the reduction in the standing – and purse – of the sovereign had placed the livelihood of many in the artist community in jeopardy. Various groups pushed for more recognition and influence but one in particular – based at the Foundling Hospital in Bloomsbury, London – showed the way forward. After the hospital had been bequeathed significant donations of artwork, small exhibitions were held to raise funds and in consequence artists were appointed governors of the hospital. The success of the Foundling Hospital exhibitions led to calls for a larger, more ambitious ones in order to promote the standing of artists more generally. As several of the Foundling Hospital governors were also members of the Society of Arts and as the Society had by this point already begun its system of technical promotion in new, larger premises, applications were logically made there for a room for an artistic exhibition.

What happened next was symbolic of, and highly significant to, the understanding of the Great Exhibition. For one thing, the Society of Arts, which had been set up very much under the aegis of the Enlightenment and its educational motives, reduced the direct financial profit artists were to gain from the exhibition by making entry free of charge and linking any profits to the sales of catalogues. It also appointed a special independent exhibition committee on the matter, which broadened the scope of the exhibition to make it national rather than restricted to members of the Foundling Hospital committee. Despite its apparently 'haphazard' layout, in 1759 the first national exhibition of contemporary art in Britain was therefore less connected with any one interest and was more universal and objective in its selection. Though the success of the exhibition was in part due to the fact that the public had been comparatively starved of access to artwork, it also lay in the Society's insistence on such a disinterested exhibition.

However, this emphasis on the educational and informative conflicted with the immediate interests of the artists involved in the project, who sought their own advancement and that of their profession. The insistence by some that there be an increase in the price of the catalogue and that its purchase be a condition of entrance forced a split. Those who parted company with the Society of Arts included William Chambers, whose influence with King George III would lead to the alternative Royal Academy exhibitions begun in 1769. Importantly, however, those who remained in the Society formed a rump of artists in an organisation overwhelmingly committed to production techniques rather than fine arts. This would be crucial in 1851.

Nevertheless, the main point to note about the Society's exhibitions of contemporary arts is that they were enormously popular and generated profits for artists in terms of their social and financial positions. As Kenneth Luckhurst noted, 'exhibitions, by enabling them to make their names known and to sell direct to the public, gave them their independence, and at long last ensured a market price for British works of art which was commensurate with their worth'.[9] The Society of Arts' tradition of exhibitions was strengthened, as was the belief in providing an authoritative overview of products. Meanwhile, the public's appetite was nurtured by this new form of access to art and the financial rewards of combining exhibitions with privilege, thus making viewing seem like social advancement, were to be obvious to anyone organising exhibitions in the future.

There were, then, several different ways in which exhibitions emerged in the eighteenth century. Mention should also be made of sporadic efforts to extend these in the direction of industrial exhibitions. In Paris, in 1683, for example, an exhibition of machinery took place which attracted a great deal of unexpected attention; though restricted to the products of one man, the exhibition was notable in that it resulted in an illustrated catalogue. Another, albeit rather improvised, exhibition took place in Weltrus, near Prague, in 1754, in order to promote Austrian industry; it involved a display by several producers to promote education by comparison. A more substantial industrial exhibition followed in Prague in 1791.[10] However, although various traditions of exhibitions developed and became familiar parts of the cultural landscape, all remained restricted to particular organisations or themes or lacked permanency.

It was only after the French Revolution that these diverse experiences became united into a whole and magnified to grander proportions. Though it had been embedded in much that had been present before, a new tradition of exhibitions emerged that was to have a much more direct influence in 1851. First, the Revolution swept away the system of aristocratic patronage in France, which had supported artists and upheld a large luxury goods industry employing artisans and designers. In order to survive, the art industry, one of the most important sectors of French production, now found itself cast upon the patronage of the public rather than that of a small élite. The fact that art could sell well – probably due to its continued associations with privilege in the public mind – was made obvious by street bazaars and shops in Paris which now traded in previously coveted works. There was also the example of the Foundling Hospital group and the Society of Arts in Britain to draw on. Moreover, the financial rewards of associating themselves with the high art exhibitions in the Louvre had already been experienced by the state-led silk and porcelain industries.

Against this background it is not surprising that the Marquis d'Avèze, the former head of the state-run Gobelins manufacturers, organised a French national exhibition in 1797 as a way of reviving the domestic art industry. Neither is it surprising that, despite

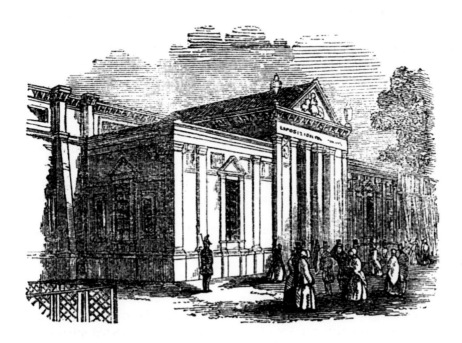

The French exposition of 1797 on the Champs de Mars, Paris – the first national exhibition.

a rather uncertain start, Napoleon's government quickly recognised the value of such exhibitions to national industry and adopted them in 1798 as regular state-led affairs under the direction of the Minister of the Interior, the Duc de Neufchatel; as of 1801 they were based at the Louvre, rather than in the Champs de Mars, where they were initially held.[11] On the one hand they helped revive French industry and revenues, which was all the more necessary now war with Britain and a continental blockade had begun. Industrialists were suddenly viewed as working in the national interests rather than against them and exhibitions began to be important demonstrations of the unity of industry and government. New innovations could be celebrated as great national successes, and useful in promoting the patriotic cause. In order to support the war effort, visitors to the exhibition of 1801 were persuaded of the 'honneur du travail', and a 'temple of industry' inside the exhibition transferred much of the symbolism that had previously been attached to the church to industrial production. Meanwhile, the exhibition borrowed from the tradition of public festivals in order to celebrate the new ideals. Industry was thus glorified and a form of rhetoric produced that would register with the masses and could unite the establishment. On the other hand, exhibitions helped underpin the new political and social *status quo* of Napoleonic France and prevent the recurrence of revolution. The generation of national wealth was aided by improvements to techniques of production as well as increased market awareness, and the government was only too conscious of the Revolution's roots in the economic catastrophes of the 1780s. Moreover, exhibitions promoted an ethos of property and consumption, now including the masses, that ran counter to ideas of social revolution. It was now seen to be good to own, just as it was good to produce, and the state, by demonstrating its own wealth at the exhibitions – in terms of trophies gained in war and through demonstrations of national museum collections – could set the pace. Exhibitions also allowed the state to be seen to be doing something for the masses and also fitted in to an extent with the Revolution's heritage of education and democratisation.

Exhibitions enabled French producers to accommodate themselves to the new concept of mass consumption and fulfilled an important role in the process of economic modernisation. Through exhibitions, consumers could become familiar with producers whose goods were previously bought only by an élite. Yet it still proved vital that consumers' attention should be directed in some way – and art proved to be the main determinant of what was desirable. The population still connected art with privilege and things that were classed as artistic appeared to sell well. The state, as the inheritor of national art collections and the harvester of artistic treasures from its foreign campaigns, was more able than any other body to demonstrate its power through art – a mode of communication with a long tradition behind it. This was also an area in which intellectuals, artists and aristocrats could stand to gain from their special knowledge and collections. The presence of an important art industry in need of consumers made it all the more necessary. Moreover, design, and in particular artistic design, proved to be an area in which French producers could still compete with their British counterparts. Through introducing systems of juries, medals, classification and reports, French exhibitions increasingly aimed to inform the new mass consumers that it was artistic goods which should be bought. The education of public taste became part of the programme of encouragement of industry and in particular in France it was art that was made fashionable.[12]

The French exhibitions were promoted by a new alliance of interest groups, including the state, which was united in its commitment to property and ownership and wished to gain wider acceptance of these values. The promotion of bourgeois values was to be a recurring part of the exhibition tradition. Yet the exercise of putting on an exhibition also involved the harmonisation of this alliance's views into one didactic whole that could be broadcast to the wider public and in order to do this, experts were drawn from all its constituent parts – industry, the educational establishment, the civil service and the aristocracy – for the juries of selection and awards. Moreover, as the exhibition revolved round art and design, as well as technical innovation, people and ideas were drawn from galleries and museums already in existence, as well as from the world of science. These early French exhibitions already showed a tendency that would become more marked in 1851 – that of producing an image of the world binding them together but also destined for the wider consumption of the population. This was an image that bore much resemblance to the encyclopaedic view of a museum. It was communicated by the system of classification an exhibition adopted, by the way prizes were awarded and by the manner in which reports on the exhibition were worded. In France, at least, this was an image coloured by the glorification of industry and artistic design.

That the French exhibitions did indeed serve the interests of their promoters was demonstrated by the fact that they were repeated on an ever greater scale in 1802, 1806, 1819, 1823, 1827, 1834, 1839, 1844 and 1849 – the latter lasting for six months and involving some 4,532 exhibitors.[13] Though transferred via Napoleonic occupation in some cases, the widespread introduction of exhibitions to other continental countries after 1815 demonstrated that the French model carried advantages with it. Once again, industrial growth had to take place largely by exploiting the market and by specialising in design rather than in cheapness of production (Britain's monopoly), and in both areas exhibitions were of use. By the 1840s, almost all of continental Europe had developed traditions of exhibitions for the purpose of promoting industry that owed much to the French model.[14]

Continental exhibitions were shaped by the particular circumstances of the time. In France, at least, the presence of a large art-producing sector meant that displays tended very much to focus on aesthetic issues. In the German states they were more educational, aiming to raise the standard of production of the state industries and agriculture, as well as of the ailing artisan sector. The French exhibitions were national from the start and tended to incorporate patriotism into their message. German exhibitions, on the other hand, remained largely regional. Indeed, for a long time the holding of a national exhibition remained the dream of national economists like Friedrich List and it was not until 1844 that the first all-German exhibition was held in the Armoury (as opposed to the aesthetic French Louvre!) in Berlin. In the German states it was only after 1830 that industry developed which could see the point in gaining access to a wider market via national exhibitions. Even then, regional exhibitions remained strong, as artisans found them far more useful as places where they could carry out direct sales.[15]

Across the European continent, where there had been a long tradition of state-led industry, exhibitions were held under the aegis of the state rather than by the private sector. They were seen as part of the panoply of measures states used to promote

The Berlin Exhibition of 1844 – the first all-German exhibition, and the focus of aspirations for unity among national economists in German states. It was housed in the Prussian Armoury.

industrialisation – a tradition which owed as much to eighteenth-century absolutism as it did to nineteenth-century protectionism in the face of British commercial strength. In fact, the state's leadership appeared to be a prerequisite for getting businessmen involved in exhibitions: without it, the displays appeared to lack authority and their prizes held no financial incentive.[16]

This is revealing: though the continental exhibitions after 1798 appeared to be a symptom of the fact that certain sectors of the economy and of the state were now pushing for industrial production based on mass consumption, the path towards this was still blocked by substantial obstacles. Artisans, for example, often opposed the development of larger-scale production and saw no need to reorientate themselves towards mass consumption. Some resisted any attempt to apply new aesthetic models drawn from art for the sake of sales; instead they continued to insist on solidity of production and traditional designs, and remained aloof from exhibitions.[17] Industrialists, meanwhile, frequently remained suspicious of any attempt to open up communication about techniques of production and about markets. Exhibitions, after all, marked a sharp break with a previous age of industrial espionage and limits on the flow of information. For example, many interests in the German states, including many governments, opposed the movement towards a national exhibition as a step that would undermine the local state. Nationalists and protectionists across Europe opposed any attempt at internationalising exhibitions – though in fact goods were already crossing borders to some of the exhibitions being held. Until the mid-century, at least, it also has to be said that the means of transport were not really conducive to holding large-scale exhibitions on the continent: the costs and difficulties of transporting large numbers of men and goods remained prohibitive.

For all these reasons, staging exhibitions on the continent remained something of an uphill struggle and it was perhaps no accident that they did best in the most industrialised and economically integrated states. Neither, perhaps, was it a coincidence that as industrialisation produced wider and wider markets, calls for an international exhibition nevertheless became ever more frequent: in Belgium, which had most nearly followed the British industrial lead and which had early on developed a dense network of railways, the idea of internationalising an art exhibition to be held in 1833 was raised; however, it was opposed by industrialists. Similar noises were made in the jury reports of the all-German exhibition of 1844 in Berlin but quashed as the German governments held fast to protectionism. Finally, in 1849, during the French national exhibition, the government consulted the chambers of commerce as to the benefits of an international exhibition. Here again the protectionist tradition remained too strong, and the idea was put on ice.[18]

II

Though there was a thriving tradition of exhibitions on the continent in the first half of the nineteenth century and though the British-based Society of Arts had had a hand in instigating this tradition, there was, astoundingly, nothing comparable in Britain at this time. The Society of Arts' artistic exhibitions had suffered greatly from the divisions over the issue of catalogues and profits, resulting in the setting up of a far more successful rival at the Royal Academy devoted to the fine arts. The Academy's exhibitions, beginning in 1769, succeeded in becoming popular fashion-setting occasions in a manner reminiscent of the French exhibitions. This was achieved mainly by dint of royal patronage through which they became the haunt of the aristocracy. They moved first to William Chambers' Somerset House and in 1837 to even more spacious accommodation at the King's Mews, Trafalgar Square (site of today's National Gallery). But the Academy's success also prevented art exhibitions from developing into wider industrial exhibitions as had happened in Paris. The Society of Arts' industrial and technical exhibitions instead became less and less popular with catastrophic results for its profile and finances.[19]

With a few exceptions – Wedgwood porcelain production for example[20] – that appealed to the upper echelons of society, British industrialists, it seemed, did not need art in order to sell and felt little compunction to educate themselves regarding design. The strength of British produce was its cheapness, based on mass production in the factory. As a result of the Napoleonic Wars, which cut off continental Europe from the global market and prevented the development of large-scale industry, British pre-eminence in this sector was secure. Mass production was also based on relatively simple technological advances: Watt's steam engine, Richard Arkwright's water frame and James Hargreaves' Spinning Jenny (developed around the 1760s) were certainly important, even revolutionary, in terms of their impact on the way the economy functioned, but they did not need an enormous amount of technical expertise to construct or operate. At this stage in technological progress machines for industry could still be developed by the producers and operators themselves. As the economic historian Peter Mathias has pointed out:

> innovation and invention was more a question of great determination, intense curiosity, quick wits and clever fingers, getting a backer to survive the expensive

period of experimenting, testing and improving, which all tended to be more important than a scientific education . . . Most innovations were the product of inspired amateurs or brilliant artisans trained as clockmakers, millwrights, blacksmiths, carpenters, or in the Birmingham trades . . . They were mainly local men, empirically trained, with local horizons, often very interested in things scientific, aware men – but men responding directly to a particular problem.

If anything, there developed a reluctance in British industrial circles to allow scientists and academics a say in the way things were manufactured, and a belief, tending towards the kind of hero-worship demonstrated by the writings of Samuel Smiles, in the self-taught industrialist. The ideas the Society of Arts was promoting – better knowledge of innovations in art, manufacturing and science – remained useful to a restricted group of academics and manufacturers. But for the majority of industrialists they did not warrant the vast educative exercise of a national exhibition.

The state, meanwhile, did not show any interest in taking up the matter. After the end of war in 1815 the political debate revolved around the subject of cutting back the burden on the public purse. Exhibitions were tainted by their connection with Bonapartism and seemed anti-patriotic, but they also smacked of the paternalistic state, something that important political interests wished to avoid. Aristocratic Whigs, mainstream liberals and radicals inspired by Jeremy Bentham were beginning to dominate the political agenda and push for a system of *laissez-faire*. The superiority of British manufactures had so far been developed through the domestic market and outside Europe and the issue of widening continental markets was not yet significant. Industrial interests did not feel their markets were sufficiently threatened at home or abroad to warrant a push for exhibitions; perhaps as a consequence of their superiority, neither were they organised enough to make such a move. Artisan and agricultural interests, meanwhile, remained strong and did not necessarily wish to promote industrial interests. The series of economic crises after 1815 kept protectionism against Europe high on the agenda and the tradition of suspicion about foreign competition remained strong: there was a statutory limit on the emigration of British artisans to Europe until 1825 and one on the exportation of machinery until 1843.[21]

The Society of Arts' decline in the early nineteenth century appears to be symptomatic of a wider situation in Britain. In France, a group of interests generally defined as the bourgeoisie, and including civil servants, academics, artists, industrialists and consumers as well as the state, had found a common cause in exhibitions, could appreciate the values of property and ownership they promoted and spoke a common language of aesthetic values. However, in Britain these classes appeared to have moved further apart. The threat of revolution, as well as the economic duress of war, appeared to forge the alliance in France. In Britain, however, the economy continued to grow and factory production streaked ahead without the aid of the state or intellectuals, leaving the bourgeoisie more disunited than ever by the 1830s. It would have been difficult to mount a national exhibition in Britain that united manufacturers' plain aesthetic sense and emphasis on cheapness with the scientific and artistic predilections of academics; and in addition while the issue of the state's role in the economy deeply split political opinion.

This is not to say that there were no exhibitions at all. In the art world, for example, the Royal Academy exhibitions established themselves and helped develop a tradition lasting down to the present. In 1805 the British Institution for Art opened as an exhibition of art works for sale. Its example was followed and improved on by the foundation in 1823 of the (now Royal) Society of British Artists in Suffolk Street, London. Other specialised art societies were formed and held exhibitions, like the (Royal) Society of Painters in Water Colours after 1805, while regional organisations, for example the Birmingham Royal Society of Arts after 1825, followed suit.[22]

In the technical realms, George Birkbeck's establishment of cheap courses of lectures for workmen in Glasgow gave rise to the Glasgow Mechanics' Institution, the inspiration for the London Mechanics' Institution. Soon, a number of provincial institutes had been founded and were putting on exhibitions to help raise funds. The mechanics' institutes also gave rise to the Society for the Diffusion of Useful Knowledge and through this the foundation in 1828 of a National Repository for the Exhibition of New and Improved Productions of the Artisans and Manufacturers of the United Kingdom on the upper floor of the King's Mews, Trafalgar Square. The British Association for the Advancement of Science was founded in 1831 which also held regional exhibitions.[23] In 1830 the 'fantastical' idea of holding an exhibition on a ship for the purpose of promoting British exports abroad was put forward by J.S. Buckingham.[24] There was also an increasing number of popular exhibitions, for example the Royal Adelaide Gallery in Charing Cross and a similar institution in Regent Street, which would later become Quintin Hogg's Polytechnic.[25]

Yet these exhibitions, while useful in introducing a limited exhibition tradition back into Britain, did not amount to the same kind of integrated event as was being held in France. They remained regional rather than national and their subject matter pertained only to one sector or subject. The National Repository failed to attract the same interest as the fashionable Royal Academy with which it shared a building and was forced out to the less salubrious Leicester Square, finally to become bad publicity for exhibitions under the title 'The Toy Shop'. The mechanics' institutes barely held their own until the Society of Arts came to their rescue in 1849. As Kenneth Luckhurst has concluded, 'generally speaking . . . and compared with that of almost any other western country, the record of England's exhibitions during this period is not at all impressive – not through lack of ability but through complete lack of interest'.[26]

Until the 1840s, therefore, more factors worked against a large-scale exhibition in Britain than for it. Even after this date, strong forces continued to oppose the holding of a national exhibition. Yet the idea did not die completely and the need for a national exhibition became increasingly clear to a small minority – a vanguard of interests. Britain had failed to make inroads into the continental market after 1815 to the extent which had been hoped. While this was compensated for by growth elsewhere in the world, recurrent economic crises together with Benthamite investigations into how to reform and reduce the state's tariff so as to work more efficiently, focused attention on this failure. One result of these investigations was the conclusion that Britain needed to liberalise its own tariff if it were to get the continent to open up its markets – in other words, free trade. Another conclusion was that British goods simply did not have the necessary quality of design and aesthetic standard to compete with continental – and in particular French – counterparts.

In the early 1830s John Bowring's reports on the French textile industry, focusing in particular on silk manufacture, strongly underlined the fact that training in design, and a culture which appreciated aesthetic values, were central to French success and needed to be emulated in Britain if there was to be any hope of competing with France. In 1834 Bowring's reports led to pressure from a newly reformed Parliament for the Prime Minister, Sir Robert Peel, to set up a parliamentary committee (1835–6) given the task of enquiring 'into the best means of extending a knowledge of the arts and of the principles of design among the people (especially the manufacturing population) of the country; also to inquire into the constitution, management and effects of institutions connected with the arts'. In a typically Benthamite fashion, and echoing the continued influence of Enlightenment thinking, this committee concluded that Britain's problems could be solved by education. As a result, a government school of design was set up in Somerset House, with regional counterparts in the main industrial centres. At the same time, however, the committee's discussions marked the beginning of a more explicit debate among Benthamite reformers regarding the aesthetic weaknesses of British produce. This was kept alive by the issue of the schools of design and would lead ultimately to the Great Exhibition.[27]

The problem was becoming universally obvious in the nineteenth century but nowhere more so than in Britain: mass production in factories had led to a revolution in the way products looked. Previously, production by craftsmen had allowed for at least some artistic creativity. Now, however, goods were being manufactured with little or no thought for design. Or else – what was worse in the eyes of some – the principles of design were not understood by the manufacturer and were simply being abused for the sake of sales. The comparison with France simply made known to wider circles what those with an eye for design had already noted: Britain's products lacked taste. The solution, however, demanded the education not only of the producers but also of the consumers.

Interest in exhibitions was also generated in another quarter. Bowring's reports did not just focus on the aesthetic side of design but also on its technical attributes. Bowring pointed in particular to the system of technical education that existed in Prussia and owed much of its existence to exhibitions that had been held there. He called for something similar to be set up in Britain in order to maintain its commercial lead.[28] This was a call that was being echoed at the mechanics' institutes and the British Association for the Advancement of Science which were both well informed about the success of continental exhibitions in raising technical awareness.[29]

The problem was also, therefore, one of industrialisation having outstripped science. Where previously the 'cult of the amateur' had sufficed to attain commercial supremacy and science's only obvious contribution to industry appeared to be the steam engine, by the 1840s the situation had manifestly changed. One of the things that had secured Britain's industrial advance over the continent had been its capacity to build machines. However, the types of machines now being demanded – ever larger engines, ever faster movements – meant a new call for precision, measurement and science. Interest in electricity was growing, with the electric generator and the telegraph both coming into commercial use in the 1830s. New production methods involving scientific knowledge were in demand, for example for dyes, glass, rubber and steel. New materials themselves made possible previously unattainable methods of construction, for example in bridge- and ship-building, which in turn required scientific expertise. This change of emphasis was becoming a concern for those directly affected – scientists – and for those worried about continental – in particular French – strength in relation to Britain.

The Adelphi buildings of the Royal Society of Arts in London. The Adam-designed building remains one of the architectural gems of this area near Charing Cross station, and still houses the Society.

Given that production in Britain had distanced itself from artistic design on the one hand and from science on the other, it was perhaps no accident that it was at the Society for the Promotion of Arts, Manufactures and Science that this situation made itself most obvious and where the strongest commitment lay to do something about it. The Society's state of financial and organisational disarray owed much to the dislocation of industry from science and design: the kinds of funds at the disposal of the Society no longer served to attract the attention of manufacturers and its system of prizes, therefore, did not act as an efficient incentive to technical development as it had in the eighteenth century.[30] Meanwhile, it had allowed the work of promoting fine arts to go to other organisations, most notably the Royal Academy. If the Society's fortunes were to be saved then it would have to find a way of reviving industry's interest in art and science. Just as in France, exhibitions would be an area in which the three bourgeois pursuits of art, science and industry could be harmonised. They fulfilled not only the long-term goal of making the Society useful again to a broad spectrum of bourgeois interests but also the short-term one of replenishing its coffers.

This was also an organisation whose membership overlapped with several of the other societies in Britain that had experimented with exhibitions and one that was international in its outlook: a long-standing tradition of contacts between scientists, artists and manufacturers in Britain and their counterparts on the continent helped focus attention on what was going on abroad, and members of the Society of Arts were frequently present at the continental exhibitions. Though by the 1840s, the idea of an exhibition was nothing new, even in Britain, it was probably the success of those in Paris and Berlin in 1844 that provided the immediate spur to Francis Wishaw, the Society's Secretary, to propose a small exhibition of painting and 'useful inventions' to be held on 6 December 1844 in the lecture room of the Adelphi buildings with a prize fund of £300 out of his own pocket. It was only visited by 150 people but the Society's enthusiasm for exhibitions led to another being held under its auspices in January 1845. It also inspired the entrepreneur and pioneer of telegraphy William Fothergill Cooke, spurred on by Wishaw, to propose at the Society's Miscellaneous Committee on 21 May 1845 'that a National Exhibition of the Products of Industry in Arts, Manufactures and Commerce in connection with this Society be forthwith established' and to put up £500 on loan to pay for it.[31] A week later, a meeting of the committee took place to discuss the matter in more detail; it was resolved:

> that the experience of foreign countries has proved that great national advantages have been derived from the stimulus given to industrial skill by bringing the manufactures of different establishments into competition with each other, and by presenting Honorary rewards to those who have excelled in each department, cheapness of production and excellence of material, both in execution and durability being assumed as the criteria of superiority. That by carrying out a similar principle in this country founded on such experience of the past, but with more extensive views, still greater benefits may be anticipated.[32]

Much later, there would be a series of rather unseemly disputes among those who had promoted the idea of an exhibition, especially regarding the role played by Prince Albert, who was often presented as its originator – in particular in the *Official Catalogue's*

Prince Albert, pictured in 1843,
shortly after his arrival in Britain.

history of the Exhibition, written by Henry Cole[33] – and also with regard to the *coup de théâtre* the internationalisation of the Exhibition which he was likewise believed to have suggested.[34] This crossing of swords had much to do with the hurt pride and competing ambitions of those linked with the Great Exhibition's foundation once its success became clear. Nevertheless, it was also highly revealing of something else: Prince Albert, though he never claimed the role for himself and always found hero-worship repellent, was attributed with having originated the idea since for some of those involved it might have seemed disrespectful to claim otherwise, because of a desire by certain individuals to ingratiate themselves, and also as a way of ensuring the Exhibition's success by tying it more firmly to Albert's name and using his authority.[35] However, the wording of the resolution passed by the committee at this point clearly demonstrates that in 1844–5 at least Albert was not the originator of the Exhibition. Rather, the success of continental exhibitions, together with the growing enthusiasm among the learned societies in Britain for them, led the Society of Arts back to the idea. Between 1844 and 1851 many individuals would contribute to the final outcome. Indeed, Albert, the Society's President from 1843, was only informed of the resolution by the Secretary after the annual prize-giving ceremony on 4 June 1845 when 'the subject of the proposed national exhibition was discussed at great length'. Though he personally had good reasons to support the idea – he was a moderate liberal, favoured educational exercises, had direct experience of exhibitions in the German states and could possibly already appreciate the beneficial effects on the monarchy of connecting himself with such a scheme – Albert was also far too astute to get involved with a project that as yet had no popular backing, other than that of a small London-based clique. He was also still far from popular with a large section of the public, which still viewed him as a foreigner and an intruder into British politics. Thus, from the beginning, he maintained a reserved stance towards the idea of an exhibition – an attitude maintained until popular support for it was really beyond doubt. His response, therefore, to Wishaw was to ask for a mature plan to be drawn up.[36] Two days later, at the Wednesday meeting of the Society, a subcommittee was set up to look into the whole idea of an exhibition. It included some of those who would continue to be important figures in the development of the Great Exhibition – William Fothergill Cooke, politician Charles Wentworth Dilke, London property agent Francis Fuller, engineer John Scott Russell, patent lawyer Thomas Webster and silk merchant Thomas Winkworth.

This subcommittee deliberated several issues which are significant as they recurred later and indeed its meetings can be regarded as one of the main stages on the way to 1851. One of its first decisions on Monday 16 June 1845 was to send a memorandum to the British Association, informing it of the intention of holding an exhibition and asking for its cooperation. This again recognised the fact that exhibitions were being held by several different organisations and that this one would serve not only as a Society project, but as one that might unite all in ensuring its success. Two weeks later the subcommittee discussed the issue of prospective sites for the Exhibition. A deputation was sent to look at the Baker Street Bazaar, where there were potentially 2 acres for their use 'in the event of being unable to obtain the use of ground-space sufficiently large scale from the government' – but the hope was at this point that state help might be forthcoming. However, the Bazaar was only the second choice, as 'the Committee was unanimous in the opinion that such an exhibition should take place in a temporary building enacted either in Hyde Park or another convenient place'.[37] In other words, even at this early stage the idea of Hyde Park as the location for the Exhibition was being raised and it was already mooted that a building should be constructed specially for the purpose. The suggestion was put forward that, in order to mobilise for the Exhibition, committees should be set up in every large manufacturing town in Britain – again a taste of things to come in 1851. However, before any of this was begun, the subcommittee wisely decided to send out deputations to find out exactly how feasible the whole project was.

Unfortunately, it was soon found, as J.S. Russell later put it, that though the Society was keen, the subcommittee 'did not meet with sufficient cooperation in money, or encouragement, from public sympathy, to warrant their undertaking the grave responsibility of carrying the matter into effect . . . the English public were as yet imperfectly acquainted with the value of exhibitions of this kind both as regards their influence on the character of the people and the commerce of the country'.[38] One problem was the naivety of the Society, which had clutched rather wildly at the idea of an exhibition along the lines of France or Belgium as a way of raising its own profile and finances but without much regard for the likely shape a British version might take. Another was the issue of the market: though the educated élite of London's societies might appreciate the value of exhibitions, the wider public had had less contact with them, and manufacturers in particular were likely to be suspicious of such ventures. The conclusion was that if the Society of Arts was still going to aspire to a national exhibition, it had to focus its ideas more clearly on British needs. It also, however, needed to publicise the value of exhibitions more widely – in particular among manufacturers and in the business world. This was in effect what the Society did over the next four years. An ongoing discussion took place in which the original plans of the Society were developed and made more consistent, and further attempts were made to configure exhibitions in such a way as to make them more popular. In addition, some important factors came into play perhaps resulting partly from the Society's actions, but probably also connected with the industrialisation that had made exhibitions themselves desirable. These also now helped make a national exhibition possible, as well as opening up further possibilities, such as that of an international exhibition.

John Scott Russell's role in bringing about the Great Exhibition has been very much underrated, to some extent because he managed to alienate the rest of the group that promoted the project – in particular the royal party – and was as a result not accorded his rightful recognition afterwards when most of the other organisers were given awards and knighthoods. This was partly because of the flamboyance of many of those with whom he was connected, who were often much more willing to seek personal glory, and also because Russell constantly had other claims on his time, particularly as his career in ship-design soared in 1850–1. Later he became involved in the building of the *Great Eastern*, ironically a project also much more connected with the name of I.K. Brunel than with Russell. When he was brought into the Society of Arts in 1844, Russell was a firm devotee of technical education and well aware of the potential of exhibitions. After graduating from Glasgow University in 1825, he had made a name for himself through his lectures at the Leith Mechanics' Institute, the British Association, the Royal Society and the Society of Arts in Edinburgh. He had been personally involved in steam engine innovation, having successfully built steam road-coaches until they were forced off the highways by legislation protecting horse-drawn coaches. He was also obviously well aware of the value of connecting science with industry: one of his main contributions to naval architecture was the 'wave-line', a scientific theory of ship construction that would revolutionise ship-travel after 1851.[39]

Having served on the subcommittee for the exhibition, Russell succeeded Wishaw as Secretary of the Society of Arts in July 1845 and ensured that exhibitions remained on the agenda. It was in the second half of 1845 that Russell decided to add the issue of artistic design in industry to the exhibition plans. Apart from being a natural field of Society activities, this held out the prospect of being much more popular and accessible and therefore helpful to the cause. During this period, while working as editor of the *Railway Chronicle*, Russell had considered for publication some maps of London for foreign tourists suggested to him by C.W. Dilke. These were produced by Henry Cole, together with the three artists Mulready, Horsley and Redgrave. They were just one of many examples of Cole's entrepreneurial efforts to exploit the commercial possibilities of artistic design in an industrial sense. Russell and Cole soon became close friends and it was this acquaintance that resulted in Russell's offer of £50 in December 1845 to help expand the system of prizes to include 'models and designs of useful objects calculated to improve general taste' and to use the money generated from the exhibitions of these 'to collect and exhibit models of the most exquisite works in Art for the improvement of the Taste of Workers and Manufactures in metal'.[40]

Charles Wentworth Dilke, art publicist
and leading member of the Royal
Society of Arts.

To further consolidate the Society's commitment to the issue of artistic design, Cole was asked to draw up the criteria of awards for the first prize-giving in 1846, a list credited as being the first definition of what would become known as 'art manufactures', the promotion of which would eventually form a crucial part of the Great Exhibition's purpose.[41] In order to set the tone – and in what appears in retrospect to be an example of stage-management – Cole entered himself into the competition with a tea-service produced under his pseudonym of Felix Summerly; he was awarded a first prize. This piece, produced with his porcelain manufacturer (and Society of Arts member) Herbert Minton, became highly popular and was on sale for years to come; it formed the start of Cole's entrepreneurial career with his Summerly's Art Manufactures.[42] The award not only confirmed his authoritative position in the realm of art manufactures, but also brought him into the Society of Arts and, at the request of Cole himself, to the attention of Prince Albert.

The Cole–Albert relationship was to be of great importance: Cole's exuberance would often become too much for Albert, who was in a position of much greater responsibility and had to tread much more carefully. Cole often appeared to be driven by personal ambition, while Albert tended to be more idealistic. But there was indeed a meeting of minds on the subject of the need for an improvement of public taste and the harmonisation of art once more with industry. As a recently arrived foreigner, Albert was able to compare British produce with that of continental Europe. In 1844, he had been Chairman of the Royal Commission that was formed to choose frescoes to decorate the inside of the New Westminster Palace (the present Houses of Parliament) and was party to its discussions about public taste. He and Cole also shared a love of the

Renaissance style and its introduction in Britain by sculptors like John Bell and artists such as Richard Redgrave.[43] The Society's new direction was confirmed finally by Prince Albert himself in 1846, when he informed a deputation which met him to discuss further exhibitions that 'to wed mechanical skill with high art is a task worthy of the Society of Arts and directly in the path of its duty'.[44]

Where Russell had succeeded in broadening the Society's exhibitions, the admission of Henry Cole to the Society of Arts clarified its educational mission, turned it more towards art and design, and also made it more ambitious and significant. Cole had been a civil servant since the 1830s, had been involved in setting up the Public Record Office in 1838, had helped create the design of the first penny post of Rowland Hill in 1840, and had been a participant in the push for Benthamite reforms. His thoughts on art and design reflected the conclusions of Bowring and the Parliamentary Committee of 1835–6 that British industry needed more aesthetic production, and he believed that education on this point for consumers as well as manufacturers would go a long way towards the moral and spiritual regeneration of the masses. Yet while he also shared the Benthamite belief that the state should expand its activities in order to rationalise and democratise society, Cole did not believe in unlimited state expansion. Other reformers, who not only wished to see the creation of central institutions in order to cope with a rapidly industrialising country but also wanted to avoid a tyrannical state, spoke only of legislating to yield the utmost happiness for all or of the rights of the individual. For Cole, the rule of thumb was that institutions should be 'self-supporting'. This encapsulated the notion of independence from the state – and many of Cole's plans were quasi-public in nature – and also conformed with his own entrepreneurial spirit: if an institution could be profitable, as well as educative, then so much the better.

Despite the distance of Cole's theories from pure *laissez-faire*, involving as they still did the idea of state action, they were in fact generally very much in tune with free trade and were to prove an important conduit between the Great Exhibition and the growing free trade movement. As Cole's ideas sat somewhere between the mid-century British distaste for state-intervention and French *dirigisme*, they perhaps allowed his study of the continent, through frequent trips there, to be more fruitful back home than they might otherwise have been: interest in what the French were doing at exhibitions only grew now Cole was in the Society of Arts. In addition the Benthamite idea of improving society, as well as making it wealthier, through artistic education, attracted the attention of social reformers and allowed the project to spill over into the area of supporting the 'working classes'. And as art was still connected in the public's mind with privilege, it also meant that the Exhibition project became more associated with the propagation of a certain 'lifestyle'. This proved to be a powerful force in drawing support from all classes – to be involved with, or to have visited an exhibition would prove to be as much a matter of social standing as anything else. This was astutely recognised by Cole, who saw in it an answer to his 'self-supporting' principle, as well as, no doubt, his ambition, and he worked hard to persuade Queen Victoria and Albert to lend artefacts from their collections to the first exhibitions at the Society of Arts.

Cole's plans often outstripped the resources at his disposal: a plan to found a 'self-supporting' National Gallery of Fine Art in 1849 fell on its face, and occasions would often arise where his ideas went far beyond what others thought feasible.[45] However,

Francis Fuller, one of the originators
of the Exhibition and a main
influence behind fund-raising.

Cole's enthusiasm and commitment, as well as his entrepreneurial acumen, were also invaluable at certain times: with Cole now also in the Society, plans were put on a more ambitious footing with schemes to hold the first Annual Exhibition of Select Specimens of British Arts and Manufactures, in the Great Room at the Adelpi in March 1847.

Even the Society officially admitted that as preparations advanced 'the exhibition was in imminent danger of turning out a total failure, and was only rescued from extinction by a couple of individuals making it a matter of personal favour with a few great manufacturers to be permitted to select from their stores a sufficient number of articles to place in the rooms of the Society and make a show'.[46] In order to secure a favourable impression at this first exhibition, Cole, Russell, and another member of the Society, the property agent Francis Fuller, concentrated on travelling round London in cabs, personally cajoling manufacturers into participating, in the firm hope that once a start had been made, the commercial benefits of exhibiting would lead others to follow. The combination of education and profit was indicated in the catalogue to the exhibition, which stated that:

it is a universal complaint among manufacturers that the taste for good art does not exist in sufficient extent to reward them for the cost of producing superior works: that the public prefer the vulgar, the gaudy, the ugly even, to the beautiful and perfect. We are persuaded that if artistic manufactures are not appreciated, it is because they are not widely enough known. We believe that when works of high merit, of British origin, are brought forward they will be fully appreciated and thoroughly enjoyed. We believe that this Exhibition when thrown open gratuitously, will tend to improve the public taste.[47]

In the event, the men managed to scrape together 200 exhibitors. To everyone's amazement, however, the number of visitors exceeded 20,000. Such unexpected numbers made obvious to recalcitrant manufacturers the commercial possibilities that were being missed in terms of advertisement and when the second annual exhibition took place in March 1848, there was no problem finding exhibitors: this time 700 took the opportunity of displaying their produce. Moreover, 73,000 visitors entered the Society's building in the Adelphi – a colossal number to visit such small premises in the space of three weeks. It demonstrated both the sagacity of John Scott Russell's plan of gradually building up exhibitions by educating the public and the astuteness of Cole's decision to exploit their economic potential.

The popularity of the events, however, allowed the Society to start thinking about expanding its project. Shortly before the second exhibition in 1848, Henry Cole had already suggested to the Council of the Society of Arts that its exhibitions be made the focus of a new national system of art education by being linked to the schools of design. The best exhibits from the Society's exhibitions should be circulated to the regional schools as a way of broadening their educational impact and creating the type of centralisation in the schools of design system that the Benthamites were demanding, as well as – in typical Cole fashion – reaping some rewards in terms of profile and publicity for the Society. In addition, however, Cole proposed that the best exhibits be collected and 'that at a period of three, four or five years a large building should be provided for a National Exhibition'. He suggested Trafalgar Square as a venue for the Exhibition – possibly drawn to this by the presence of the Royal Academy and the example of the National Repository, but also as 'it is the most convenient place for access by land and water, from all parts of the metropolis. It may be approached closely by carriages, it affords abundant space and a provision of water for specimens and models best exhibited in connection with water; and it offers facilities for a structure of the most economical character, inasmuch as there is already a good pavement, and three sides more or less available in a building for the purpose'. This event would gain in significance by being the culmination of a longer-term cycle, but Cole's plan also represented an answer to the Society's original intention of holding a national exhibition. He finally suggested that the Society make contact with the government and ask about getting its support for the acquisition of a building.[48]

In January 1848, shortly before making his suggestion, Cole had in fact tried to enlist Prince Albert in getting government backing for his plans. Once more Prince Albert, rather than spurring events on, poured cold water on them: there was still too little evidence of support for the Exhibition for him to be able openly to attach his name to the project and informal enquiries had revealed the government unwilling to commit itself, possibly because the whole direction of its policies was geared towards free trade. Even Cole admitted this was 'discouraging'.[49] Yet the Society of Arts was committed to this course, Cole was pugnacious, and he had begun to form his own contacts in government. In 1847 he by chance met Sir John Shaw Lefevre, the Permanent Secretary of the Board of Trade, on a Chelsea steam-boat. Lefevre invited him to collaborate on the schools of design and eventually offered him the paid job of drawing up a report on the subject for a select committee that had been formed to sort the schools out. Through Lefevre, Cole met Henry Labouchere, the President of the Board, and also Lord Granville, its Vice-President. The large numbers at the exhibition of March 1848 convinced the Society to back Cole and also warmed the Board of Trade to the project. Cole's suggestions were welcomed – Walter Ruding Deverall, the Secretary of the government school of design at Somerset House accepted the idea of a national circulation of exhibits; Cole's plan was officially endorsed by the Select Committee on the Schools of Design's report, which recognised that a 'national Exhibition of Decorative Manufactures, if properly organised, might be made to a considerable extent, if not wholly, to repay its expenses'; and the deputation, while not being allotted Trafalgar Square, was at least given provisional accommodation for any future national exhibition in the quadrangle of Somerset House.[50]

In order to give the Society's efforts more direction, a Committee for the Management of the Exhibition of British Manufactures was set up under the chairmanship of Henry Cole. This decided to focus its energies on the exhibition of 1849 and to use this as the starting-point for Cole's plans for both the provincial and the national exhibitions. The discussions of this committee added more detail to the Society's plans and revealed an increasing confidence about the way exhibitions should be organised, as well as a precedent of sorts for the Great Exhibition. Rules about exhibiting were drawn up in detail with the express purpose of creating a national system of education through the schools of design. The committee was specifically to include a representative from the Society's Committees on Arts and Manufactures – underlining the continued centrality of their union to the project. The committee spent much time discussing what should be included in the exhibition and the emphasis was on manipulating the artefacts shown so as to heighten their educative nature. Much of this strategy was about building up contacts with manufacturers who were viewed as fulfilling the requirements of arts manufacture, and thus promoting them and knowledge about them. This was also a task that Cole, together with Richard Redgrave (also a member of the committee), would continue in 1849 with the *Journal of Design*.[51]

The committee further exploited commercially the sense of privilege inherent in exhibitions. Cole negotiated for artefacts belonging to the royal family and the nobility to be exhibited. A system of entrance admission was set up which allowed members' acquaintances and others who could afford it to see the show first, with prices only being reduced after several weeks. Moreover, evening promenades were organised, for a restricted, ticket-only audience, allowing the same kind of fashionable feel as the Royal Academy's *soirées*. To underline the sense of occasion and novelty, the Society's rooms were lit up for the first time by the Electric Light Company.[52] These *soirées* foreshadowed a later tradition that would reoccur in different forms in projects connected with Henry Cole and finally evolved into events like the Promenade concerts at the Albert Hall.

When it opened in March 1849, the third annual exhibition of the Society surpassed the previous two in scope and popularity and had to be extended due to popular demand until the beginning of May. On the basis of this success, in April the Society sent a petition to Parliament calling for the setting up of a national exhibition. Henry Cole used Thomas Milner Gibson, a notable free trader and Chairman of the Select Committee on Schools of

Matthew Digby Wyatt, later Slade
Professor of Art.

Design to submit the petition.[53] On 16 June, at the prize-giving ceremony for the Society of
Arts, John Scott Russell, the Secretary, finally formally announced the intention of the
Society to hold a national exhibition and, following the French example, made these a
quinquennial event – meaning that counting from 1847, the beginning of the annual
exhibitions, the next would be held in 1851. The Society of Arts had been aiming for this
moment for over three years and Russell's announcement was no surprise to anyone. The
idea of an exhibition did not suddenly appear in 1849. Rather it had developed slowly.

Similarly, one cannot pinpoint any particular person to whom the idea of throwing
open the doors of the exhibition to foreign countries can be attributed. The Paris
exhibition opened on 4 June 1849 and, as their own project was now becoming a
reality, several people involved in the Society hurried over the Channel to get more
detailed knowledge of the French exhibitions. It was here that the French Trade Minister,
Louis-Joseph Buffet, put forward the idea of an international exhibition. Though
manufacturers present at the meeting were still too protectionist to accept this, Francis
Fuller, Henry Cole, Matthew Digby Wyatt (the architect and writer on art, whom the
Society commissioned to write a report on the Paris exhibition), and Herbert Minton
were only too aware that this was an idea that would more than suit their purposes in
Britain. Here, after all, was a unique opportunity to carry the Society of Arts' art
education scheme to a far grander and potentially more effective level: British producers

would be pitted against those of the continent and elsewhere and their defects, as well as their strengths, could be highlighted while foreign goods might serve as an educative device. National competition could be used as a spur to economic improvement.

The time also now seemed much more propitious: from the 1830s onwards the free trade movement sought to reform the bloated state and its Byzantine post-1815 tariff, to get rid of the Corn Laws, which had been introduced in 1815 to prevent cheap continental corn coming into Britain after the Napoleonic blockade but which were increasingly viewed as keeping food prices high and propping up the landed aristocracy, and to allow Britain to import agriculture and export industrially produced goods more freely. This was led by Richard Cobden's Anti-Corn Law League and supported by a wide variety of Benthamite reformers, radicals, liberals, manufacturers and consumers. Many free traders believed in the cosmopolitan economic model of Adam Smith, where countries traded with each other freely in order to focus on the most profitable form of production. There was also a widespread belief that industrial growth in continental Europe was connected to Britain's protectionism and that the sooner the Corn Laws were abolished, the better. British superiority in the sector of manufactured goods and its military supremacy after 1815 allowed cosmopolitanism to develop to a much greater level than might otherwise have been the case, however, and economic theory was soon accompanied by political and religious schools of thought supporting internationalism. By the time Sir Robert Peel – a Tory Prime Minister and therefore supposed defender of landed interests – abolished the Corn Laws in 1846, free trade and cosmopolitanism had become widely popular. Even if the country was still deeply divided over the issue, and the Tories threatened to reintroduce protectionism at the first opportunity, for the moment the fact that the government was Liberal suggested the idea of an international exhibition would receive its blessing. Meanwhile, public support for free trade and cosmopolitanism, as well as the manufacturers' new-found interest in making themselves known in continental European markets, suggested it would be a successful venture. The situation became all the more promising when 1849 resulted in a boom in economic terms, while continental producers were still laid low by the revolutionary year of 1848. At such a time there was less likely to be xenophobic protectionism.

On returning to Britain from Paris, Fuller by chance met Thomas Cubitt, the building developer, in Dover. Cubitt was currently working with Prince Albert on the buildings at Osborne on the Isle of Wight. Travelling back to London together, Fuller informed Cubitt 'that we could do a much grander work in London by inviting contributions from every nation; and said, moreover, that if Prince Albert would take the lead in such a work he would become a leading light among nations'.[54] Cubitt duly reported this to Albert.

After arriving in London, Fuller sent Russell a letter, two days before the previously mentioned prize-giving ceremony, telling him that 'you will be glad to hear that my journey to Paris results in an opinion that we can get up an infinitely better Exhibition in London than the one now under inspection', and he began to look into ways of financing such an event.[55] Cole, meanwhile, had returned from Paris on 8 June and conferred with Russell on the subject. After Russell's speech, announcing a national exhibition on 16 June, Prince Albert also spoke to the Secretary and then called a meeting at Buckingham Palace on 30 June to which Russell, Fuller, Cole, Cubitt and the Prince's Private Secretary, Colonel Charles Phipps, were invited. When Cole turned up the day before at Phipps's rooms at Buckingham Palace, ostensibly to find out about the time of the meeting next day, Albert was there, and the three had a long preparatory discussion on the issue. In Cole's diary and memoirs it seems he suggested internationalising the Exhibition; Albert agreed.[56]

In the same way as the question of the origins of the Exhibition itself was fought over, the issue of who had inspired its international character was the subject of much controversy – partly because this too was attributed to Prince Albert. But as in many areas, it appears originality of thought was not Albert's strength; rather his ability lay in accepting advice and ideas from all sides and helping a working group reach agreement. On the face of it, it was Cole and Fuller who injected the idea of an international exhibition into discussions. Nevertheless, it must be remembered that they had themselves drawn the idea from France. Moreover, many other people were having similar ideas at the time: in Birmingham in 1849 the Mechanics' Institute considered opening up its exhibition to foreign competitors. At a discussion at the Society of Arts on 26 June, where no communication of Cole's or Fuller's ideas had yet been made, it was independently suggested by Thomas Winkworth that he 'did not consider that the Exhibition would answer if confined to the manufactures of England. It must be on a large scale if thrown open to the world to exhibit and compete for prizes &c then all Europe would come over to England, English manufacturers would exhibit, & the Exhibition would become of great value as the National Fair of all Europe'.[57] It seems, in fact, that by 1849 industrialisation had got to the point where there were so many interests across Europe which saw a need for the internationalisation of markets and information that the time for an international exhibition had simply arrived. Moreover, the fact that Britain's manufacturers appeared assured of their superior position, and the country was just entering a period of free trade, meant that it was probably here more than anywhere that an international exhibition was likely to emerge. Cole and Fuller can perhaps take some credit for having brought the idea across from France and having seen its potential in Britain. However, the scheme would no doubt have come to fruition at some point, even without them.

Even if Albert cannot be credited with having originated the idea of the Exhibition, or that of its internationalisation, his contribution in terms of putting his weight behind the project at this point has to be recognised. He allowed his connection with the project to be known, which gave it some authority in a generally monarchist country and facilitated communications between the Exhibition's organisers and some of the top political decision-makers. There were, perhaps, several reasons for this. In general, since his marriage to Victoria, Albert had been in a position of uncertainty with regard to his constitutional role and this had attracted some merriment in the press. He had gradually found his way out of the situation both by becoming invaluable to Victoria as her personal secretary and by taking on more and more public functions, including becoming President of the Society of Arts, Chairman of Royal Commission on Fine Arts for the New Parliament in 1843 and Chancellor of the University of Cambridge in 1848. The prospect of the Great Exhibition offered him the tantalising opportunity of further making himself useful in the public eye.

The decision to put himself at the head of the Exhibition project also fitted in with Albert's view of how a monarchy should function: though many of his own advisers, and certainly many continental monarchs at the time, thought that any attempt to seek popularity would simply besmirch royalty and undermine its principles, Albert held that while being apolitical, a monarch should be engaged with the country and be seen to be doing something for the people. This was a principle that needed to be applied not only in Britain, where the reign of George IV had brought the monarchy into some disrepute, but also abroad: Albert's awareness of his own position as a German Prince, with an audience to impress in Germany, should not be underrated as a reason for his involvement in the Great Exhibition. Beyond this Albert was also very much in agreement with Cole with regard to the need to raise aesthetic standards and he supported educational reform generally. At a more immediate level, he could now see from the numbers visiting the Society of Arts exhibitions that there was the prospect of success: his fears about being associated with the project were gradually being overtaken by a sense of the potential of being involved.

III

The meeting at Buckingham Palace on 30 June 1849 has been called the 'birth' of the Great Exhibition: it is often seen as having set the framework for what happened later.[58] Concentrating first on the way an exhibition would function, Albert 'considered' the option of having four categories of display – raw materials, machinery and mechanical inventions, manufactures, sculpture and fine art – and whether they should be exhibited in one event or several: 'it was ultimately settled that, on the first occasion at least, they should be simultaneous'. On the question of prizes, 'it was further settled that, by offering very large premiums in money, sufficient inducement would be held out to the various manufacturers to produce works which, although they might not form a manufacture profitable in the general market, would, by the effort necessary for their accomplishment, permanently raise the powers of production, and improve the character of the manufacture itself'. Seemingly drawing on Cole's suggestion, Albert 'pointed out the vacant ground in Hyde Park on the South side, parallel with, and between, the Kensington drive and the ride commonly called Rotten Row, as affording advantages which few other places might be found to possess'.[59] Prior to this, Albert had been seriously considering the option of a permanent building in Leicester Square, until Cubitt, who had some experience in the business of squares, having developed many of London's most famous quarters, portentously told him 'Your Royal Highness proposes to accomplish a great public good by the Exhibition, but if you build on a square in which the public has a moral, if not a legal, right, you will do a great wrong, and set a bad example'.[60]

Then, turning to the international question, the minutes of the meeting record that 'it was considered that, while it appears an error to fix any limitation to the productions of machinery, science, and taste, which are of no country, but belong, as a whole, to the civilized world, particular advantage to British industry might be derived from placing it in fair competition with that of other nations'. With regard to strategy, Cole's ideas appear to have been accepted, and 'it was settled that the best mode of carrying out the execution of these plans would be by means of a Royal Commission, of which His Royal Highness would be at the head'. However, as the Exhibition was to be held on Crown property and as international exhibitors would have to deal with British customs regulations, the Commissioner of Works and the Board of Trade were to be consulted. Meanwhile, in order to get the necessary funds, a system of subscriptions, as proposed by Fuller, was to be adopted, and 'it was suggested that the Society for the Encouragements of Arts under its Charter possessed machinery and an organisation which might be useful, both in receiving and holding the money, and in assisting the working out of the exposition'.[61]

Rather than being the 'birth' of the Exhibition idea, this meeting in many ways represented the coming together of the various strains of thinking that had gone before. The Society of Arts' educative aims stood centre stage and had been expanded once more to include all the scientific and technical aspects it had originally wanted. Artistic instruction, however, still enjoyed pre-eminence, and the classification system chosen – raw materials, machinery and mechanical inventions, manufactures, sculpture and fine art – appeared to recognise the priority given to art as the top of a chain of production. The Exhibition was to be international but this was to be exploited for the Benthamite aim of allowing British manufacturers and designers the chance of comparing their own products with foreign ones, rather than for market reasons. Meanwhile, the Society of Arts' system of prizes, which had been exported to France, was to be reimported and boosted to cope with the new industrial situation. In addition, the continental model was to be emulated by the setting up of a Royal Commission that would have the authority of a state institution – and thus command the respect of manufacturers and prevent any idea of partisanship – but would also be a body independent of state finances and untainted by political connections. These ideas appear to have arisen as a result of discussion, and the wording of the minutes of this meeting suggests that Prince Albert did not originate them but rather acted the role of facilitator.

Neither should the meeting be seen as having set in stone the parameters of the Great Exhibition: in fact, the decisions on prizes and funding would later be rescinded altogether, those on classification and foreign comparison would be altered entirely, and even the decision on Hyde Park would come close to being cancelled. The problem was that up until now all the discussion on exhibitions had taken place among a small group of activists, in other words those groups, as represented at the Society of Arts, who saw the need for change. Their priorities – in particular the need to realign art and science with industry through education – dominated and as yet no one had really consulted the manufacturers themselves or the wider public. This meant that the project as defined at Buckingham Palace on 30 June 1849 was still rather abstract and there was no concrete evidence that such a dry educational exercise, particularly with foreign participation, would have any kind of popular or financial success. The whole thing still seemed rather risky.

As the government would have to be consulted over the issue of a Royal Commission, as well as over the practicalities of customs, Albert contacted two old political allies: Sir Robert Peel, who was not a member of the current government, but by dint of being the originator of free trade legislation retained strong contacts with it, and whose opinion and outlook Albert trusted implicitly after Peel had helped him built up a public role for himself in the 1840s; and Sir Henry Labouchere, President of the Board of Trade, someone with whom Albert had had close contacts already through the Fine Arts Commission of 1843, who sympathised with Society of Arts' educational crusade and who had already been appraised of the Exhibition plans by Cole. At a meeting at Osborne on 14 July, Albert asked Cole, Cubitt, Russell, and Fuller to go over the whole plan again, this time in the presence of Labouchere. Labouchere, obviously worried about committing the government to the venture, proposed that instead of setting up a Royal Commission, the Society of Arts should simply continue its guiding role and set up a managing committee, of which government ministers could be part. This was turned down by Cole, Fuller and Russell, however, who wanted to retain a financial and executive role for the Society – after all, the exhibitions had been started with that body's pecuniary woes in mind – but thought a Royal Commission should have legislative and judicial functions, as

> one of the requisite conditions for the acquirement of public confidence was, that the body to be appointed for the exercise of those functions should have a sufficiently elevated position in the eyes of the public, and should be removed sufficiently high above the interests, and remote from the liability of being influenced by the feelings of competitors, to place beyond all possibility any accusation of partiality or undue influence; and that no less elevated tribunal than one appointed by the Crown, and presided over by His Royal Highness could have that standing and weight in the country, and give that guarantee for impartiality that would command the utmost exertions of all the most eminent manufacturers at home, and particularly abroad: moreover, that the most decided mark of *national* sanction must be given to this undertaking, in order to give it the confidence, not only of all classes of our own countrymen, but also of foreigners accustomed to the expositions of their own countries, which are conducted and supported exclusively by their governments.[62]

This was an important statement. It recognised the need to compromise with the continental system of state-led exhibitions and the influence of the foreign model. It revealed the concern of the Exhibition's promoters not to be seen to be involved in 'jobbery' – or dishonest financial profiteering – something which would become of great concern later. It also now transformed royalty from being just a symbol to be exploited in an educational and commercial sense at exhibitions, to an objective, over-arching authority, standing at the centre of the whole project. All of this also explained why the Society of Arts now began to lose its grip on the Exhibition project as it moved steadily into the public domain.

The worries about limited support for the plans, however, were serious. Before the meeting, Peel had informally contacted the government about the chances of getting a Royal Commission, and communicated the reply that while ministers were in favour of the idea of an exhibition, 'its great magnitude would necessarily require some time for maturing the plans essential to secure its complete success'. Labouchere now agreed and suggested that, as Parliament was having its summer break, the time should be used to consult more widely to find out whether manufacturers and commercial interests in particular would support the project and subscribe to it financially.[63] As a result of this meeting, the Society of Arts was forced not only to relax its hold on the control of the Exhibition project but also to open it up more widely to public consultation, in particular with manufacturing and commercial men.

Albert, perhaps now worried once more about being involved with a project that might drag him and the monarchy into disrepute, backed the idea of consultation wholeheartedly and when Cole, who was as headstrong as ever, informed him that one should strike while the iron was hot and send a deputation immediately to the Prime

Henry Cole in 1851, ambitious promoter of art in industry and a driving force behind reforms in art education in the nineteenth century.

Minister, Lord John Russell, asking for a Royal Commission,[64] he was rebuked: Phipps informed him that the Prince did not agree with his 'doctrines', that the Society of Arts, rather than sending any deputations, would do far better by 'feeling more extensively the public pulse,' and that 'if the plan is to be matured under [Prince Albert's] auspices, he must be the person to treat with the cabinet ministers upon it (which indeed is his place as President of the Society of Arts) and that he must be guided by his own discretion (willingly receiving all suggestions and advice) as to the urgency of the time of the decision of the question'.[65] Cole, for the moment thoroughly put in his place, answered that if he had known Prince Albert's views, he would not have said anything. He added ruefully: 'the great personal interest which the Prince obviously takes, even in organising the details of this matter, are convincing omens of the future success of the undertaking, & I feel ought to inspire all of us'.[66] On 1 August, Albert set the matter in progress his way by requesting the Home Secretary, Sir George Grey, the brother of his own secretary General Charles Grey, to raise the matter of a Royal Commission with the government.

Where Cole had thought of getting an early Royal Commission as a way of attracting support among manufacturers and in the country, Russell now pressed Fuller to sort out the financial aspects in the hope that if a loan could be raised to secure monies for prizes, manufacturers would be encouraged to take part. Several days before the meeting at Osborne, Fuller had already found a potential financier. This turned out to be his father-in-law, George Drew, acting as agent for the building contractors G. and J. Munday.

Cole and Russell corresponded with Fuller over the issue during the weeks after the Osborne meeting, and at the Society of Arts council meeting on 31 July Russell informed the Society of Drew's offer. This consisted of a loan of £20,000 for the prize fund and one of approximately £10,000 for costs, and the provision of a suitable building. In return, the contractor would expect repayment of the loans, plus a cut of the profits made. It was highly indicative of the uncertainty which still surrounded the project's success when Wishaw commented that if the contractor was indeed going to take upon himself the whole risk then 'even the whole profits might be fair – certainly two thirds would be fair for such a risk'. The success of the Exhibition was still far from assured. The council eventually agreed to allow the contractor half of the profits plus 5 per cent interest on the loan but when Prince Albert heard of this agreement at a meeting at Osborne next day he 'expressed it as his opinion that such a risk on the part of a contractor seemed to bear rather the character of generous cooperation in the object than of an ordinary commercial enterprise'. Moreover, at a council meeting on 7 August, the Society of Arts was informed that the contractors now demanded two-thirds of the profits in order to ensure that they would have a say in the running of operations, and in return the £20,000 could be paid back out of gross receipts, while they would pay all expenses and the wages of workers out of their portion. Though the Society eventually negotiated this to mean £20,000 plus the 5 per cent interest out of the gross receipts, the final settlement did express quite clearly the fact that no one really imagined the profit would be enormous.[67]

At a meeting at Osborne on 1 August, when the Society presented Albert with the details of this agreement, the Prince, to his credit, did query it. However, his main worry was that having secured the money for the Exhibition, the amounts of subscriptions would be low.[68] Henry Cole was perhaps more financially experienced, as well as more confident: as he recounted; 'at a very early stage of the business, I had felt the great likelihood that as the idea became understood, public opinion would prefer some other mode of carrying out the Exhibition than by contract'. It was thanks to Cole that at the last minute a clause was inserted into the deal allowing for the termination of the contract by arbitration, if desired by the Royal Commission once it was set up. However, even Cole pointed out that 'at the time, as Mr Herbert Minton remarked to me, the contract was the right thing to have had made',[69] and the wording of the decision regarding termination suggested the fear was that there would be a complete absence of public support, not an abundance of it.[70]

As a result of the financial issue being resolved, an executive committee was formed to manage the affairs of the Society of Arts' exhibition fund. It consisted of Cole and Fuller, two other Society members, and the contractor and his nominee; a board of trustees for the fund was nominated and included the Marquis of Northampton, Baron Goldsmid, Sir J.P. Boileau and George Drew. It had already been agreed that the views of manufacturers were to be sought. Now, however, this could be extended in order to show that financial arrangements had been made and some concrete decisions had been reached through showing manufacturers the minutes of the meetings held with Prince Albert. It was decided that, beginning in late August, Cole, Fuller and Wyatt should visit the north of England. Russell, meanwhile, was to be sent to the German states. In order that they be given access to important manufacturers, the men were to be furnished with introductions from Prince Albert personally, repeating the pattern of using royalty to promote the project. Yet the tentative nature of the whole venture was still apparent – Prince Albert was quick to point out to the men before they left that though they might use his name, 'care should be taken that they should not be misinterpreted as published officially or by authority'.[71]

This was, therefore, the moment at which the Exhibition idea was to be launched upon the public. Until this time, in fact, it remained a scheme that had been hatched by a small group of men and influenced by their concerns. Their ideas had drawn on a long tradition of exhibitions, both in Britain and abroad, but in particular the art exhibitions of revolutionary France and the subsequent tradition which developed there. The notion that the standards of design could be raised by tapping the commercial potential of art's social value was attractive to Benthamite reformers, while exhibitions were believed to be useful as a means of raising technological standards. For this reason, perhaps, it was logical that the Society of Arts, an organisation devoted to arts, manufactures and science, spearheaded the Exhibition project. Yet its ideas were essentially still those of an élite – activists who wished to educate the wider populace – and their plans were still rather dry. In order to secure success – and in particular in financial terms – this élite was forced to seek not only the sanction of royalty, and in this respect they were remarkably similar to their French predecessors, but also that of the state and the public. It was this next stage in the dialogue about the way the Great Exhibition should look that probably secured its success.

There's a big show coming boys, a big show coming,
When every man will do his best
And for the prizes wilt contest, at the big show coming.
'Tis a novel thing no one disputes
It has caused a great sensation,
And may the best men reap the fruits
Of the produce of their nation, at the big show &c

CHORUS:
At the big show coming boys
The big show coming,
Yes, the big show's coming boys
Only wait a leetle longer.

H. Wood, 'The Big Show Coming', EX.1851.107, NAL

2

THE ROYAL COMMISSION

In September 1849 as the main promoters of the Exhibition toured manufacturing towns in Britain, the concept was still very much confined to a small élite and focused on educational aims. Moreover, it was still dominated by ideas about raising standards of artistic production. However, by 1 May 1851, when the Great Exhibition opened, it had become something quite different, far more complex and all-encompassing in scope but also much more significant to the population at large and was capable of inspiring awe in both its supporters and opponents. The question of how this transformation took place is difficult to answer: there appear to be several reasons rather than one. Perhaps never again would all these factors work together to produce such an impact for an exhibition. The Great Exhibition has proved a difficult act to follow because the road that led to it is unlikely to be replicated.

For one thing, 1849 marked the beginning of an economic boom in Britain, with industrial exports taking off once more. This meant that the previous recalcitrance of manufacturers to get involved in exhibitions, which had been noted by the Society of Arts, abated: protectionism and commercial suspicions were less sustainable at a time of expansion and the Great Exhibition was now to offer the chance of showing wares to foreigners. The introduction of free trade in Britain in 1846, via the abolition of the Corn Laws, also heightened this interest and, coupled with the boom, strengthened the manufacturing sector's support for cosmopolitanism.

However, while the benefits of economic growth did filter through into the wages of many industrial workers and tradespeople, they did not reach many of the poorest labourers and agricultural workers, and the differences in means between different sectors of the British population, which were in any case extreme, threatened to become larger. British society was deeply divided at the mid-century. The threat of revolution stemming from the combined forces of Chartism and the Anti-Corn Law League was headed off at the pass by Peel's abolition of the Corn Laws in 1846, which separated the economic from the political discontents by aiming to reduce the price of bread. However, the abolition dealt a sharp smack in the face to landed aristocrats and the threat of some kind of political reaction hovered unfavourably in the air. So, too, did the threat of revolution, which had not yet quite gone away. In March 1848, revolutions swept across continental Europe as a result of frustrated liberalism in France, and the dual effects of industrial and agricultural collapse elsewhere. Though the Chartists who convened on Kennington Common in April 1848 were frustrated in their attempt to march on Parliament, contemporaries could not yet say that the movement had completely died.

It was against this uncertain background that the Society of Arts appeared to have discovered an answer to the problem of attracting interest in exhibitions by linking them to art and making use of the social prestige connected with it. This course of action seemed proven already by the increase in numbers coming to the exhibitions in 1848 and 1849, and many aspects of the Great Exhibition were to hark back to a belief on the part of the Society of Arts that it was this combination that had worked. However, with success finally in reach, the time had come to reorientate the project in order to reflect the aims of the whole of the Society rather than just its artistic side. Advice was drawn from the continent and efforts were now made to draw in experts from all the fields of manufactures, science and art.

Yet government members, politicians, and aristocrats – even, albeit so far indirectly, royalty – were also involved, not just manufacturers, academics and intellectuals. And at a time when revolution or reaction seemed close, the possibilities of such an integrative exercise as an exhibition were explored more deeply. Through such an event, the values that this alliance shared, namely moderate liberalism, constitutional monarchy and the sanctity of property, could be demonstrated and, with luck, strengthened in the wider population. The Great Exhibition would be about proving to themselves and to their revolutionary and reactionary opponents, as well as to the rest of the world, that the alliance's values were the best. The new *status quo* – the post-Corn Laws alliance of manufacturers with liberals and Whigs – could be strengthened and confirmed. The Exhibition was to be a vehicle for the establishment of a new order founded by a newly configured élite and characterised by its commitment to the principles of ownership and property, as well as production. In this respect, the goals were remarkably similar to those in France in 1798.

One of the central issues binding this new élite together was the theory of free trade. Manufacturers, as well as the general public, were beginning to believe in it as the boom progressed into the 1850s and food prices fell, and many felt its introduction had saved Britain from revolution. Yet at home there was still opposition to free trade. In addition, foreign countries by and large – Belgium and Switzerland being notable exceptions – held to protection. The Great Exhibition therefore became more and more about demonstrating the truths of free trade.

Yet the fact that the Exhibition now became not just educative, and not just the province of reformers and experts in art, science and industry, but also the project of this new, more politicised élite made it the centre of a veritable hurricane of debate. The Great Exhibition also generated debate abroad, where the British lead in free trade was being studied closely by other industrialising powers and their manufacturing communities. The revolutions of 1848, followed by the reactions of 1849, had polarised things outside Britain politically too. As any modern publicist knows, all coverage can be good coverage and the provocative nature of the Exhibition, even before it opened,

The Royal Commission. Left to right: Charles Wentworth Dilke, John Scott Russell, Henry Cole, Charles Fox, Joseph Paxton, Lord John Russell, Sir Robert Peel, Robert Stephenson. Seated left to right: Richard Cobden, Charles Barry, Lord Granville, William Cubitt, Prince Albert, Lord Derby. This picture is an idealised one, erroneously showing Fox and Paxton as members of the Commission. (V&A Picture Library)

ensured that it had entered the minds of the widest possible audience; almost everyone had an opinion on it.

Two additional factors explain the Great Exhibition's high profile when it opened. Firstly, in order to secure financial success, and because the political élite was interested in involving the public more in governance with a view to winning them over, the organisation of the Great Exhibition was made a public concern. The public decided the extent of the Exhibition and also what went inside it. Though this was only representative rather than full democracy, and though the public involved was that part which sympathised with the principles of ownership, it did serve to make the Exhibition a publicly owned affair. Debates were carried out regarding the nature of the Exhibition which included the public. The people increasingly treated it as 'their' Exhibition.

This may make the Exhibition organisers sound like textbook project managers but in fact nothing could be further from the truth. They were a diverse group, often with competing ambitions; many were so unused to public decision-making, and what they were doing was so new, that many mistakes were made along the way. In fact, much of the way in which the Royal Commission for the Great Exhibition of 1851 operated was the result of hard-learned lessons and on the way to the opening many large public-relations mistakes were made. This statement runs very much against the grain of contemporary literature about the Royal Commission, much of which was propaganda in sympathy with the Exhibition's aims. It also contradicts historical literature, which glorifies the Royal Commission as some kind of model of bureaucratic decision-making, always meeting deadlines and recording its actions to the last detail. The second factor which made the Exhibition familiar to the general public by the time it opened was, therefore, the *faux pas* of the Royal Commission. Ironically, some of the Exhibition's greatest successes turned out to be the result of the Commission's mistakes.

I

In August 1849, the promoters of the Exhibition project were still thinking very much along Benthamite lines – aiming to raise the standards of British manufacturing design, now also including science, through comparison. Though the scale of the project had grown, it still reflected very much the concerns of this small group to reunite designers and scientists with industrialists, and neither the public's nor the government's views had been directly involved in the discussion. With regard to the Society of Arts' relations with the wider populace, its exhibitions had been promoted by tapping the public's demand for social advancement, as well as the manufacturer's ability to sniff out profit, and to this extent their organisers – in particular Henry Cole – had already noticed that some accommodation of the demands of those they were trying to entice was necessary to the success of their didactic mission. However, till now the use of this tactic had remained relatively limited and adequate only, perhaps, to ensure success in the localised setting of London.

With regard to the Society's relations with government, state involvement had been viewed as ultimately necessary for the carrying out of a national exhibition, since Benthamites generally viewed the state as the most rational and effective institution at the national level. Nevertheless, though the involvement of the state might be required, it should ideally be kept to a minimum and, according to Cole's dictum, exhibitions should be self-supporting rather than publicly funded. The Society's efforts to make exhibitions an adjunct to the government schools of design illustrated the way in which many of its members viewed the question of cooperation with the state.

The state, for its part, remained guarded towards the Exhibition. There were already those, such as Albert, Sir Robert Peel, Henry Labouchere and the Prime Minister, Lord John Russell, who were perhaps beginning to realise the potential value of such an event: it could serve to unite the disparate forces of the bourgeoisie; perhaps it could raise the levels of the country's production and thus help the labouring classes; it might strengthen the industrial sector and make it a bulwark against the reactionary landed classes that had been so grievously alienated by the abolition of the Corn Laws in 1846; and thus it could generally help guard against revolution and reaction. Nevertheless, until now, the whole project had seemed rather tenuous and likely to end up as a financial flop. Such an outcome would have consequent negative effects for a political élite which at present – in the immediate wake of the severe ructions of 1846 and revolutions on the continent – felt sensitive to anything that might undermine its position still further.

The situation was beginning to move into a new phase, however, and gradually the Society of Arts, the state and the public began to enter into a dialogue. The Society of Arts now became more desirous of state involvement. The numbers achieved at the 1849 exhibition had made not just a national but an international exhibition a possibility. As Digby Wyatt's report on the French exhibition showed,[1] state leadership was necessary to the success of any venture at this level, as manufacturers were suspicious about bias and profiteering under any other circumstances. State – and especially royal – patronage ensured not just some kind of objectivity, but also profit when goods were accorded official merit. It would be necessary at least to echo this to attract foreigners to Britain and, as events would prove, British manufacturers were just as worried as their overseas counterparts about the fairness of an independent, unofficial body like the Society of Arts. There was in any case a strong tradition of looking to the state in Britain to act at the national level and even Benthamite liberals, while they opposed state interventionism and sought state reform, viewed it as the most rational and effective actor when it came to operating nationally. The value of having royalty attached to an exhibition had already been demonstrated at the Society's rooms in the Adelphi and some Society members were already aware of the fact that circumstances on the continent would be repeated in Britain and make state-involvement – preferably via a Royal Commission – just as much a necessity here.

To encourage public backing for the Exhibition, Henry Cole had already turned to Sir Robert Peel in July 1849 for a demonstration of his support. He told Albert, 'we have reason to know that Sir Robert Peel is interested in the proposed Exhibition and we think it might be very useful if he would make some slight public sign in evidence of his good wishes. If the Commission is issued, *that* fact testifies [*sic*] the good will of the present government. The unanimity of all parties would be complete by having some outward sign of the late Premier'.[2] Government support for the scheme would bolster the Exhibition's status as a national undertaking rather than the progeny of one unofficial body.

Cole's application to Peel in particular is significant. As a Conservative who recognised the need to accommodate the manufacturing sector – as opposed to the landed gentry – at the heart of the state, and who had therefore jettisoned much of his own party support in 1846, and as the son of a northern manufacturer and someone who was on familiar terms with Victoria and Albert, Peel seemed an ideal spokesperson to be linked to the Exhibition. He represented the state in its entirety, as opposed to any party affiliation. In addition, in many people's eyes, in particular those of the vast swathe of political opinion that supported free trade, he was the epitome of honesty and integrity because he had given up the prejudiced support of 'vested interests' in the Conservative Party. Yet it is important to recognise that the approach to Peel was also a political choice: it showed that the Society of Arts did not just want the patronage of the state for the Exhibition, but the state as represented by Sir Robert Peel: Peel embodied not just neutrality and probity but a neutrality and probity as judged by a particular part of the British population – the broad band of political opinion that opposed revolution and reaction, and supported manufacturing and free trade instead to feudalism and protectionism. The Society's approach to this particular configuration of the state was no surprise: after all, many of its members were drawn from the manufacturing classes, and there was a general political concentration in the Society upon liberal beliefs. Indeed, many Society members were also Liberal politicians. In other words, the Society was beginning to reach out to the state, but only to the state in its newly-configured, post-1846, pro-manufacturing, liberal form.

However, neither Peel, nor anyone in government, felt sure enough of the Exhibition's success, even at this stage, to openly commit themselves to it. Peel informed Albert –

possibly on the basis of his own political instinct, possibly on that of Russell's Liberal government, with whom he was acting as unofficial intermediary – that first of all the views of manufacturers should be sought out round the country and efforts ought to be made to get promises of subscriptions for the Exhibition as proof of the public's desire for it.[3] This was a highly astute instruction: not only did it allow Albert and the government to pull back from the project should the public turn out to be against it, it also meant that members of the Society of Arts, who were to serve as the deputies to the provinces, would come into contact with the public, learn more about their ideas and perhaps end up shaping their own to fit more the general demand. In other words, though the Society of Arts' educative mission had already had to be bent to fit popular public interests to a limited extent by involving art and royalty, it was the need to ensure the Exhibition's success, and in particular the fears of the members of the élite for their own positions, that really opened the flood gates and began the process of public consultation.

The deputations began on 27 August 1849, with Cole, Fuller and Digby Wyatt setting off on a massive tour, visiting between them manufacturers in the Potteries, Manchester, Sheffield, Bradford, Huddersfield, Leeds, Nottingham, Derby, Kendal, Newcastle, Edinburgh, Coupar and Braemar. They then had a short sojourn together at Balmoral on 3 September, where they reported their findings provisionally to Prince Albert, before splitting up again to visit Dundee, Perth, and Stirling, and reuniting in Glasgow to go via Greenock to Belfast and Dublin. After the Dublin meeting on 7 September, the three returned via Birmingham on 15 September to London, and from there visited Ashford, Canterbury, Dover, and other areas in the south. Perhaps in order to provide more objective corroboration, Henry Labouchere was asked to go once more to Birmingham and the Potteries.[4] Meanwhile, foreign governments and manufacturers also needed to be consulted, for their involvement appeared even less certain. Once again in order to prevent the impression of official support for the Exhibition, rather than the Foreign Office making contacts, John Scott Russell was sent as a sort of semi-official emissary with letters of introduction from the Foreign Secretary, Lord Palmerston, to manufacturers and governments in Brussels, Cologne, Hanover, Berlin, Leipzig, Munich and Frankfurt.[5] Familial connections – Colonel Phipps was the brother of the British Ambassador in Paris, Lord Normanby – were used unobtrusively to sound out the views of President Louis Napoleon regarding the attitude of the most important foreign participant to the Great Exhibition.[6]

Given the rather *sotto voce* character of these moves, the results were quite unexpected and of great significance, both to the way the Exhibition idea progressed and also more generally. For one thing, though the idea had indeed been to widen the discussion about the Exhibition to include 'eminent persons', by which the Society of Arts significantly meant manufacturers and not merchants or others 'less directly concerned in actual *production*',[7] it was soon discovered that many others also wanted to be involved. Economic confidence, the popularity of free trade and cosmopolitanism, the general sympathy with the values of property and wealth and the desire for social advancement which participation in the Exhibition offered, the potential for advertisement and profit, and royal patronage, meant that the visits of the commissioners to the towns often became public events and those that could not attend rushed to read about them in the newspapers.

The unexpected level of public interest was to make this episode a first lesson in public relations for the Exhibition organisers. There were difficulties in controlling journalists, who pushed into meetings intended to be private in Manchester and created embarrassment through their reportage. Henry Cole's persistent use of the royal tag to sell the Exhibition to the public also landed him in trouble with Prince Albert when the press reported that at the meeting in Dublin, which had become something of a semi-public rally chaired by the Lord Mayor, Cole named Albert as the sole originator of the Exhibition project. Phipps, a staunch defender of royalty's aristocratic right to rule and already rankled by Albert's dalliance with the idea of popular monarchy, warned 'the meeting at Dublin seems to have been very successful but I confess that I have no confidence in the soundness or stability of opinions pronounced at public meetings, and I have a still greater dislike to hearing Your Royal Highness's praises, however just, so loudly sounded by persons going about under an authority granted by YRH. The mischievous person in even the best disposed meeting might make this a foundation for much that would be disadvantageous to the plan and disagreeable to YRH'.[8] Albert himself was worried enough by Phipps to inform Cole – perceptively – that 'praising me at meetings looks as if I were to be advertised and used as a means of drawing a full house'.[9] After the tour was complete, Cole defended his position to Phipps by explaining:

I hope His Royal Highness will make all charitable allowance for the defects of provincial reporting. With the most perfect consciousness of the liability to misstatement and of the doubtfulness of many parts of the proposal – I have myself tried very hard not to appear to overstep the precise facts at every meeting – but in vain. There seems a fatality that you *must* be misreported. I felt this ever since the Dublin meeting and so strongly at Canterbury and Dover that I spoke at both meetings as if tongue-tied and I felt quite *beaten*. Notwithstanding all my pains the reporters put things in a way I never did – I quite despair of even being able merely to read the cautiously worded minutes without saying a word and finding the facts correctly stated in provincial papers and I assure you that I am very nervous and uncomfortable.[10]

As a result of the unexpected rush of support, local politicians pushed themselves forward remarkably quickly to meet the emissaries and show them round. In Manchester Cole *et al* 'received on all sides suggestions that, for many reasons, it was expedient that we should make our visit known as early as possible to the mayor, or chief magistrate, and be guided by him as to the parties it might be most desirable to see'.[11] To an extent this was a repetition at the local level of a national harmonisation between political leaders and supporters of the Exhibition, though in places like Manchester, local politicians were often themselves manufacturers. It also meant that, on a much grander scale than had been envisaged, the emissaries began setting up a network of influential people who were committed to the Exhibition. It was a network that found its roots in the political *status quo* and in the values of industrialism, production, ownership and property which the project suggested.

The response was no different abroad, where, revealingly, Russell reported 'the liberality, wisdom and advantages of the great plan everywhere appreciated – he found every disposition in the most influential quarters, to afford cooperation; and he found at

Berlin, where already the greatest advances had been made in a similar direction, an organisation existing, well calculated to secure effective cooperation, and which the Minister expressed his readiness to put in motion for so important and interesting a purpose'.[12] Normanby, meanwhile, reported equally revealingly on 20 September that 'I breakfasted with the President the day before yesterday at the Elysée and had much talk with him afterwards on this subject. He was very much pleased with the idea and entered into it heartily; as these are points to which he has always given much of his attention one may be sure if the idea is matured of his doing all in his power to ensure its success as far as France is concerned'.[13] Despite the fact that industrialisation was not as advanced in continental Europe as in Britain, there were already many manufacturers there who saw the need to expand into the international market, as well as many liberals calling for the relaxation of national controls on commerce. Louis Napoleon needed to consolidate his position in revolution-ravaged France by presenting himself as a reformer but without conceding enormous political freedoms. The Prussian government in Berlin wished to demonstrate its position as the most progressive German power in order to steal a march on Austria and demonstrate the unity of its *Zollverein* customs union. For both governments, then, Russell's advances were welcome.

The deputations, therefore, represented the first step towards linking together all those groups who supported the kinds of things the Exhibition already stood for – industrial production, commercial liberalisation, consumption, ownership, education and the preservation of the political *status quo* from revolution and reaction. This network was to become increasingly integrated and formalised later in a system of local committees and Foreign Commissioners. The deputations also brought the Society of Arts' plans into contact with the wider public for the first time. This had two major results: it allowed a rhetoric to develop that would be useful at later fund-raising events and elsewhere to ensure the widest possible public support. It also, as Peel had envisaged, resulted in the Society of Arts' plans becoming more suitable for public consumption.

Now a surprising number of manufacturers echoed the Society of Arts' belief, and that of Benthamites in general, that, as Mr Nelson of the Manchester company Nelson, Knowles & Co. put it, 'most manufacturers have much too high an opinion of their own excellence, and it is desirable they should measure it by that of others', or that, as Messrs Thomson, Hargreaves, Dalgleish and Falconer of Edinburgh put it, 'it is very necessary that all parties should know what the French and all nations are doing, and should compare their manufactures with our own. The comparison would show what our manufacturers could do, and by generating increased knowledge and appreciation in our consumers would induce the production of a much higher class of work'. This enlightened approach was sometimes even tinged with an ethical hue: at the Edinburgh meeting, the view was put forward 'that moral good would result from that assemblage of rival manufacturers which would be induced by the Exhibition'. All of this bolstered the original intentions of the Society of Arts.

Yet the deputations also revealed new pockets of support for the exploitation of the Exhibition. Rather than just being interested in education, many manufacturers hoped more crudely to expand their international markets. The emissaries also reported their belief 'that there will be a considerable amount of national pride and exertion on the part of individuals to contribute to its success'. Idealistic cosmopolitans, meanwhile, wished to 'rub the sharp corners of many nations off'.[14]

Such contradictions stemmed from the fact that those who supported the Exhibition often had diametrically opposed interests – in this case exporters and cosmopolitan liberals versus domestic producers, patriots and nationalists. They reflected, and to some extent explained, the inherent contradiction in British liberalism at the time; it did indeed have both cosmopolitan and patriotic aspects. However, as the aim of the Exhibition organisers was to bring in as many supporters as possible from all those committed to the defence of the *status quo* and the promotion of industry, such impurities were imported wholesale into their rhetoric.

The deputations also placed on the agenda several public concerns that needed to be addressed if the Exhibition were to be a success: first, the emissaries reported that despite the generally liberal mood of those they spoke to, there was still a protectionist reluctance on the part of many manufacturers to reveal their goods to foreign competitors for fear of piracy, stemming, they believed, from the inadequacy and relative newness of the present Copyright Registration Act. This was the first mention of patent laws as an obstacle to the Exhibition and it began a discussion among the event's promoters that would lead to a full-scale campaign in January 1850 to introduce more stringent legislation. Then there was also much disagreement about the prizes to be given out at the Exhibition, with some fearing that large financial prizes would lead to corruption, others thinking that without them important manufacturers would be unwilling to compete, and many views in between. This, too, lead to later discussions, but at least for the present, it warned the Exhibition promoters that this was a touchy subject and persuaded them to stay quiet on the issue in order to maintain wide support: Fuller was told off in no uncertain terms by Phipps for appearing to say, at the meeting in Dublin, that money prizes would be given.[15] A memorandum by Cole entitled 'Suggestions for Prizes to be awarded to Exhibitors of the Most Meritorious Works', written one month later, was quashed.[16] Similarly, there was much worry expressed about what exactly would be rewarded at the Exhibition. Would manufacturers receive merits for having produced cheaply? Or would quality be the main focus? The deputations in Britain revealed that all thought the two should not be directly in competition, while from Paris Normanby also communicated President Napoleon's concern on the same subject[17] – France, after all, was known for its quality produce and artistic design. Much of the rest of European production was similarly artisan in nature. Once again, these messages warned the Exhibition promoters to remain silent on the subject, if important supporters were not to be alienated. But they were also a first sign that the Society of Arts' original plans to reward only design would have to be expanded eventually, if the participation of the industrial north as well as that of foreign countries was to be assured.

One area in which there did appear to be unanimity, and which did have an influence both on the rhetoric used in campaigning and in later organisational discussions, was over the financing of the Exhibition. Here, it was reported that 'the preponderance of opinions we heard was certainly in favour of *wholly* supporting the Exhibition by voluntary subscription'. (In order to emphasise the point, the deputation went to the lengths of recounting how 'a lady of nearly eighty years of age, who probably would not be able to travel to London even to see the Exhibition said, – "I will subscribe my crown if no part of the expenses comes out of the taxes, but not otherwise."') Such acute public distaste for government-aided projects stemmed partly from liberal reformers' demands that the state be severely restricted and partly from the public obsession that existed at the time with regard to 'jobbery'. The preoccupation with this latter subject had much to do with liberal reformers' calls for an end to what they viewed as the corruption of the state in the past, the fact that a new group of wealthy industrialists was now coming into British political life for the first time, and the increased religious zeal of the mid-century in the face of modernisation and industrialisation. There had already been several notorious instances of 'jobbery' relating to public buildings in London, the most prominent being the new Houses of Parliament, when the contract was almost handed to Robert Smirke, a former architect at the state Board of Works.[18] The liberal reformist MP, Joseph Hume, had led a campaign at that time against this – incidentally with the involvement of Peel – which had resulted in calls for a public competition and a Royal Commission to oversee the work. Such a way of doing things was more – to use what had become a catch-phrase in Victorian Britain – 'disinterested' and in tune with the liberal reformers' ideas of competition leading to a more moral result.

Voluntarism smacked of the same elements: by throwing themselves at the mercy of the public, rather than being dependent on the state, the Exhibition organisers would end up with a more efficient, suitable and worthy event. As in several other instances, this public sentiment chimed with the plans of the Society of Arts, which had from the start considered voluntary subscriptions as the way forward. The fact that there were still differences between the Society's and the public's views of what should happen to the money made with these subscriptions would only become apparent later. For the moment, the voluntary aspect of the Exhibition was to be stressed on all occasions.

Furthermore, according to the deputations, 'the most remarkable evidence taken' was the unanimous view that any tribunal which judged the prize-giving had to be completely impartial and that a Royal Commission 'was the only means of securing the utmost practicable impartiality, and that its appointment was indispensable to securing public confidence'. Again, this had much to do with the public debate about probity, as well as the example of the Houses of Parliament campaign. It also mirrored the experience of continental countries where royalty and the state were looked to as the final arbiter of such issues. At this point, however, the call for the leadership of a Royal Commission represented an important signal to Prince Albert and his political contacts that the public demanded state involvement. This – coupled with the overwhelmingly positive response in general to the idea, the crucial agreement of France to participate and signals of support from other important potential participants like Sir Archibald Galloway, Chairman of the East India Company[19] – now encouraged Albert to move.

Already by the middle of September 1849, Albert had decided on the basis of provisional reports to go one step further and hold a major meeting with representatives from the City of London. This would not only seal the question of financial backing for the Exhibition but would also represent a much more public unveiling ceremony in the presence of important political figures and the national press.[20] Phipps, once more alarmed by Albert's attempt to get popular support, warned his master that, especially in view of Cole's débâcle in Dublin, 'a public meeting in the City of London upon a subject at present only under consideration would give an opportunity for all kinds of wild suggestions, and would probably add little to the real progress of the undertaking . . . I have a general distrust of committing to any person the deputed power of *making a speech* bearing, or being supposed to bear, Your Royal Highness' Authority'.[21] However,

Albert's determination to go ahead is clear from the fact that on the same day Phipps sent Cole letters of introduction to the Lord Mayor in order that he might arrange the event. However, even while writing the letters Phipps continued to grumble that:

> I do not however myself consider that anything in the form of a *public* meeting is the best method either of advancing business, or even of obtaining the verdict of public opinion. One bold and troublesome agitator will usually gain the day over a dozen well informed, practical men. *I* should not advise anything in the shape of a public meeting in London; but this is only *my own* opinion. The question of expense, particularly, though really, I believe, of easy arrangement, is one that might be very disadvantageously treated at a public meeting; and there are in the City of London orators who object to every thing, and would sacrifice any undertaking to the pleasure of making a smart speech.[22]

The meeting with the City of London took place on 17 October in the Egyptian Hall of the Mansion House. Even though his connection with the scheme was by now common knowledge, Albert still adhered to Phipps' way of thinking to the extent that he did not personally attend. Nevertheless, present, in addition to many of the most important members of the Society of Arts and the press, were between 300 and 400 of the most influential merchants, financiers, politicians and officials in the capital, including the Governor and Deputy Governor of the Bank of England, the Chairmen of the National Bank of Ireland and the London and County Bank, the Chairman of the Hudson Bay Company Sir John Henry Pelly, the Lord Mayor Elect, the afore-mentioned Joseph Hume MP, as well as many other Members of Parliament.[23]

Though Cole would later recount quaintly how, as this was his first public speech, he sent Dilke's father to the back of the hall to signal to him whether he was loud enough, in fact it was nothing of the sort: Cole and his fellow emissaries had by this point travelled round the country, and worked out what worked best in public speeches. Cole's speech in particular demonstrated the results of this experience.

For one thing, before he gave it and in view of earlier mishaps, Prince Albert impressed upon Cole 'the necessity of clearly stating that everything hitherto said and done, was only to be accepted as provisional'. Cole therefore took care to make it clear that plans were by no means final. Nevertheless, more true to form, Cole knew that royal patronage tended to sell the Exhibition project and as a result he still peppered his speech with references to the success of the latest exhibition of the Society of Arts, and the fact that Queen Victoria had supplied 'the chief specimen'. He further recounted, ignoring all those who had been involved in initiating the project so far, how the success of that exhibition was so great 'that Prince Albert considered himself warranted in endeavouring to mature his plans for the much more extensive and important exhibition which he contemplated'. He stressed the voluntary nature of the project, which he now knew to be essential to its acceptance, but cleverly combined this with patriotism and liberalism by telling those present: 'we all know that in other countries, projects of this kind have been carried out by the governments; but we also know that in other countries, governments are accustomed to do many things which I, for one, believe that the English people do much better for themselves than any government can do for them'. He also, and in a much more forceful way than previously, announced the intention of setting up a Royal Commission, which, as he explained, would prevent the Society of Arts being open to accusations of jobbery. Drawing on all the views heard in the provinces, Cole presented a picture of the Exhibition promoting education, increased international trade, a stronger economic position for Britain in the world economy and so on.[24] All of this was well received.

The meeting was an enormous success for the Exhibition's promoters. The plans of the Society of Arts as presented by Cole were fully endorsed: Hume stood up and proposed 'that the cost of the Exhibition should be provided by voluntary subscriptions, and not by the general taxation of the country and that a Royal Commission is necessary to invest the undertaking with a national sanction, and to give the world the utmost confidence that the prizes will be awarded impartially' – a motion that was heartily welcomed.

After other resolutions of support, the London MP J. Masterman initiated a vote that led to the setting up of a powerful committee in the City to aid the collection of subscriptions; it consisted of the Lord Mayor, Lord Mayor Elect, the Aldermen, the Governor of the Bank of England, the Chairman and Deputy Chairman of the East India Company, notable financiers such as T. Baring, S. Jones Loyd, Barons Goldschmid and Rothschild, as well as many other influential figures. The financial success of the Exhibition seemed more secure than ever, and the network of powerful sympathisers further solidified.

In addition, the national press gave the plans a positive reception, even if it still seemed nervous about such a large venture. It also now took up many of the rhetorical themes in support of the Exhibition heard at the Mansion House. In its leader of the 18 October, *The Times* commented: 'The proposal yesterday submitted, at the suggestion of Prince Albert, to the magnates of the city is one against which nothing but its grandeur can be objected. An exhibition of the industry of all nations speaks for itself, if it can only be accomplished without signal failure or inequality of execution, and if, as has, indeed, been suggested, it is not engulfed by its own magnitude . . . ' Taking the cue from Cole, and like him echoing the contradictions of the vast body of moderate public opinion which it spoke for, *The Times* was able to support the Exhibition's cosmopolitan and educational nature, but largely because it was confident and patriotic enough to believe that British producers could match up to the competition and that the exercise would, in the long run, benefit Britain's economy and standing in the world. It was also able to see important political benefits in allowing foreigners to view British institutions. Cosmopolitanism, as a result, could be made a national cause. It concluded melodramatically: 'Nothing can be so proper to London as an exhibition which shall represent the genius and invite the attendance of all nations. This peaceful metropolis is the asylum of the outcast and unfortunate. All parties find refuge here; the Absolutist here meets his Republican foe, and the Imperialist the rebel to whom he is indebted for his own exile. We have recently opened our ports to the produce and the ships of all nations. What place so appropriate for the mutual aids and intercourse of peace as this free and open metropolis?'[25]

II

The most striking message from the deputations to the provinces and abroad, therefore, was the fact that not only was the Exhibition widely supported – and the City meeting was the icing on the cake as far as this issue was concerned – but also that it had the potential to unite a surprisingly broad cross-section of the public. This unity was inspired by a variety of causes – promoting industrialisation, education, extending markets at home and abroad, raising British standards of production, cosmopolitanism – all of which had begun already to modify and expand the Society of Arts' rather dry didactic plans. It was an alliance that obviously encompassed large numbers of the working classes, merchants, manufacturers, City men, moderate liberals and conservatives, local politicians as well as parts of the aristocracy. It was also characterised by its support for the maintenance of the political *status quo* and moderate liberalisation, and a support for industrialisation and the values which upheld it – profit, ownership and consumption.

This alliance bore remarkable similarities to that which had supported the introduction of free trade – and thus it was no surprise that free trade continued to crop up in discussions connected with the Exhibition, the more so as the Exhibition seemed to underpin the cosmopolitan economic model which lay at its heart. Yet at the same time the alliance went further: by promoting national strength and patriotism, and by defending the principle of property, the Exhibition could reach out to conservatives and aristocrats who had been alienated during the free trade dispute. It could also gain the sympathy of radicals and the working classes by pointing to the improvements in general prosperity that would result from industrial advancement. On the one hand, then, the Exhibition promoters were tempted to identify the event with the free trade cause in order to tap the broad seam of public support for the issue which was left over from 1846. On the other, if the true integrative potential of the Exhibition was to be achieved, and conservatives and aristocrats were to be kept on board, the event's organisers had to be careful to play down the importance of commercial liberalism.

For the moment, just as local politicians obviously recognised the political potential of the Exhibition and came rushing forward to offer their services in its promotion, national politicians also began to recognise the benefits of being involved with such a popular cause and the uses to which it could be put. Albert, as we have seen, had been committed from the beginning to the aesthetic aims of the Exhibition and for some time had looked for ways in which he could boost his own, and the monarchy's, popularity. The revolutionary wind of 1848 had also probably quickened his mind on the subject. As he wrote to his brother, Ernst, in April 1849: 'At present the democratic and social evils are forcing themselves on the people. The unequal division of property, and the dangers of poverty and envy arising there from, is the principal evil. Means must necessarily be found, *not for diminishing riches* (as the communists want), but to make facilities for the poor. But there is the rub'.[26] Not only did he now see popular monarchy as a way forward, he also thought more deeply about ways of reducing working-class radicalism. The Exhibition presented the opportunity for Albert to reach out to that part of the working classes which supported the maintenance of property and the political *status quo*, to advertise such values to those who did not, and, with any luck, also to raise the level of income generally. It was clearly also massively popular. Albert now pushed forward with an application for a Royal Commission and discussions about how this should be structured.

The political establishment – in particular that represented by Peel and the government of Lord John Russell – now proved itself to be much more accommodating.

There were hard political reasons for this: the Liberal government had only come into office because Peel had split the Conservatives over free trade and it was therefore extremely weak in Parliament and dependent on its new-found Peelite allies. Judging by the Society's reports, the Exhibition now presented the hope of associating the government with a vote-winner. The administration would also be seen as doing something widely connected with free trade, thus binding the Liberals and Peelite Conservatives more closely together in Parliament and, with any luck, preventing a protectionist backlash.

At the same time, however, there were deeper, more sociological considerations. The Exhibition obviously had the capacity to gain support from most quarters of British society, bridging the divide that had opened up between the classes. Like Albert, many politicians were deeply concerned, in particular in view of what had happened on the continent, about the polarisation that had come about in British society through Chartism and free trade. For Peel especially, the alienation of the country from its aristocracy had created a dangerous situation. Despite the fact that he hoped to establish the free trade, pro-industry *status quo* in Britain more firmly, Peel also hoped to regenerate some consensus in British political life – and not just for the sake of his own political career. The Exhibition represented a valuable opportunity to extend an olive branch to the landed aristocracy, for it allowed the latter to collaborate in a mainstream political event that upheld the values of art and property, was led by Albert and had patriotic overtones. In order to keep this back door open, however, it was important that the free trade aspects of the Exhibition, while recognised in government and in private, were not spoken of openly. On this point, Peel and Albert were of one mind.

It was not only the political establishment's attentions that were focused by the success of the deputations and City meeting. The Society of Arts also began to extend its plans. From early on, Cole had foreseen links between the various societies in London and the country to create a more efficient, and a more effective, educational organisation, and to give more prominence to the Society and its exhibitions.[27] This had been supported because it resolved what many in the Society viewed as a schism that had opened up between scientific, artistic and industrial societies and bodies. Now that the Exhibition seemed a real possibility, and public support – in particular for the demand for education in industry – had given the Society and its plans more clout, these expansionist schemes could become more ambitious and extend to the national, and even international, level. Once again, what this amounted to was an attempt to unite all those who supported industrialisation but who wished to see it accommodate science and art rather than destroy them. Inherently – because these were issues that linked intellectuals, the bourgeoisie and the aristocracy – this meant strengthening the social and political *status quo*. At a different level to the politicians, therefore, the Society was aiming for the same goal. The fact that so many different groups were simultaneously striving to defend the *status quo* says much about the sense of fear that existed at the mid-century as a result of the onslaught of industrialisation and the threat of social and political revolution.

Thus a whole variety of factors fed into the discussions between Albert, Phipps, Peel, Lord John Russell, Labouchere and the members of the Executive Committee for the Exhibition at the Society of Arts (Russell, Fuller, Cole and Dilke) resulting in the proclamation of a Royal Commission on 3 January 1850. In July 1849, Cole had already set the ball rolling by suggesting to Albert, after discussions at the Society, that the Commission be one of inquiry like the Fine Arts Commission, yet that it also include representatives from sectors of commerce, science and art – on the French model – to create what he termed 'the stamp of nationality'[28] and objectivity. It was perfectly natural to seek a commission of inquiry at this point as the best mode of progressing, even if it seems strange at first sight since the Society of Arts still proposed undertaking concrete work through the profit-orientated services of Messrs Munday. In addition, the Fine Arts Commission's status as a body investigating the best means for improving artwork had been popular with Benthamites and had given it an air of probity that would be essential to the Exhibition. Perhaps more importantly, however, this was a political suggestion by Cole, as the Fine Arts Commission had been Peel's creation. Indeed, many of its members reappeared in Cole's list of nominees. However, for the moment all had had to wait until the deputations to the manufacturers had taken place.

On 24 October 1849, with the support of manufacturers and the City apparently secure, Cole, Russell and Fuller travelled to Windsor for a meeting with Albert and Phipps where the matter was further discussed. Albert now proposed formally underpinning the link with government by having two secretaries to the Commission – one from the government and one from the Society of Arts.[29] More significantly, and possibly after discussion with Peel, he now also proposed extending the Commission to include the Duke of Richmond – one of the most notorious aristocratic opponents of free trade in the House of Lords but one who also headed the Agricultural Society and could therefore be approached in his capacity as representative of one of the country's main sectors of production.[30]

In pursuance of this idea, Albert first tried wielding his own not inconsiderable influence, together with a large dose of flattery, in a letter to the Duke which pointed out the latter's value as a means of finding out the attitudes of the agricultural sector.[31] Having opened up communication, Albert then sent Cole on 7 December to a personal audience with the Duke, during which Cole recorded rather hopefully that the Duke was tempted to join the Commission but would have 'to manage the Agricultural Society'.[32] As Cole recorded in his diary, this possibility caused some excitement among the Exhibition's supporters.[33] However, in the event, Richmond obviously recognised the devious intentions behind all this (he later claimed Cole was 'worse than O'Connor', the Chartist!)[34] and rejected Albert's overtures.[35]

Another important contribution to the discussion came from Henry Labouchere at the Board of Trade, who, in view of the popularity of the Exhibition among manufacturers, wished to extend their presence in the Commission, which, according to Cole's plan, was weighted more towards experts than industry. Albert still worried that support might not be as great as Labouchere seemed to suggest and asked him to do more research on the subject.[36] Cole, meanwhile, fought his corner, pointing out views that insinuated manufacturers did not necessarily know their own interests and warning that 'if manufacturers &c are to be on the Commission – it would I think be well to obtain confidentially some opinions on the names proposed. Trade jealousies are very keen indeed. It must be recollected that the Commission in England represents the Minister of Agriculture and Commerce in France and that the various interests are represented by a sort of election of persons'.[37] In other words, the Commission, according to Cole, might be representative of the country's economic sectors, but only in

Stafford Northcote,
government Secretary to
the Royal Commission and
unofficial auditor.
Northcote's responsibilities
were increasingly taken
over by Edward Bowring
because of family illness.

a way determined by those promoting the Exhibition. There was still, therefore, a strong whiff of Benthamite elitism about Cole's attitude to industrialists.

By the time it was proclaimed, however, the Royal Commission obviously bore the hallmarks of an attempt to integrate the demands of all those with an interest in the Exhibition. In terms of structure, there appeared to be power-sharing: a Commission drawn from political circles and representative of different interests in the country was faced by an Executive Committee drawn from that of the Society of Arts. Prince Albert, President of the Society, was Chairman of the Commission. Moreover, as had been discussed, one Secretary came from government (Stafford Northcote, the personal secretary to the President of the Board of Trade) and the other from the Society (John Scott Russell). This all meant that the state could now be involved in judging and inspecting the Exhibition and could give the project the authority necessary to encourage the participation of foreign competitors without being obliged to support the event financially or be seen to be in control of it. Meanwhile, the Society would be guided by the Commission and thus prevented from any 'jobbery'. It also placed nominal control in the hands of Prince Albert, maintaining the connection with royalty.

In terms of membership, the Royal Commission obviously represented a conglomeration of the demands of its promoters. The Society of Arts' concern to include representatives from science, art and technology in pursuit of its educational objective, to create a body of objective experts, and to forge links with other learned societies was obvious. Representing art were Charles Barry, Sir Charles Eastlake and Sir Richard Westmacott – all leading members of the Royal Academy, and celebrated architect, painter and sculptor respectively. Science and technology, meanwhile, were represented by the President of the Royal Society Lord Rosse (of telescope fame) and successive Presidents of the Geological Society Sir Charles Lyell and William Hopkins, the builder and President of the Institution of Civil Engineers William Cubitt and the engineer Robert Stephenson. In order to extend the Commissions's 'stamp of nationality', there were representatives from the aristocracy and landed wealth (the Duke of Buccleuch and Lord Rosse), from the City (Thomas Baring, Lord Overstone and Alderman William Thompson), from agriculture (Philip Pusey – brother of the Oxford Movement leader) – and, according to Labouchere's wishes, from industry the Manchester cotton producer and Chamber of Commerce leader Thomas Bazley, the Leeds textile manufacturer John Gott, and the London silk industrialist Thomas Field Gibson.

Albert and Peel's efforts to integrate the Commission politically were also accommodated, and it included representatives from all the main political groupings; the

Thomas Bazley, President of the powerful Manchester Chamber of Commerce, and one of the few direct representatives of industry on the Commission.

Richard Cobden, the promoter of free trade and – with John Bright – the leader of the Anti-Corn Law League. Cobden by this point was enjoying the laurels of legislative victory and had broken links with Chartism.

Conservative and protectionist leader in the House of Lords, Lord Stanley, the radical Richard Cobden and, most importantly, Sir Robert Peel and Lord John Russell, of whose membership *The Times* commented 'these are the two pillars of public affairs in England, and of course without them the Commission would fall to the ground'.[38] Ministerial – and in particular Board of Trade – presence was ensured by the membership of William Gladstone (former President of the Board of Trade) and Henry Labouchere; Lord Granville was Vice Chairman of the Commission. Granville, the Vice-President of the Board of Trade, was a particularly important influence; he was an aristocrat with free trade sympathies and strong links to manufacturing through his family estate, and had linguistic skills (which were viewed as being necessary in the future) and sociability.

The Commission represented a combination of the integrative programmes of the Society of Arts on the one hand, and Albert, Peel, and Lord John Russell on the other. Thus, as Haltern has pointed out, it was an attempt 'to create a carefully considered whole out of representatives of different social and political groups, and leading representatives of all those interested in an industrial exhibition'.[39] Nevertheless, though integration was the Commission's main characteristic, it is also important to note two weaknesses in its attempt to build harmony. First, that it did not contain any members directly from the working classes, but was rather a group of aristocrats, experts, politicians and manufacturers. An attempt had obviously been made to reach out to the masses through the inclusion of Richard Cobden, but Cobden was the respectable face of working-class radicalism, and had been willing to support Peel's abolition of the Corn Laws and break ranks with the Chartists. Secondly, although the Commission did attempt to include all political persuasions, and *The Times* praised it for welcoming protectionists, it still showed a heavy bias towards the forces of free trade. Stanley was the only protectionist worthy of note on the Commission, and even he appeared less committed to economic doctrine, and was soon to recant. Both of these factors were to be important in the long term.

And will they spoil our noble ride,
The ladies' joy, the Guardsmen's pride,
Who love to gallop side by side?
For thee, will none an effort make, –
For thee whose life has been at stake,
Since thy fell doom Prince Albert spake?
But if on thee he builds his show,
Defiance in his teeth we'll throw,
And wail our famous Rotten Row.

Anon, 'The Three Complaints', EX.1851.147, NAL

3

'AN ORDEAL OF DOUBT, DISCUSSION AND EVEN OPPOSITION'[1]

The period between the formation of the Royal Commission and the opening of the Great Exhibition on 1 May 1851 was crucial to the success of the project. There were two main reasons for this: first, the public became directly involved in discussions about how the Exhibition should look. Though, as had already been shown, the need to include public desires and interests had been recognised from an early date for a variety of ideological and financial reasons, the willingness on the part of the Exhibition's organisers to do so had remained limited and their own objectives still dominated. After January 1850 this changed. In what was, as Albert recognised, a rather unpleasant eye-opening 'ordeal', the Royal Commission was forced to take on board public demands to a far greater extent and the Great Exhibition became a much more 'publicly owned' affair. The second reason for the importance of this period was that the Exhibition now succeeded in becoming the focus of public interest and debate. This was the result of several factors – the original intention to generate public discussion, several major errors of public relations management, but, perhaps more importantly, the provocative message of the Exhibition that began to emerge in this period.

I

The dialogue of the Royal Commission with the wider public had initially been intended as a limited affair in which the interests of the former would dominate. This was reflected in the draft guidelines from the Executive Committee which, so far, was still dominated by the Society of Arts and its educationalist ideas. It stipulated that 'the whole Kingdom should be thoroughly educated to understand the several objects and scope of the Exhibition, and have their sympathies properly aroused towards it; and that the local committees ought to be the machinery by which this object is to be accomplished'.[2] However, the Royal Commission was soon listening carefully to the wishes of the local committees and making much more use of them than was originally intended, to the point where they became the backbone of its campaign to promote the Exhibition. In order to explain how this situation came about, it is necessary to turn briefly to the two months preceding the formation of the Royal Commission.

Towards the end of November 1849, a newspaper article had appeared in the *Daily News* which mentioned that the Society of Arts had signed a contract (i.e. with the Mundays) to erect a building for the Exhibition. The contract, as we have seen, was necessary at the time as the public refused to allow any government support and someone needed to carry the risk. However, in its dealings with the public, the Society of Arts had omitted to mention this fact and had dwelt on the issue of voluntary subscriptions as the means of financing the Exhibition. Much support had been acquired on this basis – including that of Joseph Hume, the scion of probity in British politics, who had helped set up a finance committee at the City meeting. Hume was now surprised and even horrified to think that a private speculator might be profiting from public charity and in order to correct what he assumed was an error he wrote to the *Daily News* stating that 'I cannot believe that any members of the Society of Arts would take the step you inform the public they have done of incurring so hastily so large an expenditure, or indeed any expenditure, without the careful consideration and previous sanction of the committee appointed at that public meeting'.[3] In order to rectify things, John Scott Russell was sent to Yarmouth to explain to Hume personally the circumstances that had necessitated the contract, to reassure him of the fact that the Society was not involved in 'jobbery' and to show Hume the relevant documents.[4] Hume declared himself completely satisfied that the Society had done nothing wrong.[5]

Albert, however, alerted to the public relations dangers inherent in the contract, asked Drew and the Mundays if they would submit to arbitration to reduce the amount of profit they would make from the Exhibition. Drew, in the face of royal pressure, obliged – though he rightly defended his position with the point that 'in July there was no evidence at all to indicate how far the public would respond to the proposal; and there was no pecuniary guarantee whatever to secure its eventual success, as indeed there is none certain even now . . . If they had viewed this proposal simply as tradesmen, they would probably have declined it.'[6] Albert then also pressurised Cole and the Executive Committee into publishing the contract and the correspondence to demonstrate his own, and the Society's, honest intentions.[7] This took place in several publications, and *The Times*, at least, admitted that when the plan was being drawn up 'instant action was necessary, and under these circumstances it appears to us that the Prince Consort and the Council of the Society of Arts have resolved upon a course to which few, if any, rational objections can be urged. It is certainly a pity that the element of private speculation should be mixed up with a high national object, but, as matters stood, could it be avoided? and, if so, in what manner?'[8]

Despite this piece of crisis management, however, the cat was out of the bag. On 27 December 1849, John Potter, the Mayor of Manchester, wrote to Lord John Russell to warn that the contract's publication had caused great consternation in the north and 'concurring that some of the arrangements are calculated to detract from the *national* character of the undertaking and to lessen its claims on public sympathy and support,' a deputation, including the President of the Chamber of Commerce, Thomas Bazley, wished to speak to him.[9] A day later, Potter wrote once more to reiterate that 'the terms, though since modified . . . appeared to us objectionable as they might be supposed to give to what was announced as, and intended to be, a "Great National Undertaking" the character of an "Interested Speculation" or even a "Private Job"'.[10] Though Labouchere wrote back a few days later that nothing of the sort was intended and tried to calm the Manchester men by pointing to Bazley's inclusion on the Royal Commission, Potter would not be put off.[11]

The press was beginning to point the finger at the Society of Arts' contract. On 29 December, the *Patent Journal* carried the headline 'The Exhibition of 1851; Is it to be made a "Job"?' It said:

> There is a trite, but true adage, that oftentimes 'PROVIDENCE provides the meat, while the devil sends the cooks', and the metaphor may, we think, be applied with great propriety to the recent proceedings in connection with the proposed industrial exhibition of 1851. A more noble purpose – a more befitting occupation for the nation to engage in, could not, we may venture to say have been proposed . . . How important it was, then, that all the preliminary proceedings for carrying out this national purpose should be worthy of the object, and befitting the nation; – that every act should be in unison with, and proper to the purpose in view. It is with regret, that we are compelled to say that the reverse has been the case, – and that we are obliged to give our unqualified disapproval of the proceedings lately taken in the matter

Noting the City meeting speeches in October, which had stressed the voluntary nature of the project, and comparing them to the contract in *The Times*, the article continued:

> Does this look like a *public* subscription? – Is this the manner in which a '*national*' object should be met by a wealthy nation? . . . We do not hear that all other means had been tried, and had failed. We are not told that the City men would not subscribe! We have yet to learn that some thousands of pounds would not have been subscribed in Manchester; but on the contrary, on the 17th of October, one of the parties to the deeds tells an influential meeting that there was no question of their being able to raise the funds by public subscription. Yet in November this deed is sealed, before an effort had been made so to obtain the money in a proper manner; and that which should have formed a source of profit to the Society of Arts is converted into a money making transaction for the befit of two enterprising traders . . . A Munday Exhibition it will be – MUNDAY prizes, and MUNDAY profits.

The article then went on to pronounce that as 'a clique' at the Society had advertised the project as a voluntary one, 'it is but justice that they should bear the odium of this transaction'. In what was basically a Victorian example of 'naming and shaming', Cole, Fuller, Stephenson, Dilke and Drew were accused of promoting their business interests through the Society of Arts:

> Mustering in strong numbers in the 'Council' of the Society, they have adopted the policy of 'clanship', and hang together like Scotchmen in India, or the English at

Boulogne. They ride rampant at the Society of Arts. The Council in its constitution is formed on the model of a select vestry, and the councillors, who elect one another, never take the advice of the members of the Society . . . in fact, there is a partnership deed between the above gentlemen and the Society of Arts whereby the name of the Society is used whenever, and for whatever they please.[12]

The issue of 'jobbery' was now threatening the whole project. Demonstrating the level of this threat, and using once more the royal card to gain support for the Exhibition, Labouchere now arranged for the Manchester deputation to be met by Albert at the House of Lords. This, he thought, 'would have a most excellent effect, and would probably ensure the cordial cooperation of the town, which appears to have taken alarm at some of the proceedings of the Society of Arts'.[13] Meanwhile, Stafford Northcote, governmental secretary to the Commission, drew up a memorandum detailing action the Commission should take at its first scheduled meeting on 11 January. He proposed immediately setting up a committee to renegotiate entirely the Munday contract. This, he thought, 'will satisfy the deputation, as they seem to have confidence in *the Commission*, but to be apprehensive lest the acts of *the Executive Committee* should have fettered the free action of the Commissioners, which is not the case'. In other words, it would help distance the project from the Society and its executive committee as they were now tainted by the 'jobbery' brush.

However, Northcote's suggestion also threw the project more entirely upon public charity. On this point he pointed out that 'the Exhibition being wholly self-supporting, its success must depend on the universality of the interest felt in it, and this again will depend upon the share which every person must feel that he has in its management. Hence the importance of having as many local commissions as possible, and these the offspring of the choice of each locality . . . Nearly the same remarks, *mutatis mutandis*, may be made on the establishment of relations between the Commission and foreign countries and the Colonies'.[14]

At the first meeting of the Royal Commission at Westminster Palace, Sir Robert Peel and Lord Overstone pushed through the decision not to renegotiate the contract but to ask the Treasury to cancel it entirely (an option available due to Cole's prescience),[15] pay off the Mundays with compensation and organise a guarantee fund as a fail-safe if the Commission should be unable to pay back the government. Labouchere – the Board of Trade's representative on the Commission and, as such, a type of auditor – remarked on the whole issue that 'it is good example of how public misunderstanding can arise. We must now consider as soon as possible what is to be done about subscriptions.' He continued: 'I am inclined to think that nothing had better be said to the public about a guarantee fund, which might only perplex them.'[16]

The issue of the cancellation of the Munday contract has been overlooked in most histories of the Great Exhibition and yet it is crucial in understanding how and why the whole project opened out to involve the public. One major consequence of the whole affair was that the Royal Commission and the state now began to establish themselves as the controlling forces in the Exhibition project; they started to disentangle themselves from the Society of Arts and its rather élitist educational views. Partly this was the result of the Society being connected in the public mind with 'jobbery'. This connection was now magnified by the rather unseemly tussle at the Society, where many members resented the aspersions being cast on the Munday contract and, understandably, realised with horror that the profits it had promised might now be lost. Prince Albert, as President of the Society *and* Chair of the Royal Commission, was in an embarrassing position. At first still defensive of the contract, he amended the cancellation notice with the explanation that he did not believe 'the words as they stood did sufficient justice either to the motives which had actuated the Society of Arts in framing the contract, or the liberal spirit which the Messrs Munday evinced in agreeing to it'.[17] By March 1850, the triangular arbitration process between the Society, the Commission and Mundays had taken its toll on Albert's patience. While remaining adamant that the Society had done no wrong, he had become cooler towards it and observed that he would 'not anticipate that the Council of the Society will allow any personal feelings on their part to interpose needless difficulties in the way of this settlement being speedily and satisfactorily determined'.[18] In the event, the Mundays were repaid by the Treasury in July 1850 but the arbitration over compensation, led by Stephenson, dragged on acrimoniously,[19] rubbing salt into the wound until July 1851 when £5,170 plus costs was awarded.[20]

Such psychological separation from the Society was, however, also underpinned formally. The Treasury's willingness to step in and buy out the Mundays was bought at a price: a Finance Committee was set up to look at the whole question of funding, which removed control of the financial dealings of the Commission from the Society and the Mundays. Two Treasury officials were appointed to 'assist' the secretaries – an addition which boosted the Commission's auditing capacity and helped the government keep a tab on expenses. More importantly, the subcommittee of the Finance Committee, which had been set up to look at the cancellation of the contract, recommended – supported strongly by Peel – that the Commission 'appoint some government officer, perhaps from the commissariat or audit departments', to oversee the work of the Executive Committee.[21] The inference was clear: the Executive Committee, which was still the old one formed by the Society of Arts, had got the Commission into too much hot water. It needed to be controlled. As Northcote told Albert's secretary, the Executive Committee 'will require a strong hand over them, or they may bring His Royal Highness and the Commission into serious embarrassment. It may be very unjust, but His Royal Highness ought to be informed of the fact that there is great distrust of some of the Executive Committee; and the scheme is one which can only succeed if there be full confidence in those who are working it. When one thinks what an opening there is for jobbing, it is quite clear that the responsible managers should be like Caesar's wife'.[22]

The man chosen to control matters was Colonel William Reid, one of the least known figures involved in the Exhibition and yet a man who was actually crucial to its success in a practical, unobtrusive fashion. Reid was a unique combination of military commander, enlightened and effective civil servant, scientist and academic. He had served heroically in the Napoleonic Wars, been Governor of the Bermudas and West Indies, had a reputation as a surveyor and author of treatises on meteorology. He was also a vice president of the Royal Society. He came highly recommended by both Labouchere and Peel,[23] and seemed to fit the role of the 'strong hand'. Reid's appointment represented a sharp demotion for the Executive Committee which included the main promoters of the Exhibition, and was a blow in particular to Cole, who had been so instrumental in forming the plans. It also could be seen

THE INDUSTRIOUS BOY.

"Please to Remember the Exposition."

Punch's view of the financial problems faced by the Royal Commission and the role of Albert in fund-raising. (*Punch*, Volume XVIII, 1850)

as a personal affront to its chairman, Stephenson – a fact that was exploited by Cole in order to persuade him to join the others in a joint resignation.

However, the existing administration of the Royal Commission made continuity of staff essential and in particular required the continued presence of Cole, who, despite his ambition, was seriously committed to the project. Northcote worked hard on Albert to persuade him to keep them on.[24] Stephenson was calmed with an offer of a place on the Royal Commission. Cole decided to withdraw his resignation after a heavy dose of flattery and once it became clear he was still needed; he was also possibly persuaded because the Finance Committee offered him a paid position at £800 per annum.[25] As Northcote explained regarding Cole, 'I have had a great deal of conversation with him, and think he is not so much annoyed at the appointment of Col Reid, as at the retention of the Executive Committee in a shape which gives him no other position than that of Mr Fuller and Mr Drew who nevertheless do not intend to, and cannot render the services that he can and will'.[26]

The cancellation of the Munday contract helped reduce the élitism of the Great Exhibition in another way: it threw the whole project upon the charity of the people and made the outcome dependent on their commitment. As Albert – who was evidently somewhat piqued by the press campaign against what had, at first, seemed like a good plan – announced, it was now 'absolutely necessary that the public should clearly understand, when the contract has been abandoned in deference to their supposed wishes, and a certainty thus exchanged for the chance of what a general subscription may produce, that the success or failure of the proposed exhibition now rests with them, and must depend entirely on the manner in which they come forward with their contributions'.[27]

The Royal Commission, it was decided at the first meeting, would set about constructing as extensive a network of local committees as possible, building upon the contacts already made through the deputations of 1849 and upon the groups already formed. This network had now become a financial imperative and the Commission was perturbed by initial reports from the Executive Committee at the end of January 1850 that of 350 invitations to set up local committees, only 4 had been taken up; 25 had been declined and the rest had gone unanswered. The reasons, the report maintained, were partly to do with the fact that invariably the approach 'will be viewed as an obvious solicitation for subscriptions only' and the views of manufacturers being ignored, and partly to do with the enormous amount of ignorance about the Exhibition's aims. 'Indeed,' the report concluded, 'the Executive Committee think it necessary to say, that their confidence in their ability to form local committees is diminished'.[28]

One response to this was the decision that deputations should be sent out, directed by a newly formed Subscriptions Committee, to educate and explain the Royal Commission's plans and set up local committees. Another was the formation of a Correspondence Committee, consisting of Cole and Dilke, which would answer incoming letters from the localities and 'arrange for bringing all important points of principle before the Commission in the most convenient shape for their decision'.[29] This allotted the two men a policy-making role directly influenced by the public. Thus, the sudden need to gather subscriptions had forced the Royal Commission to set up a dual structure for finding ways of promoting support and listening to public demands.

During the following months, approximately ten Subscription Committee deputies travelled extensively around the country and had already visited some 200 towns by the end of March.[30] Initially, the primary aim was to increase the flow of subscriptions to the Royal Commission. However, one of the deputies to the north reported:

I should not be doing my duty if I omitted to convey to you my belief, founded on what I have seen and heard, that the work of organising these towns is only now *begun*. Even where committees are formed, they will *do* nothing of themselves. You or your representatives must supply all the motive power; the secretaries will all wait for instructions, and will then carry them out very imperfectly, unless under the eye of one charged to guide and control them. I endeavoured not to find the necessity for me to initiate anything, but practically I found I had to do all the work, write the resolutions, suggest the members of committee in many cases, and get up the whole steam. Every town that I have been at, will need to be visited again, except Blackburn and perhaps Hull. The history of the Blackburn agitation is suggestive. At my first visit I met six or seven cold and indifferent persons; not one of them disposed to move a muscle in the matter. I talked with them, interested them; they asked me to come again. I promised, and the second time met some sixty of the magistrates of the district. So good a feeling was produced as to cause them to wish to hold a great meeting in the Theatre. This was done last Thursday with the best results, as the subscription list, I confidently expect, will prove. The Theatre was crowded to excess, and very great interest was excited . . .

The people are ignorant and apathetic in the matter to a degree difficult of realization. They must be informed, interested, excited, before any good can be done with them; this is up-hill work, and ought to be done with zeal. The first and greatest difficulty is to get any one *to listen to you*, that done, however, half the battle is won.

Thus, the need for subscriptions necessarily led to a campaign to win over the minds of the wider public on an informal, educational level. The Subscription Committee began to bombard the country with circular letters – by mid-February 1850, 17,000 had been sent out, advertisements were placed in relevant publications and newspapers, fancy receipts were designed as rewards for subscribers, important looking books for promising subscriptions were circulated. Central to this campaign were local dignitaries and people of influence in each place, a network that had been explored already by the deputations in 1849.

Local meetings were held, led by the town dignitaries, at which familiar rhetorical themes were exploited – the Prince's role at the head of the project, social harmony between the aristocracy and the working classes, patriotism and the superiority of Victorian culture, cosmopolitanism, the social and philanthropic benefits of education, etc. In this regard, the Subscription Committee led the way by organising another Westminster meeting at Willis' Rooms ostensibly 'to take into consideration the best means of furthering the objects proposed', but in reality to set up a committee for Westminster, raise more money from the City and set the tone for the hundreds of similar, lesser meetings round the country.

The speeches at the Willis' Rooms meeting on 21 February 1850 provide an insight into the way the Exhibition promoters linked the Exhibition to significant mid-Victorian public preoccupations, and many of the themes used there recurred and grew in the Exhibition movement. The reformist Liberal, Lord Carlisle, began by stressing the long tradition of festivals that lay behind the Exhibition and originated in ancient Greece. In those days, Carlisle pointed out, such festivals were based on feats of physical strength. The Exhibition, however, was to celebrate industry. He continued:

. . . it seems but natural and but becoming that in this period of the world at which we have arrived, industry, skill, enterprise, should have in their turn their own ovation, their own triumph, their own high holiday [applause], when the workmen and the workwomen of the world may enjoy a day's pause from their engrossing toils for the purpose of seeing what their fellow-workmen are doing, and can do all the world over [loud applause] – when they may see, no barbarian rites, but useful inventions – not exhibitions of physical prowess in the prize-ring or the foot race, but to witness results which interest the mind and elevate the soul [applause] – not suppliant provinces and chained captives, but the pursuits of peace and civilisation – not in the crowded saloon or the heated theatre, but in an arena where all ranks may mingle, where all may learn, and all may profit by what they see [loud applause].

Education and free trade were both, he implied, supported by the Exhibition: 'I believe,' he said:

that in this world consummate excellence is only to be obtained – save in those rare developments which form the exception and not the rule – by strenuous effort, by the light of free competition, and by the force of that reaction which follows on each occasion of disappointment [applause]. But in order to secure that universal interest which we hope to be inspired, and those benefits which we hope to be derived from this undertaking, it is obviously necessary that the accommodation provided, both in its dimension and its conveniences, should be on an adequate scale; and in order to make the undertaking worthy of the accomplished Prince who made the suggestion – worthy of the eminent personages to whom its development had been confided – it is essential it should be met by a corresponding amount of public support and liberality [applause].

Carlisle's speech was notable for introducing Pope's 'Windsor Forest' in connection with the Exhibition. This poem, repeated time and again at meetings round the country, expressed the cosmopolitanism of the Exhibition, but also gave it a sense of the historic, even the millennial. As Carlisle put it:

I feel I cannot better sum up all that may be said in this behalf than in words written, nearly a century and a half ago, by a poet who always expressed himself with more point and completeness than any other man – I refer to Alexander Pope. He says –

> 'For me the balm shall bleed, and amber flow,
> The coral redden, and the ruby glow,
> The Pearly shell its lucid globe unfold,
> And Phoebus warm the ripening ore to gold.
> The time shall come' –

Listen, ladies and gentlemen, and see if Pope was not almost as good a prophet as he was a poet –

> 'The time shall come when, free as seas or wind,
> Unbounded Thames shall flow for all mankind,
> Whole nations enter with each swelling tide,

And seas but join the regions they divide;
Earth's distant ends our glory shall behold,
And the new world launch forth to seek the old' [loud applause]

Carlisle's clarion call was followed, significantly, by a speech from Charles Blomfield, the Bishop of London, who explained his adherence to the project by pointing out the Exhibition's benefits in terms of peace and Christianity; 'for what could be better calculated to propagate the Church of Christ, and to diffuse Christian principles – what could be better calculated to lead men to regard themselves as friends and brothers than their being engaged in a common pursuit, and their being bound to assist and encourage one another in those pursuits?' Increasing interdependency among nations was – according to the Bishop – 'Heaven inspired and Heaven directed', and as if to prove the Exhibition's divine credentials, speeches were given by the Ambassadors of France, Prussia, Belgium and the United States.

One of the most influential speeches at the event was given by Samuel Wilberforce, the Bishop of Oxford. Published later under the title *On the Dignity of Labour* the Bishop's speech repeated the same argument on the heavenly nature of progress as that of his London colleague. Wilberforce also now introduced a new theme – the idea that the laws of nature and laws of art were the doing of God. The Exhibition, by improving man's grasp of these, was helping the Christian cause: 'I think it, therefore, my part,' he explained, 'holding the place which I do hold in the Christian Church, to come forward, not with any secret misgivings – not with any cold ungenial doubts or hesitations, but to come forward heartily, and I may say, rejoicingly; not in spite of my Christianity, but because of my Christianity, to aid in the development of science and the mechanical arts'. The most important part of the Bishop's speech, however, was about the theme of work. Here he had tuned in to a subject associated with the Exhibition which, if approached from the right angle, could unite manufacturers, Christians, philanthropists, and also reach out to the working classes:

What can be nobler than industry and work? It is surely better to work than to talk [applause]. It is better to lie down at night and feel that we have worked something, if it were but the least article – the smallest button on any part of our dress – it is better to feel that we have worked that, than to lie down at night with the consciousness that we have done nothing [applause]. So this Exhibition, as promoting the industry of nations, is a great and a noble work. It calls attention to the dignity of labour – it raises incalculably the dignity of the working classes – it makes other people feel the dignity which attaches to the producers of these things. In more than one way, the same happy result will follow . . .

In a theory of labour relations that would be increasingly used in support of the Exhibition he continued:

No man can shut his eyes to the fact that the long and lasting struggle which has existed, and which must still continue to exist, between skill and capital – that never-to-be-thoroughly-adjusted struggle, as I think it – every one must see that there are certain features in the present position of that struggle not of the most pleasant aspect [hear, hear]. Now, nothing can tend more to soften the necessary asperities of that struggle, to introduce the amenities and the courtesies of life into the hardness of the strife, than such an exposition as that which is now proposed.[31]

While the Subscription Committee's deputies whipped up support round the country, forming an Exhibition 'movement', the Correspondence Committee worked at bringing the local committees' queries and grievances to the attention of the Royal Commission in order to prevent public alienation. Though begun as a means of getting subscriptions, the devolution of administration to the local committees soon became a point of principle, especially once the sheer volume of queries Cole and Dilke were meant to deal with became apparent. In what was a shining example of making a virtue out of necessity, the local committees were informed by the Correspondence Committee that 'abroad such exhibitions are supported wholly by the governments, and by them managed in all the details. In the present case the Exhibition is to be established, not by the government, but by the country voluntarily coming forward with its aid.' As a consequence, the local committees were not only being asked for money, but also being consulted on a range of crucial issues, such as who was to select the exhibits, whether they should be limited and who by, etc.[32]

In immediate, practical terms, this consultation exercise highlighted several important public worries. It succeeded in finally changing the Royal Commission's intentions regarding giving out money prizes: several influential figures – the famous engineer Isambard Kingdom Brunel on the Royal Commission's Machinery Committee and some leaders of the powerful Westminster local committee[33] – thought money prizes would be unworkable and unhealthy and the committees for the four sections ultimately agreed. The consultation exercise also allowed the Royal Commission, by means of a declaration, to counter the rumour that sales would be allowed and the fear that the Exhibition would become a grand 'bazaar'.[34]

The principle of consultation was then extended to the issue of the size of the building and the selection of goods: local committees were asked to indicate which goods they would like to send to the Exhibition and, on the basis of this indication, an estimate of the building's size was made. After the size of the Exhibition was fixed, each local committee would be then allotted a certain amount of space and, in conjunction with the Royal Commission, select the actual specimens sent. Thus, out of the need for the Royal Commission to go cap in hand to the local committees arose the principle of self-administration. This turned out to have the benefit of allowing the Royal Commission, through national newspapers, to 'name and shame' local committees that appeared to be backward in organising themselves. It also allowed the Royal Commission to funnel regional rivalries – which were still remarkably strong – into the Exhibition. More importantly, devolution of administration ultimately secured the involvement of the public in the Exhibition project: many people would go to the Exhibition just to see how 'their' committee had turned out.

II

The Royal Commission had, in the meantime, continued its task of organising the event. Its discussions now reflected a compromise between the Society of Arts' plans and experience, governmental members' views, and the input of the public via the Correspondence Committee. To begin with, four committees were set up to look into the question of sub-divisions for each of the four sections – raw materials, machinery, manufactured produce and fine arts. This prioritisation, as has already been pointed out, reflected the Society of Arts' educational plans by placing art uppermost. It was also decided that the fine arts section was to include 'sculpture, but not oil or water-colour paintings generally nor portrait busts'[35] – as the Exhibition was to promote the use of art by industrialists and new techniques by artists rather than aesthetic understanding. Also reflecting the Society of Arts' desire to cooperate with other bodies, the committees were made up of members of the Royal Commission plus other recognised experts – most notably Lyon Playfair, already known to Peel through his reports on Ireland and established at the Royal College of Chemistry and the College of Mines, and I.K. Brunel. At a meeting at Buckingham Palace on 13 February, chaired by Albert and with Russell, Cole, and Dilke present, the chairmen of the committees and subcommittees drew up an outline of which goods would be displayed in the four great classes.[36] In order to explain this list to the local committees, and help them fulfil its requirements, Playfair, who enjoyed the backing of Peel and was recommended by him to Albert, was appointed a paid position as Special Commissioner to the provinces.[37]

In late January 1850, a Building Committee was formed to look into the question of housing the Exhibition. Its membership again reflected the Society of Arts' agenda – marrying architecture with engineering, two ways of designing buildings which had become differentiated from each other in consequence largely of the Industrial Revolution. It consisted of the Duke of Buccleuch, the Earl of Ellesmere, Charles Barry, William Cubitt, Robert Stephenson, Charles Cockerill, I.K. Brunel, T.L. Donaldson, and John Scott Russell as Secretary.[38]

After considering the relative merits of the Crown properties in the north-eastern part of Hyde Park (near Marble Arch), the north-western corner of Regent's Park and the southern part of Hyde Park on Kensington Gore, the Building Committee plumped for the latter. The only problem with this site appeared initially to be the trees – a small clump opposite the Prince of Wales Gate, as well as other, more substantial ones. Lord Carlisle, the Commissioner of Woods, the government officer in charge of Crown lands, would allow the clump and others to be removed. One mature tree however, would have to stay, and any plans for the building would have to accommodate it.[39]

The Committee, following the past example of the Houses of Parliament and preempting any accusation of 'jobbery', proposed holding an international design competition.[40] There were to be no monetary rewards. Rather, the competition would 'rely upon the desire which men of all countries will feel to forward the objects of the proposed Exhibition'. The specifications, entrants were told, were 'to be strictly observed'. The building was to be one storey high, approximately 700,000 square feet in size and light was to come from the roof. However, it was also specified that the trees should be preserved, the building should be built of fire-proof materials and certain general principles were added: '1. Simplicity of arrangement. 2. Economy of space. 3. Capability of extending or curtailing the building, without destroying its symmetry as a whole, or interfering with the general arrangement, – it being impossible to determine the exact extent of roof required until a late period of construction. 4. Adaptation for the erection of separate portions of the building at different periods.'[41] These principles revealed that the Royal Commission was only intending a temporary building. They also expressed the new reality that the extent of the Exhibition was to be determined by public support. Not included in the instructions to contestants, however, but mentioned in the Building Committee's report to the Royal Commission, was the suggestion that 'the Committee think it probable that, when the plans are received, they may not be limited to the selection of any one plan, but may derive useful ideas from many; and that the best plan may be determined upon by the help of this general assistance'.[42]

The Royal Commission also strengthened its network of supporters, both at home and abroad. Abroad, it had put out feelers – once again via the consular service, demonstrating the quasi-official nature of the project – to similarly minded societies and people who would be willing to organise exhibits and be involved in the project.[43] In France, the leader of exhibitions there, Charles Dupin, reconvened the 1849 juries in order to select French produce, creating some continuity between the Great Exhibition and its continental forebears.

At home, meanwhile, more contacts were being made with societies in order to get their support: a particular boost to the Exhibition project was the agreement of the Royal Agricultural Society to cancel its own plans for an exhibition in Hyde Park in 1851, and instead allow that part which concerned implements to be subsumed into the Royal Commission's plans, and the part concerning animals to be held elsewhere.[44] This

The Mansion House Meeting, an exercise in pageantry and symbolism.

not only guaranteed visitors but also held the possibility of persuading rather suspicious agricultural interests over to the Exhibition's cause.

On 21 March 1850 the Commission recognised the importance of the network of local dignitaries to the success of the project in the provinces by holding the first of several banquets in connection with the Exhibition. Here, some 140 mayors were the guests of the Lord Mayor – other distinguished guests at this first dinner included Albert and the representatives of many foreign states.

Like the local meetings, the Mansion House dinner demonstrated that an Exhibition 'movement' was beginning to emerge, bound together by a rhetoric, or what has been called an 'Exhibition ideology'.[45] This could be seen in the special decorations put up: the Egyptian Hall was decked out in shields and coats of arms, as well as implements of industry, from around Britain and the world. These symbolised geographic but also social unity. Above Albert's table, at the eastern end, a window was 'filled in with two colossal figures, representing Peace and Plenty encircling an immense globe of the world with a wreath of laurel; and beneath this group was a large picture representing the Port of London, with ships arrived from every quarter of the earth, disembarking the produce of the several countries'. On the western side, meanwhile, facing those at the top table, was:

a colossal allegorical figure of Britannia, holding in her hand a ground-plan of a building for the approaching grand exhibition. Four angels surrounded Britannia, and trumpeted forth to the various parts of the world that she was willing to receive the works of art and manufacture of all nations, and to reward the most meritorious. Beneath these figures was a large picture of an elevation of a portion of a proposed building, with one of its grand porticoes. On the outer walls were subjects painted in fresco or encaustic; and surmounting the whole was seen an immense dome or sphere, (emblematical of the universality of the exhibition,) surrounded by groups of statues.

The speeches, too, called on familiar themes: John Bird Sumner, the Archbishop of Canterbury told the audience that 'while we are ministers of religion we are at the same time citizens, and we do not cease to be patriots [cheers]; and as citizens and as patriots we take a lively interest in whatever tends to promote the national prosperity . . . I rejoice in this the more because it will tend to carry into effect one of the most glorious characteristics of our holy religion – Good will among men [loud cheers].'

Peel, after rising to thank Lord Palmerston for his speech, stressed the political unity between Conservatives and Liberals which lay at the heart of the Exhibition project. Then, combining a sense of national superiority with cosmopolitanism, theology and pacifism, he told the audience that 'we propose to gratify the people by other agencies more in harmony with our civilization and our Christianity – to teach them gratitude to the Almighty Creator, by exhibiting the wonderful contrivances of nature for the happiness of man, and to draw closer the bonds of amity and general intercourse by the honest rivalry of industry and skill'. The French Ambassador, Monsieur Drouyn de Lluys, on behalf of the foreign contingent, flattered British pride and reinforced the moderate liberal connections of the project by pronouncing the Exhibition 'the House of Commons of English industry'.[46]

It was Albert's speech, however, which was most significant, for although it borrowed on the same familiar themes in support of the Exhibition, it now fused them into a whole, locked on to a sense of disorientation and wonderment widely held by the public in the face of industrialisation, and gave the affair far greater historical and philosophical importance. Albert began by noting the enormous changes that were taking place in everyday life, the new cosmopolitan, or 'modern' system which was emerging, and the benefits this system brought to man's knowledge of the world around him:

... Nobody ... who has paid any attention to the peculiar features of our present era, will doubt for a moment that we are living at a period of most wonderful transition, which tends rapidly to accomplish that great end, to which, indeed, all history points – the realization of the unity of mankind. Not a unity which breaks down the limits and levels the peculiar characteristics of the different nations of the earth, but rather a unity, the result and produce of those very national varieties and antagonistic qualities.

The distances which separated the different nations and parts of the globe are rapidly vanishing before the achievements of modern invention, and we can traverse them with incredible ease; the languages of all nations are known, and their acquirement placed within the reach of everybody; thought is communicated with the rapidity, and even by the power, of lightning. On the other hand, the great principle of division of labour, which may be called the moving power of civilisation, is being extended to all branches of science, industry, and art.

Identifying himself as a 'moderniser', yet harmonising modernisation with Christianity, Albert pointed out that industry, and the education it brought, should be supported, as it empowered and enriched a wider number of people, and brought man closer to knowing God's laws:

While formerly the greatest mental energies strove at universal knowledge, and that knowledge was confined to the few, now they are directed on specialities, and in these, again, even to the minutest points; but the knowledge acquired becomes at once the property of the community at large; for, while formerly discovery was wrapped in secrecy, the publicity of the present day causes that no sooner is a discovery or invention made than it is already improved upon and surpassed by competing efforts. The products of all quarters of the globe are placed at our disposal, and we have only to choose which is the best and the cheapest for our purposes, and the powers of production are intrusted [sic] to the stimulus of competition and capital.

So man is approaching a more complete fulfilment of that great and sacred mission which he has to perform in this world. His reason being created after the image of God, he has to use it to discover the laws by which the Almighty governs His creation, and, by making these laws his standard of action, to conquer nature to his use; himself a divine instrument.

The Exhibition, by revealing more about the laws of God, would have religious significance, and could be supported by Christians everywhere.

Yet it was the final theme in Albert's speech which would perhaps be the most important. The Exhibition, Albert argued, by involving experts and striving for universality, would become in itself a scientific experiment, and reveal man's progress in relation to what he believed were God's unchanging laws:

> Science discovers these laws of power, motion, and transformation; industry applies them to the raw matter, which the earth yields us in abundance, but which becomes valuable only by knowledge Art teaches us the immutable laws of beauty and symmetry, and gives to our productions forms in accordance to them.
>
>   Gentlemen – the Exhibition of 1851 is to give us a true test and a living picture of the point of development at which the whole of mankind has arrived in this great task, and a new starting-point from which all nations will be able to direct their further exertions.[47]

Albert's speech, like many others, tied together cosmopolitanism, pacificism, industry, commerce, education, moderate liberalism and Christianity into one cause. It had an enormous effect – with countless letters to Albert afterwards swearing allegiance to the Exhibition. However, perhaps the unique feature of the speech was that it made the Exhibition into a gigantic experiment, one with Christian, but also millennial, overtones. This was a theme that would attract an enormous range of Victorian movements to the Exhibition.

It looked like a work of genius on Albert's part; the speech was published many times over and won praise in many quarters. However, the idea of the Exhibition as an 'experiment' actually owed much to the ongoing discussions about classification, and the attempts to make sense of the variety of categories to be displayed. As in France, the aim to make the Exhibition universal seemed to lead towards a museum-like solution and to an attempt to classify the whole world according to one principle. It was also, however, the logical outcome of Albert's connections with the Benthamite statistical movement made popular and necessary by industrialisation. Albert was personally involved in this through his connections with William Whewell at Cambridge, and his old tutor, the famous Belgian statistician Adolphe Quetelet.[48] He had consulted the latter regarding the Exhibition's system of classification in January.[49] From now on, the attempt to make the Exhibition into an 'experiment', a stock-taking exercise of man's progress, would influence many aspects of its organisation and reception.

The problem was, however, that the Royal Commission and the organisation set up in support of the Exhibition were to determine the methodology and define the objectivity of this experiment. This decision-making process did not include, however, that section of the working classes which rejected bourgeois values and demanded a greater economic and political slice of the cake. The Royal Commission and its committees were dominated by aristocrats, intellectuals, and businessmen. Local committees were under the suzerainty of mayors and usually made up of manufacturers and merchants. Moreover, any attempts to gain more say for the working classes, to allow their plight to be explored on its own grounds, to democratise proceedings, were quashed: the desire to avoid any autonomous working-class representation probably lay behind the Royal Commission's rejection of any proposal to set up a unitary committee of selection for London that might undermine its own position.[50] It was certainly reflected in the refusal of the Royal Commission to exhibit artefacts meant 'to ameliorate the condition of the working classes, and to raise an independent subscription for that purpose'.[51]

The most glaring example of the Royal Commission's failure to bridge successfully the gap between itself and radical working-class demands was the dissolution of the Bishop of Oxford's Central Working Classes Committee. From the start this body had caused much worry among several important members of the Royal Commission – including Peel, who opposed its existence. It was only allowed because it was hoped the committee would successfully attract subscriptions. For safety's sake, it had been stuffed with MPs, clerics, publicists, literary figures like Dickens and Thackeray, who had a sentimental, rather than a political attachment to the working classes, and Cobden. These were people who were popular and influential with the working classes but hardly social revolutionaries. With luck, they would dilute the presence of the two unpalatable Chartist radicals, William Lovett and Henry Vincent.

The Commission had also only allowed it to be an affiliated body rather than directly part of the Exhibition structure. The members of the committee obviously felt they were putting their heads on the block for the Royal Commission, without gaining any solid rewards for the working classes – and at the first meeting they demanded their organisation be given equal status to other committees. This, however, would have alienated the Conservatives and aristocrats in the Commission, in particular Lord Stanley,[52] who, according to Cole 'would have bolted' had this been accepted.[53] As a consequence – perhaps with relief on both sides, though also with some disappointment among those such as Albert who had hoped to tie the working classes into the Exhibition project – the committee was disbanded. From this moment the Exhibition lost any hope of being in tune with radical working-class demands. The Royal Commission now decided what was good for the working classes and the educational, bourgeois approach dictated its decisions.

The Commission also struggled to win over the protectionists, a group that included landed aristocrats, farmers, many small-scale producers and artisans, and staunch Conservatives. This latent body of political opposition already made itself obvious in Lord Brougham's rather surprising attacks on the Royal Commission in the House of Lords on 19 and 23 March 1850. At the Willis' Rooms meeting a month previously, Brougham had spoken in support of the Exhibition. However, even then – rather like the evil witch at the Christening – he warned strongly of the dangers to British manufacturers of competing against foreigners in an Exhibition devoted only to luxury rather than virtues of home produce such as 'the texture of the fabric . . . the wearable and durable nature'.[54] Rankled, perhaps, that he had not been invited back to speak at the Mansion House meeting and sensing that real protectionists (as opposed to Stanley) were being muzzled, Brougham now demanded that the proceedings of the Royal Commission be laid before Parliament, and launched what seemed at first like a rather improbable attack on Hyde Park as the site for the building. Attacked by Granville for his inconsistency, Brougham replied that:

> He still believed that the Exhibition would do great good. The manufacturers would gain by the exhibition of foreign ingenuity, which would enable them to strike out new lights, and add fresh improvements to their former inventions. Their gain, however, would only be gain in the long run; presently their profits would be

diminished, as prices would be reduced, but ultimately they might be benefited by the result . . . It was invidious in men of their lordships' rank in life to subscribe towards that which would be immediately beneficial to themselves, and which must for a time be prejudicial to all manufacturers and shopkeepers.

In the first exchange, Brougham had the wind taken out of his sails with a declaration by Lord Carlisle – importantly, as events would show – that the building would only be temporary. In the second, Lord Stanley's witty and derisory riposte served as adequate defence.[55] Brougham's attack had been rather unsure: he, after all, was less zealous in the protectionist cause than many others and possibly motivated by a sense of being slighted. Still, it served as a shot across the bows. Granville certainly recognised it as an attempt 'to enlist the prejudices of every class against the undertaking'.[56]

Protectionist forces were beginning to regroup after the initial dilemma over the Exhibition. The arch-nationalist, protectionist paper *John Bull*, for example, began to express 'an apprehension, lest its objects should be misconceived, and its practical working made subservient to party views and party aims'. Though, patriotically, it could not believe that Albert had intended it so, the paper referred to a description of the Exhibition in the *Morning Chronicle* as 'the inaugural festival of free trade' – a description that revealed much about where the Exhibition drew its support from. It warned that 'if the project had been put forth in that sense, and for that purpose, instead of being received with cordial approbation throughout the kingdom, it would have been scouted as a piece of political charlatanry; and to this low and discreditable level it will infallibly sink down, unless the attempt so to represent it be at once discountenanced as it deserves to be'.[57] By the beginning of April, the conspiracy theory had developed: Lord Grey, as Lord Lieutenant in Northumberland, set up a meeting there to raise subscriptions and failed to get more than six signatures. *John Bull* reported jubilantly 'the gentlemen of the county considered, and very properly so, that the occasion was not such as to warrant a county meeting, and they declined to subscribe money, because the organs of the government "let the cat out of the bag", and characterised the affair as the "great inaugural festival of Free Trade"'.[58]

The basic problem was that the Exhibition movement had developed into something very similar to a political party devoted to the cause of modernisation. Its aims were pro-industrial and its agenda was very much a bourgeois one – in support of the principles of political *status quo* and moderate liberalism, profit and property. Radical working class people and many protectionists could not agree with its aims. But they were not the only opponents. Many religious zealots, unyielding reactionaries and supporters of localized or rural life spoke out against it. Then there were also those – understandably in the mid-century, when much of Britain was still pre-industrial – who were ignorant of the aims of the Exhibition and whose first reaction was fear.

Despite the Royal Commission's efforts, these pockets of opposition and ignorance still amounted to a considerable hurdle to the Exhibition's success, a fact that was made plain by the extremely slow advance made in the realms of gathering subscriptions: only £39,249 had been taken by mid-April (according to Cole, the Exhibition needed at least to raise £160,000 – an alternative estimate done by Barry put the costs at £293,000!).[59] The extent of the problem was laid bare by the fact that Lyon Playfair, who had initially been appointed to explain the classification system to local committees, soon found himself – thanks once again to Peel,[60] and to the desperation felt by the Commission – with the job of 'trouble-shooter', an assistant (Colonel Lloyd), and the right to sit at Commission meetings.

Playfair and Lloyd's reports to the Commission provided a vivid map of the opposition to the Exhibition.[61] Protectionism and ignorance were the two commonest reasons for the failure of the localities to support the Exhibition. In particular, agricultural interests – for example round Leicester, Doncaster and Derby and in the south – thought the Exhibition would not benefit them, while many towns with small-scale industries voiced concerns. Manchester, the most important industrial town, was less than enthusiastic about the prospect of placing its cheap, mass-produced goods next to luxurious French ones. Liverpool was indifferent. In Stockport, meanwhile, there was much radical, working-class opposition to the project, while in Coventry, Lloyd uncovered an attempt on the part of radicals to set up an alternative local committee – which was forthwith railroaded by the Royal Commission. Such reports must have been depressing reading for the Commissioners. However, assiduously, and tactfully, Lloyd and Playfair countered opposition, using personal connections, manipulation of the local press and education.

One issue, in particular, threatened to overturn the whole project: at one of its first meetings, the Birmingham local committee forced the Mayor, William Lacy, to send a letter to the Royal Commission objecting to the fact that it was not compulsory for manufacturers' names to be attached to exhibits, 'as, should shopkeepers be allowed to collect and exhibit articles under their own names only, an undue influence will be exercised over the smaller manufacturers, and the Exhibition will become a mere Bazaar, instead of accomplishing its real object of a *bona fide* display of manufacturing skill'.[62] What this letter amounted to was a potential split between merchants and manufacturers.

It was, perhaps, understandable that it originated in Birmingham, where there was a large proportion of vulnerable small-scale producers. However, without clarification by the Royal Commission of exactly why it did not want labels attached to goods, the Birmingham cause was in danger of attracting support from protectionists elsewhere. The Royal Commission wrote back to point out that there were many cases

> in which it may be extremely difficult to determine, even when all the circumstances are fully known, who is the party most entitled to claim the merit of production, or to be called the manufacturer . . . There are many articles where the original suggestion is the chief merit, and where manufacture is nothing more than a mechanical process, whereas in another case merit may lie entirely with inventor, or designer, who might not be the manufacturer, retailer, proprietor or exhibitor. In such case the Commissioners do not see how the compulsory regulation suggested would be consistent with justice, or productive of good.

The Birmingham committee was obviously not persuaded by the Commission's educationalist logic and stood its ground. The whole affair deteriorated, not least because of the Royal Commission's haughty dismissal of Birmingham's claims. The dispute led to Birmingham making a vote of censure against London and a growing national movement of independent local committees in May and June 1850 in support of the manufacturers' interests *vis-à-vis* those of design education.[63]

ALBERT! SPARE THOSE TREES.

ALBERT! Spare those trees,
  Mind where you fix your show;
For mercy's sake, don't, please,
  Go spoiling Rotten Row.

That Ride, that famous Ride,
  We must not have destroyed,
For, ne'er to be supplied,
  Its loss will leave a void.

Oh! certainly there might
  Be for your purpose found
A more congenial site
  Than Hyde Park's hallowed ground.

Where Fashion rides and drives
  House not industrial Art,
But 'mid the busy hives
  Right in the City's heart.

And is it thy request
  The place that I'd point out?
Then I should say the best
  Were Smithfield, without doubt.

There, by all votes approved,
  The wide world's wares display,
The Market first removed
  For ever and a day.

Punch's rhyming comment on Albert's plans for Hyde Park and Sibthorpe's opposition. (*Punch*, Volume XIX, 1850, p. 10)

Meanwhile, a diverse alliance of protectionists and anti-modernists had begun to galvanise itself around another point of attack; the Exhibition's proposed site in Hyde Park and the loud opposition to this emanating from the surrounding neighbourhood of Kensington. In March Brougham had already shown that protectionists might exploit this issue. The decision of the Royal Commission to display the entries for the building competition at the Institution of Civil Engineers on 10 June, the crowds that flocked to see the plans[64] and initial survey work going on in Hyde Park heated the matter up once more. It was taken up by Colonel Charles Sibthorpe, MP for Lincoln: on 17 June he raised a parliamentary question about how many trees were to be cut down in Hyde Park.

Though many at the time wrote Sibthorpe off as some sort of crank, and the epitome of the rotten-borough tradition which reformers had worked hard to eradicate from Parliament (he was the latest in three generations of Sibthorpes to have represented Lincoln), he was an old opponent of Albert, had made a name for himself by forcing the reduction of the latter's state grant in 1840 and deeply opposed any efforts to support modernisation.[65] He was also, now, obviously issuing a clarion call to all those who opposed the Exhibition: having been told, he informed the House, that only young trees would be cut down, he had inspected the site proposed and had found a clump of trees which he estimated to be around forty years old. He now wished to know:

> . . . whether there was an intention to cut down the 10 trees that had been marked in the park. The parks were the property of the people, and had always been so considered, and he asked for what were they to be cut down? – for one of the greatest humbugs, one of the greatest frauds, one of the greatest absurdities ever known – he meant the intended exposition of 1851. For such a thing as that the government were about to be guilty of the crime of demolishing public property of the most valuable kind, and all for the purpose of encouraging foreigners, who would only laugh at the English for their folly . . . If he thought that the exposition would be for the public good, he should as readily subscribe to it as any man in the country, but he would do nothing to encourage foreigners, – nothing to give secret service money to them in the shape of premiums paid to strangers out of the pockets of the people of this country. There was every reason to fear that this was only the commencement of a series of inroads upon the parks. Here they were going to expend £26,000 on this building when the Irish poor were starving . . . it might be a sore subject to some members, but he did not care for that. It might be a sore subject to the government, but nothing could be of much importance to them, for their days were numbered . . .

Like Brougham, Sibthorpe was obviously using the excuse of Hyde Park to vent a number of grievances against the Exhibition. Though it was clumsy, his attack was also embarrassing: the Royal Commission had, in fact, gained permission to cut down all but one of the trees. Lord Seymour, the Chief Commissioner of Woods and Forests (the official charged with the care of the Queen's estates), parried with the opaque statement that 'he believed that not one large tree would be removed'.[66]

As Sibthorpe had probably hoped, the opposition to the Hyde Park site began to grow in volume – not least because the Kensington lobby consisted of many influential people from the *beau monde* and the newspaper world. *The Times*, which even two weeks previously had been chastising the country for its failure to subscribe, perhaps now sensing that the protectionist cause was beginning to get the upper hand, suddenly did a u-turn and, while still covering itself with the rather false argument that it was protecting Albert's and the monarchy's interests, began what would become a deluge of criticism of the Exhibition project. Prince Albert, it maintained:

is not unnaturally identified with the Exhibition. It therefore behoves his advisers to be very careful in what manner they carry out his idea, and to be very chary of associating his name with measures which will certainly prove very unacceptable to the public . . . The whole of Hyde Park and, we will venture to predict, the whole of Kensington Gardens, will be turned into the bivouac of all the vagabonds of London so long as the Exhibition shall continue. Who can forget the spectacle Hyde Park presented during and immediately after the fair at the Coronation? The grass was trodden down, the whole place was converted into a bear-garden, reeking with pollutions of all kinds and offending every sense in turn. The difference now will be that this disreputable spectacle will endure for months instead of for days, and that the park will be disfigured in a manner that it may require years to remedy.

Turning to Seymour's performance, *The Times* remarked that this was not only 'flippant', but gave the impression that the people had no say in the matter. It prodded MPs by saying 'a member of either House of the Legislature could not make himself more deservedly popular than by pressing this point over and over again upon the attention of the advisers of the Crown'.[67]

It was in the middle of all this that the Royal Commission now committed what was probably its worst public relations mistake to date; the publication on 24 June of its final choice for the building in Hyde Park. In fact, the contest to design the Exhibition building had been a public relations disaster from the start: the Building Committee had been swamped with some 233 entries, a number that reflected the enthusiasm which the project was arousing, particularly abroad. However, apparently as the result of the great divide which existed between engineers and architects, or as Cole put it, between 'art and science',[68] the committee had failed to come to an agreement on any one of these entries, and instead had chosen to give out 'honourable mentions' as an award to those that deserved it, and to take ideas from the entries and with these produce its own design. On the one hand, it caused a storm of protest in support of disappointed entrants. On the other, there were raised eyebrows at the high number of awards given to foreign entrants: this appeared to confirm many protectionists' and nationalists' fears that the Exhibition would be about trouncing British producers and designers. Moreover, as many observers pointed out, the foreigners who had been awarded had very often produced exactly the kind of luxurious design the Royal Commission had said it did not want in its initial instructions to the competitors. As the *Athenaeum* journal put it:

It might be supposed that *he* amongst the competitors had done best who did what was given him to do: – certainly not he who did exactly the contrary. That *he* should be the prize man who gave the useful practical suggestions, – not he who built *Chateaux en Espagne*, and furnished designs which it was provided by the Instructions were to be altogether rejected. The Committee have taken a more ingenious view of the matter, – and the straightforward Englishmen who were not prepared for the eccentricity have gone to the wall.[69]

Now, however, and after much delay, the Building Committee's own design was published. This was the biggest mistake of all. Despite the Royal Commission's previous assurances that the structure would be temporary, and the furore which was going on

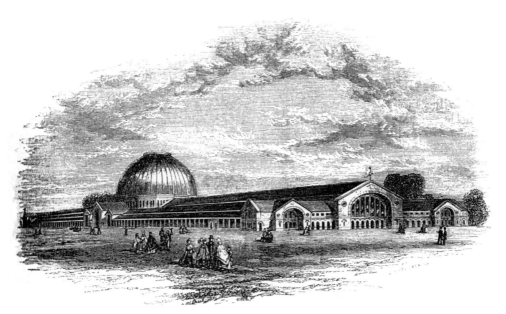

The Building Committee's design. The heavy brick construction provoked fears of the permanent destruction of Hyde Park. The dome, a recurring architectural symbol at exhibitions, was later the model for the British Museum.

in the national newspapers over the issue of Hyde Park, the plan put forward was for a brick building, with a 200 ft diameter dome, twice the size of St Paul's cathedral. The tumult among the press was predictable: *The Times* led the way:

> The case against the appropriation of Hyde Park as the site of the buildings for the intended Exhibition becomes stronger as the plans of the projectors are developed. We are not to have a 'booth', nor a mere timber shed, but a solid, substantial edifice of brick, and iron, and stone, calculated to endure the wear and tear of the next hundred years. In fact, a building is about to be erected in Hyde Park to the full as substantial as Buckingham Palace . . . By the stroke of a pen our pleasant Park – nearly the only spot where Londoners can get a breath of fresh air – is to be turned into something between Wolverhampton and Greenwich Fair. The project looks so like insanity that, even with the evidence we have before us, we can scarcely bring ourselves to believe that the advisers of the Prince have dared to connect his name with such an outrage to the feelings and wishes of the inhabitants of the metropolis . . .[70]

On 28 June, a petition from the inhabitants of Kensington was presented to both the Royal Commission and Parliament. In Parliament, the attempt to use the petition to get a vote of censure on the Hyde Park site was stalled by the government with what could, on the face of it, be seen as quite shockingly tasteless tactics: Queen Victoria had that day been attacked while leaving the Duke of Cambridge's residence, and had been left badly bruised and shaken. Lord John Russell answered each attempt to raise the Hyde Park question with a call for solidarity with Her Majesty by adjourning the House. On that same night Lord Palmerston had begun his historic, and mammoth defence to Parliament of the policy of protecting British subjects from government oppression abroad (the so-called Don Pacifico affair) and MPs were doubtless in need of a break. Nevertheless, the use of royal patronage for the Exhibition appeared now to be being taken to new extremes!

After an, at times, embarrassing stand-off between those who wanted the House to adjourn and those who wanted to tackle the Hyde Park issue, Labouchere stood and informed all present that the Royal Commission had not yet definitively discussed the matter but would do so the next day – Saturday. It therefore would be better to leave the debate till Monday. He also stated, more strongly than before, that the building would definitely be temporary, however it turned out. When the Kensington supporters tried to stand to speak again, William Gladstone stood and said that he 'would just remind the honourable gentlemen that if there was to be a dome as high as the Monument, and twice the diameter of St Paul's, there was no reasonable apprehension that the building would be erected before Monday next'. The only person able still to speak before the House adjourned was Colonel Sibthorpe. He parted with the warning that when the House reconvened he would put a question to the Attorney General about the legality of the tree-felling in Hyde Park.[71]

In the event, Parliament was kept busy on Monday with questions of supply, and the debate on Hyde Park was scheduled for Thursday 4 July.[72] In the meantime, each side prepared itself for the contest. *The Times*, for its part, was confident of public opposition to the Royal Commission, reporting on 29 June:

> The erection of the building, as proposed, is so deeply offensive to the feelings and wishes of the inhabitants of London, that even the discursive flights of the Parliamentary orators would appear to lose something of their interest by the side of this more homely topic. Dine where you will, go into what drawing room you will, enter into conversation with the first chance stranger, met on a river steamer or in a Kensington omnibus, and on all sides there rises a groan of indignation at the intended pollution of our beautiful park.

Letters against the Exhibition, the paper informed its readers next day, 'would have been alone sufficient to have filled our journal any day since the nature of the contemplated structure has been made public'. *John Bull* waxed poetic in support of the trees in Hyde Park, evoking all the patriotic feeling it could in support of English oaks.[73]

At the Royal Commission, meanwhile, there were mixed opinions on the prospects of success. Peel, for one, confidently informed the Commission meeting on Saturday: 'depend upon it, the House of Commons is a timid body'. As a result of his conviction, the Royal Commission decided that, for better or worse, 'the site proposed is the only one available for the purpose and that to abandon it would be tantamount to giving up the Exhibition'. A statement was sent to the Treasury the next day for presentation to Parliament, outlining the reasons why the Royal Commission had chosen Hyde Park – river and road access, nature of ground, and so on – and still maintaining it was the best possible site.[74] The press, however, was not to be persuaded. According to *The Times* the Royal Commission was adopting 'the three following positions: 1. There is nothing objectionable in the choice of Hyde Park as a site. 2. Hyde Park is the best of all possible sites. 3. Hyde Park is the only possible site, now that the year is so far advanced, and the time for altering the arrangements already entered into has run so short.' The *Globe*, meanwhile, usually supportive of the Royal Commission, wrote that 'if the first question – that of fitness of site – remained open, we might think it worth while to continue the argument. That being closed, we can only regret that the Commissioners did not, in the first instance, take a little more trouble to ascertain, and to satisfy, public opinion upon it'.[75]

In the face of all this, despondency reigned. Northcote, for one, thought that while victory in the Lords might be attained, in the Commons defeat was almost certain.[76] Albert, also, was less than confident. On 28 June, he had written to his close adviser, Stockmar, that 'the Exhibition is now attacked furiously by *The Times*, and the House of Commons is going to drive us out of the park. There is immense excitement on the subject. If we are driven out of the park, the work is ruined. Never was anything so foolish'. On 3 July, he added; 'I cannot conceal from you that we are on the point of having to abandon the Exhibition altogether. We have announced our intention to do so, if on the day the vast building ought to be begun the site is taken from us'.[77]

Behind the scenes, meanwhile, panic led to some interesting efforts to save the day. Northcote worked hard to influence the press in a positive direction.[78] Cole produced petitions for the local committees to sign in favour of Hyde Park, which were then sent back to the Royal Commission as proof of public support, and wrote draft speeches for Granville and Labouchere, who would be leading the defence in the Lords and the Commons respectively.[79] Secretly, the Cabinet discussed alternative sites – in particular Battersea Park – though Lord John Russell ultimately agreed with Peel that the best tactic would be to stick with Hyde Park.[80] Albert himself joined in the efforts. He tried on the one hand to persuade Seymour to build a temporary ride in Kensington Gardens in the belief that this would pacify the *beau monde*, who seemed to be so upset that their fashionable riding circuit would be given up for the Exhibition. And on the other he asked Lord Palmerston, the Foreign Secretary, to point out in the parliamentary debate 'the communications with foreign governments, and the disappointments they would justfully feel at the overthrow of the Exhibition at the 11th hour'.[81]

By the beginning of July, therefore, the Royal Commission was embattled on several fronts at once. Its modernising, bourgeois, moderately liberal and implicity free trade movement had managed to provoke a range of forces to stand against its plans, even if many of them hid behind the banner of Kensington residents. Despite the efforts of the Royal Commission to include them, much of the force behind this opposition appeared to stem from die-hard protectionists. Indeed, from the personnel involved, it was tempting to conclude that the Exhibition debate had become a re-run of the anti-Corn Law debate of the 1840s. Now, together with the many other pockets of opposition, the stage seemed set for a second show-down.

There are two points to make about this situation. The first is, that no matter what the outcome, the whole Hyde Park affair had ensured an enormous amount of press coverage for the Exhibition and perhaps allowed it to enter into the minds of a far wider populace than would otherwise have been possible. The second is that, whether the danger was real or not, the Royal Commission felt deeply threatened at this point. This was to have enormous consequences, as the steps which it took to eradicate the threat perhaps had the most lasting impact upon the way the Exhibition was set up.

III

As it turned out, however, the threat to the Exhibition had been much exaggerated. The debates in both houses turned out to be anti-climaxes, and the two votes in the Commons – one on the issue of the site, the other on the illegality of the tree-felling – were won by a huge majority (166–47 and 166–46 respectively). Peel had been correct about Parliament's opposition. Many Conservatives felt loyalty now to a project that included Stanley and Peel among its leaders. Peel and Albert had, perhaps as planned, managed to spike protectionism's guns in Parliament. Moreover, as Peel, the experienced politician, perhaps sensed, no matter how much hue and cry was raised in defence of Hyde Park in London, in Parliament it was the voice of the whole country that mattered. There the Royal Commission had indeed managed to gain supporters – as evidenced by the unanimous vote of a deputation from the provincial towns in favour of Hyde Park[82] and the commentaries of the provincial press – and there was much consternation outside London that the Kensington lobby was in danger of scuppering the whole affair. As the influential *Manchester Guardian* indignantly wrote: 'The inhabitants of the metropolis invite their country cousins up to London, to celebrate a national jubilee; and then, because they fall quarrelling among themselves as to whether they shall put us in the front bedroom or on the first floor, or in the three-pair-back, they threaten to revoke the invitation, and spite each other, by sending *us* off in a huff! Call you this your town breeding? Then give us rustic simplicity.'[83]

There was, however, another reason for the muted nature of the debate in Parliament. On 29 June, after the Saturday meeting of the Royal Commission, Peel fell off his horse, suffered fatal injuries, and by 2 July was dead. The impact of Peel's death was enormous. Though he had alienated many hard-core Conservatives with the abolition of the Corn Laws, he had also won an enormous amount of respect across the parties. Moreover, even many of those who disagreed with him respected his honesty and his attempt to forge a middle path in politics. His decision to end the Corn Laws, and thereby cheapen food, had also made him popular with the masses. The death of one so closely connected with the Exhibition, and with the Hyde Park site, focused Parliament's mind – particularly as the announcement of his demise came directly before the debate on 4 July. As Lord John Russell reported to Prince Albert, 'the feeling of the House was completely altered and all parties seemed to agree that Hyde Park was the best site. So it is to be hoped that no further interruption will take place'.[84] In a sense, the enormous national outpouring of grief over Peel's death, as witnessed by the countless memorials to him round the country, spilled over into support for what was, famously, Peel's project. A connection which had previously been a weakness, in that it made the Exhibition appear like a free trade festival, now became a source of strength, attracting support among many people who, at heart, were less committed to a political line and more connected with political personalities. For many people, from now on, the Exhibition enjoyed the sort of hushed reverence accorded to the dead. The Exhibition movement had got something it badly needed – a martyr. All this explains the impact, for example, of Albert's speech later in October at a mayors' banquet given in York when he specifically intoned Peel's name.[85] Albert himself perhaps, as he had been so closely connected with him, became imbued in the public eye with the spirit of Sir Robert Peel.

Punch's Monument to Peel. Peel was viewed by mainstream political opinion as having overcome his conservative prejudices to introduce free trade and, thereby, cheap food for the masses. (*Punch*, Volume XIX, 1850, p. 157)

PUNCH'S MONUMENT TO PEEL.

With regard to the opposition of the local committees to the issue of labelling and, implicitly, the educational purpose of the Exhibition, the Royal Commission also managed to solve this issue by the end of June. It did this partly through education, partly through flattery and partly through compromise. In mid-May, the Royal Commission had agreed to receive a deputation from the Birmingham committee on 27 June. This allowed a month and a half for Playfair and Lloyd to tour the country, educating, persuading and cajoling, specifically in order to limit the attraction of the Birmingham cause. When 27 June arrived, the Royal Commission invited not only Birmingham, but deputations from local committees across the country – ensuring that Birmingham's voice was drowned in a sea of support. In order further to ensure meekness, the audience was chaired by Prince Albert himself – once again the use of royalty to quell opposition. Nevertheless, at this point the Royal Commission was perhaps so concerned not to alienate any potential supporters that it still decided on a small compromise with the local committees: the rules of the Exhibition were altered to read 'all persons, whether being designers or inventors, the manufacturers or the proprietors of articles, will be allowed to exhibit; but they must state the character in which they do so'.[86]

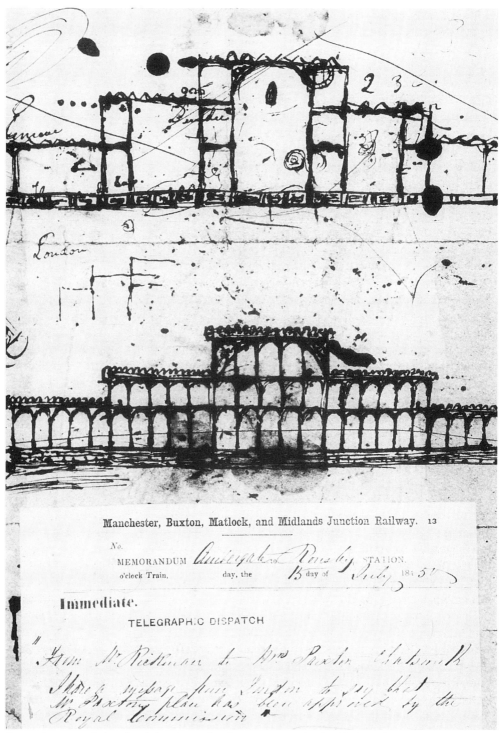

Paxton's original sketch of the Crystal Palace, apparently doodled while he was bored in a committee meeting. The sketch shows Paxton's thoughts well formed. The arched transept was a later addition.

Even though there was an element of railroading going on, the 27 June deputations from the local committees did show that the Royal Commission recognised more than ever that it must consult the local committees if it was to ensure their support. Indeed, the deputations, killing two birds with one stone, had also been called to ratify one of the most radical attempts yet on the part of the Royal Commission to enfranchise the local committees and thus secure their allegiance: the jury system.

At the end of May, Playfair, who had been involved in the original discussions about classification and who was now faced on a daily basis by the demand from the provinces for clarity on the issue, sent Albert a draft plan for a jury system. Without going into any great detail, he suggested splitting the four classes into approximately thirty sections and appointing a jury for each. The members of this jury would be chosen by those towns that were particularly strongly represented in that section and each jury would elect a chairman, who would then sit in a General Council, alongside representatives to be elected by the Royal Commission. Interestingly, in his report Playfair explicitly recognised the need to open up to the local committees, pointing out that 'the feeling of the country is so decidedly in favour of the representative system that it is expedient to start with this principle'. However, the structure he suggested would have the added benefit of still allowing the Royal Commission to lead, by giving the General Council, as he put it, 'sufficient character, high position, and impartiality secured by the infusion of the aristocratic element'. The pro-property, bourgeois agenda of the Royal Commission would not, therefore, be de-railed by introducing this democratic element. Rather, as Playfair hoped, 'such a council would command the respect of the public – a confidence in its decisions would follow'.[87] In this way, the integrative programme of the Royal Commission would be furthered and all those with a respect for social order and bourgeois values would gravitate towards it. Playfair's plan was accepted as the basis for the juries, though Albert pointed out that as foreign countries were taking part, juries would also have to include representatives from abroad.[88]

The jury system, then, still allowed the Royal Commission to have control. To this extent it was another compromise rather than a full concession to the local committees. However, it also had at its heart an important element of democracy. That the plan was accepted by the Royal Commission, and then offered to the local committees' deputation for acceptance on 28 June, probably owed much to the perceived heightened threat to the Exhibition. Though the jury system was another result of crisis management by the Royal Commission, it turned out to be a reason for the Exhibition's success. It ensured that the Exhibition commanded respect in the localities and also expanded the public's ownership of the event.

Having pointed out several different ways in which the Royal Commission tried to deal with the public opposition to the Exhibition at the beginning of July 1850, we now turn to the final, perhaps most fortuitous and certainly the most well-known concession; the acceptance of Joseph Paxton's Crystal Palace in the place of the Building Committee's own design. Paxton, who till this point was best known as the Duke of Devonshire's head gardener at Chatsworth and the designer of the Great Conservatory there, had shown no interest in competing for the design of the Exhibition building and had not submitted a plan in April. The difficulties of the Building Committee in finding a suitable design were, however, well known and on 7 June, he visited Cole and informed him, as Cole put it, of 'his flat roof of glass'.[89] Though the questions regarding

Joseph Paxton, glorified in the *Illustrated London News*.

Kensington as a location had not yet made themselves obvious at that point, Paxton's building seemed to solve several other problems. In particular it could be built and taken apart relatively quickly. Its modular structure – consisting as it did of repetitions of iron beams filled in with glass – meant it could be expanded or contracted at will, and just at this time there was much uncertainty about how many exhibitors would be coming. Cole, therefore, advised Paxton that although the competition was over, tenders were now about to be called for and Paxton should submit his design alongside that of the Building Committee. Given the fact that Paxton had not taken part in the competition, this was, at best, a highly curious piece of advice. Nevertheless, Paxton duly took his plans to London on 20 June. On the way, apparently by chance, he met Robert Stephenson in the train and persuaded him of the merits of his design – thus gaining not just an ally in the Building Committee but someone who headed a whole network of business contractors belonging to the railway industry, including Fox and Henderson of Birmingham (Fox had trained under Stephenson).[90]

Despite the obvious risk of opening the Royal Commission up to accusations of favouritism and 'jobbery', on 2 July Cole was sent to Birmingham to persuade Paxton's contractors, Messrs Fox and Henderson, to put in a cheaper tender. Already, the public outcry over Hyde Park and the Building Committee's brick edifice had caused a warmer attitude to alternative proposals in the Royal Commission. However, when the tenders were examined on 11 July, William Cubitt on the Building Committee merely recorded that a building by Paxton 'of so peculiar a character as to require a special notice' had been considered. The committee remained frosty. It pointed out that:

> Mr Paxton proposes to construct the whole building of iron and glass. From a close comparison of the tender for this project with those sent in by other parties, taking into account the omission of the dome and some other works not included in the tender for Mr Paxton's, there does not appear to be any economy effected by this plan; on the contrary, the cost would appear to exceed by nearly 10 per cent, that of the ordinary construction proposed by the Committee. In Mr Paxton's plan there would be greater facilities for adding galleries, but that mode of increasing surface has not hitherto been considered desirable.[91]

The Building Committee, after all, was being asked to consider not just the plan of a 'Johnny-come-lately'. This was also a design that rivalled its own – and Brunel in particular was supposed to have been particularly proud of the dome and called the building affectionately 'my bantling'. As has been pointed out elsewhere, Paxton's plan was 'a cuckoo in the nest'.[92] Still, by 16 July, Paxton's design had been accepted by the Royal Commission in place of the Building Committee's.[93] How had this come about?

There were, perhaps several factors that played a part. First, the pressure on the Royal Commission over Hyde Park did not immediately stop after 4 July, as Colonel Sibthorpe, Brougham and others now applied to the Attorney General Sir J. Romilly to launch an inquiry into the issue of the tree-felling in Hyde Park and issue an injunction. The press, meanwhile, became more hysterical if anything, fuelled by the fact that a new Attorney General had just been appointed (Sir J. Romilly was replaced by Sir J. Jervis on 11 July 1850) and that this issue could be used to test his nerve and that of a government, which was in any case shaky. For those in the Commission, the support of the Attorney General was by no means a foregone conclusion.[94] In the midst of this, Paxton, certainly not backward in coming forward, published an illustrated description of his design in the *Illustrated London News* on 6 July. The press now began a campaign in support of Paxton's plan, and in opposition to that of the Building Committee. By 11 July, obviously, this had failed to move the Building Committee. Yet the press campaign continued.

The pressure mounted: in order to start any building the Royal Commission needed to set up the guarantee fund for the bank loan as discussed at the beginning of the year. The difficulty was, where could it find the estimated £170,000? A major part of the problem seemed solved when, on 12 July, an offer was received from Sir Morton Peto for £50,000. However, added to it were the words: 'perhaps I might take the liberty of saying that I consider the success of the Exhibition would be considerably increased by the adoption of Mr Paxton's plan if it is not too costly'.[95] (This rather substantial vote in Paxton's favour was the result of Cole's conversation with Peto earlier in the day at the Reform Club.)[96] In addition to this, on 15 July a petition came in from Kensington residents 'advocating the erection of Mr Paxton's building in Hyde park'.

In the event, the Building Committee had already decided on that day to accept Paxton's plan, though crucially the report of the discussion noted that 'an important addition has been suggested of covering the entire length of the central portion or nave with a semi-cylindrical roof, and which being returned in transepts will include the trees beneath the glass'.[97] The arched transept of the Crystal Palace would later become one of the great features of the building and a dispute would break out between Paxton, Henderson, Barry and the Building Committee about who thought of it first. In reality, it seems that Fox and Henderson had suggested the idea of a transept as a means of strengthening the building. Once Paxton had accepted this idea he took it one stage further, realising that by making the transept arched the problem of the trees would be solved. Sir Charles Barry on the Building Committee, meanwhile, had hit upon the same idea independently as a solution to all the Royal Commission's problems. The pressure on the Royal Commission by this point more or less dictated that Paxton's building be accepted but at least the addition of an arched transept allowed the semblance of a compromise and saved some sort of face for the Building Committee. The only person left to be won over was Brunel. During a private walk in Hyde Park with Paxton, Brunel valiantly gave way: an arch would be substituted for the dome and the Exhibition could go ahead. Thus the sting was taken out of the whole press furore that had surrounded the Royal Commission for weeks.[98]

In some ways it was as if the whole episode had been a way for all those – in particular the protectionists – who opposed the modernising programme of the Exhibition to vent their frustration. Yet in the final analysis, their forces were not as strong as those that supported the Royal Commission and they were unable to keep up the momentum once the issue of Hyde Park's preservation had been sorted out. By the end of the parliamentary session in August, in fact, the movement appeared to have disbanded, leaving only hardened stalwarts like Sibthorpe to castigate the Royal Commission. In particular, the protectionists seemed to have disappeared. The liberal *Daily News* commented that 'protection, which began the session with loud preludes and threatening *rappel*, has gradually subsided into a low and drowsy hum – half malediction and half moan'. *The Times* also noted that 'everybody is asking what has become of the protectionists'.[99]

Nevertheless, it is important to recognise the seriousness of the public opposition to the Exhibition at the beginning of July, as several crucial decisions of the Royal Commission followed from this.[100] Certainly, the adoption of Paxton's design by the Royal Commission was a marriage of convenience that was only intelligible against this backdrop. The Royal Commission had to pay a high price in terms of prestige and potentially opened itself up to accusations of 'jobbery'. There was an outcry on the part of some of the competitors for the building design who now felt – with some justification – that they had been treated abominably by the Royal Commission. Several of the designs submitted bore remarkable similarity to Paxton's. For example Richard Turner, creator of the Winter Garden in Regent's Park and the Palm House at Kew Gardens, and Hector Horeau, a lesser known but highly influential builder of glass market buildings in France, had both submitted plans for buildings of iron and glass. Paxton's originality was thus questioned, as was the Royal Commission's sense of honour. It was also pointed out that Paxton's design broke the original rules of the competition – particularly that the structure be fireproof. (In fact, another criticism which could be levelled at the Royal Commission was that Cole had drawn up a report which had changed the definition of the term 'fireproof' after the competition had taken place.[101] This relaxed the rules, moving responsibility for guarding against fire from the architect

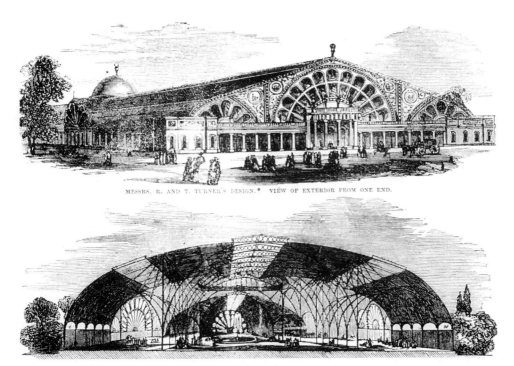

MESSRS. R. AND T. TURNER'S DESIGN.* VIEW OF EXTERIOR FROM ONE END.

Richard Turner's exhibition building. Turner remained convinced of the superiority of his building and viewed Paxton's Crystal Palace, with some justification, as unfairly chosen.

and his use of materials to the maintenance personnel, making the efficient upkeep of the building crucial. This was a change that would have dire consequences for the Crystal Palace in 1936.) Turner in particular repeatedly bombarded the Royal Commission and the Society of Arts with letters asking for an opportunity to prove that he, in fact, had first suggested the Crystal Palace – an opportunity which, predictably, was not given.[102]

The Commission also paid a high price by associating itself with Paxton himself. Paxton had not only risen from very humble beginnings on a farm, a fact that possibly irked some of the Royal Commission, he also had a tendency towards supporting the interests of the masses and exploiting popularity, which would set him against the Royal Commission on several notable occasions. His use of the press to publicise his plans for the Crystal Palace was the first of many bitter experiences for the Royal Commission in its relations with him and while the Building Committee accepted his plan, it still resented being pressurised in this way. As Paxton later put it: 'the Committee thought me a conceited fellow and that what I said was nearer romance than common sense'.[103] Not only did later pictures glorifying the Great Exhibition fictitiously present Paxton as one of the original Royal Commissioners,[104] they also led to the erroneous impression that Paxton and the Royal Commission got on.

Still, the kind of populism that Paxton represented was also a shot in the arm for the Royal Commission. While they may have been rather disturbed by his brashness, the people began to identify him as a hero; a self-made man who had risen from the position of 'gardener' to being the saviour of the Exhibition and the foe of aristocratic bureaucracy; someone who did not try and lecture others, but rather got on with things; a man whose prodigious work-rate became a lesson for all those who believed in the Victorian ethos of hard work. Plenty of myth-making was to be directed at Paxton: Dickens led the way, painting him as the embodiment of Victorian efficiency in contrast to the decadence of the eighteenth century. 'Mr Paxton – a man of high scientific attainments' Dickens wrote, 'is not a mere academic *savant*. *His* Alma Mater is Nature'. In Dickens' popular *Household Words*, Paxton appeared as a workaholic, 'whose very leisure would kill a man of fashion with its hard work'. The building itself symbolised work:

> . . . his walls and foundations are not simply walls and foundations, but ventilators and drains as well. His roofs are not simply roofs; but besides being the most extensive of known sky-lights, are light and heat adjusters. His sash-bars do not only hold the glass together, but are self-supporting, and form perfect drains for both sides of the glass, – for draining off internal, as well as external moisture, while the tops of the girders are conduits also. His floors are dust-traps, and aid in ventilation. Lastly, his whole building is, while in the course of construction, its own scaffolding. Thus he saves time as well as money.[105]

Paxton's reputed straightforwardness and efficiency contrasted sharply with what many saw as the heavy and wasteful machinery of government, thus he attracted many liberal reformers. *Punch*, for example, a newspaper that was to get much satirical mileage out of the Exhibition, picked up on the Duke of Devonshire's comment that 'Mr Paxton has never attempted anything which he had not succeeded in fully carrying out' and compared Paxton's frugality and efficiency with Sir Charles Barry's protracted and costly work on the new Houses of Parliament, which even in 1850 were not completely finished (a jibe that no doubt endeared Paxton still further to the Royal Commission).[106] For the Royal Commission, and those who opposed populist excesses, Paxton remained somewhat of a thorn in the side, and the issue of his success an embarrassment – explaining perhaps the 'minor mystery'[107] of why he was omitted from Samuel Smiles's pantheon of nineteenth-century heroes in *Self Help*. To the people, he was an idol.

It was the building, however, which was the main benefit of the Commission's connection with Paxton. This was not only because it served the practical purpose of outmanoeuvring the opposition, but also because it almost immediately attracted publicity to the Exhibition, and soon became an icon advertising the event far more effectively than the Royal Commission could have done on its own.

There are many reasons for the building's appeal. To appreciate them fully, however, present-day observers must try to forget their own long familiarity with the type of building the Crystal Palace heralded – those made of metal and glass and consisting of endlessly repeating segments – and put themselves in the shoes of observers in the mid-nineteenth century. For one thing, the materials used in the construction were highly unusual at the time. Most buildings were still erected using stone, brick or wood. Even though wrought iron and glass had by this point been used in several railway station buildings – Euston, King's Cross, Waterloo and London Bridge had all been finished in the preceding decade and a half – and conservatories – such as Decimus Burton's great glass house in Regent's Park – these were still a novelty, and Paxton's building took the

Punch's vision of the repeal of the Window Tax. The measure was viewed as a major step in the improvement of public health and became another reason for the widespread affection for Peel.

use of such materials to a scale never before tried. As recently as 1845, Peel had abolished the glass excise, which had made the material an expensive commodity, so the building also smacked of luxury – and as if to brandish the fact, a new technique was developed by the glass manufacturers, Chance Brothers, which allowed for larger panes to be constructed than was previously possible.[108] The building, therefore, looked and felt unlike anything previously known: it is interesting to note the frequency with which visitors remarked on 'lightness' and the different shades of light, as their most lasting impression of the building.

But it was not only the materials that were different; the way in which these materials were now produced was different too. One of the central features of the Crystal Palace was its modularity – the replication of each of its parts again and again. This was a form of construction that was only possible because of the improvements in machine tools which had come about as a consequence of the Industrial Revolution, because of the work of Boulton, Maudslay and Whitworth, and because of an infrastructure of industrial production that owed much to railway building. Implicitly, then, the building was an expression of how far technology and industry had advanced. Obviously one could have said the same of several other buildings round the country. Yet the Crystal Palace was different. It involved machinery in almost every possible aspect of the construction process – the creation of the pillars, the glass, the famous Paxton gutters, the wrought-iron arches, the patented trolleys that transported the glaziers along the roof – and it took the process

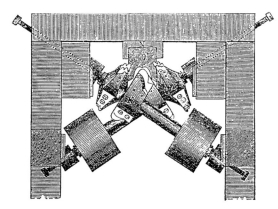

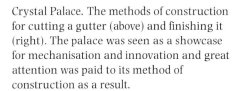

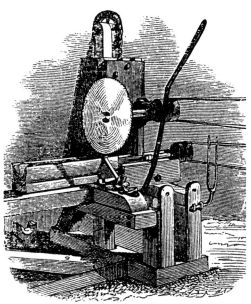

Crystal Palace. The methods of construction for cutting a gutter (above) and finishing it (right). The palace was seen as a showcase for mechanisation and innovation and great attention was paid to its method of construction as a result.

of replication to extremes – with 24 sq ft units multiplied to a vast area of 800,000 sq ft, and covered by some 900,000 sq ft of glass. The building went further than any station or conservatory and became a show-piece, an advertisement for mechanised building and for the power of industrialisation. No other building before this had gloried in its 'newness' in quite the same way. It was highly controversial.

But so, too, was the aesthetic message of the building. Many people, as has already been discussed, were concerned at the division that had opened up between design and production as a consequence of industrialisation and this was also true in the realms of architecture. Here, in the nineteenth century, functional buildings with no aesthetic attributes had proliferated – factories, stations, bridges, houses for new urban populations, and so on – and a rift had opened up in the building profession between architects – that is, those who designed buildings with aesthetic concerns in mind – and engineers, who were more and more concerned with construction questions. As has been described, Cole and his clique at the Society of Arts were one of the groups which discussed this split. They saw the solution as the education of producers and consumers regarding design, based on introducing them to a set repertoire of artistic styles – classical, renaissance, etc. This was criticised – both at the time by John Ruskin,[109] for example, and later by Nikolaus Pevsner[110] – for leading to a senseless regeneration of old styles and promoting the glut of decoration which Pevsner, for one, associated with Victorian things.

In fact, this profusion of styles – the eclecticism of Victorian design – owed just as much to the exuberance of a new bourgeoisie, able for the first time to acquire artistic artefacts whose ownership had formerly been limited to the aristocracy. Cole *et al* specifically called for decoration to correspond to the materials used and it was hoped that education in classical design styles, though it might result now in over-decoration, would eventually lead to a new appreciation of design and a new style for the nineteenth century. This was reiterated time and again in the *Journal of Design*, which Cole edited and which made a point of commenting on exhibitions and new artefacts in order to educate producers about design. It was also partly the purpose of the Exhibition, which for the Society of Arts was an opportunity to provoke comment on contemporary design, compare it with styles of the past and thereby, with luck, move towards a new, more suitable style. Hence John Scott Russell, in his address at the Society of Arts' Exhibition of Medieval Art in 1850, called for 1851 to be an occasion for contemporary designers to pit themselves against those of the past. Producers visiting the Society's rooms, he said, 'must strive to equal or to excel' what they saw. 'If they can excel in artistic design and workmanship still all they see here then they may consider themselves able to cope in the great industrial competition of 1851 for the palm of merit. But they must measure themselves with no lower standard . . . let it be their duty to see that the Englishman of 1851 can do no less than the Italian of the 15th century or the Greek of Ancient Days'.[111]

Yet where Cole's solution to the problem of buildings worked on the basis of harmonising styles of the past with materials and techniques of the present, Paxton put forward a different solution; one that pointed forward to the twentieth century and movements like the Bauhaus. This was the idea that industrial products could have their own inherent aesthetic quality and did not need to look to the styles or aesthetic ideals of the past.

Cole, at least, was far more open-minded than Ruskin and Pevsner appreciated – as well as far closer to them in ideas than either would have liked to acknowledge – and was keen to provoke debate about design. It is probably this inclination that explains

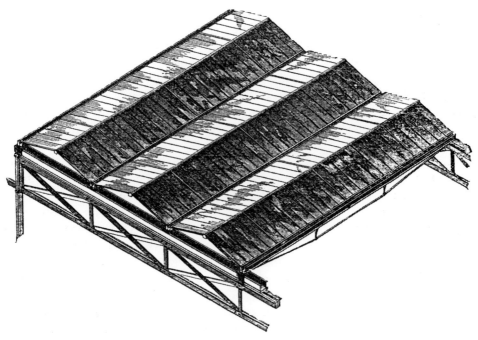

Crystal Palace. The methods of construction. A section of roof.

why behind the scenes he supported Paxton's plan. Nevertheless, Paxton's was a far more radical and provocative solution to the aesthetic question than Cole's and the Crystal Palace caused a storm of debate as a result. The building, therefore, not only gave the Society of Arts' original art education scheme a new dimension but also gave the Exhibition enormous press coverage.

The newness of the Crystal Palace, then, drew attention to it – and it is remarkable how much attention was paid to the fact that it was constructed out of glass. *Punch*, which was probably responsible for giving the building its nickname, seemed to get an endless number of images out of the fact. The building was compared to a looking-glass in which ladies were going to be able to look at the latest fashion. It was compared to a 'glass hive' in which one could see the bees at work – reflecting the Exhibition's aim to glorify labour. The 'transparency' of Paxton's building was contrasted with the shady goings-on in Barry's Parliament – 'Crystal Palace' echoed implicitly the Palace of Westminster. The term 'Crystal Palace', however, quickly became a catch-phrase – probably because it captured the sense of wonder and luxury that a building constructed from glass evoked in the public. (In a similar way, the building was almost invariably described by observers as 'fairy-like'.)

Meanwhile, the building's slender structure, in comparison with the solidity of others to date, was seized on by opponents of the Exhibition. Hence the line taken up now by the protectionist *John Bull*:

Whether such a structure . . . as this be the best adapted in the world to protect the costly and delicate objects which are to be collected within it, both from the injuries of the weather and changes of temperature, and from the designs and attempts of thieves and housebreakers, – who will, especially the latter, find a glass-house a great convenience, – is a question which does not appear to have suggested itself to the minds of the Commissioners; any more than the other and no less important question, what sort of atmosphere is likely to be created in such a building on a hot summer's day, with every part of it crammed full of visitors, and the rays of the sun descending upon it with almost perpendicular power. If the heat likely to be generated under such circumstances should have upon man's industry and ingenuity the same effect which it is known to produce upon vegetation, then, indeed, should we see trade and inventions flourishing as they never flourished before.[112]

The building profession, meanwhile, being so brazenly spurned by the structure, which was manifestly almost completely a work of engineering, also began to find fault in it. This was encouraged after the Royal Commission and Paxton engaged in a propaganda exercise in the building's support and trumpeted its technological superiority which, quite obviously, was an attempt to silence the critics and, perhaps, paper over the scandal of the design competition. After one in a series of lectures about the building at relevant institutions in London, in which Professor Cowper had tried to prove the strength of the arched transept by using feather quills, the *Builder* (which carried the significant subtitle 'An Illustrated Weekly Magazine for the Architect, Engineer, Operative, and Artist') noted that the lecture had had two main objects: '1st, to exemplify the greatly increased strength which could be obtained from materials by giving them a scientific form (a very good point); and secondly to prove what much

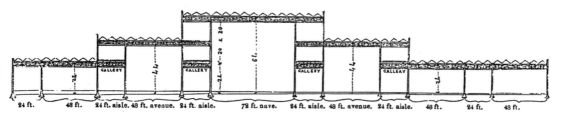

These sketches show Paxton's design together with the arched transept.

cleverer fellows engineers were than architects, – a very weak one'.[113] The publication's investigation of Cowper's statistics revealed them to be wrong, leading the Royal Commission to have to introduce new supports in the transept of the building.[114] The *Builder* had given the Royal Commission one in the eye but the debate about the structure's merits continued to grow in the building profession and erupted at two stormy meetings devoted to the Crystal Palace at the Institution of Civil Engineers on 21 and 28 January 1851.[115]

There was also, however, the aesthetic challenge posed by the building, which was seen as having substituted the rationality of engineering for the artistic craft of the architect. One letter in particular to the *Builder* summed things up:

We are told that most important consequences will result from the elaboration of this great idea: the public are fairly roused in the eleventh hour, and will, in future, be regulated by *common sense* only: the lawyers are already setting their houses in order: architecture must follow: we shall get our *quietus* at last: the public will be imposed upon no longer: the Exhibition building will be considered the *ne plus ultra* of art – the perfection of scientific combinations: iron and glass will be the only materials tolerated during the age of *common sense*: our temporary buildings will be permanent: our

Glazing the building was a novel feat of construction and was a battle against the elements. It was not completed by the due date – though repeated threats by the Royal Commission ensured Fox and Henderson finished the task. Under the transept is one of Hyde Park's elms.

permanent buildings will be of temporary construction: we shall not spend £500,000 on a work to last for centuries, but we shall spend £150,000 on the freak of a year: the conservatories of Chatsworth and Kew will be the types for our museums of art: railway sheds will furnish the most appropriate models for our ecclesiastical structures: our senators, thoroughly imbued with principles of *common sense*, will reform their ways – restrict their acts and discussions within these limits, and regulate the affairs of the nation, ranged like flower-pots in a greenhouse: all flights of the imagination will be cooled down to the standard of *common sense* . . . Had Mr Paxton's design been submitted in competition, it would have been snubbed and scouted like the rest, merely because it was a *common sense* design, and adapted to its purpose. The

Committee . . . were ransacking ancient and modern art for an idea, attempting, among a collection of permanent buildings, to find a model suited for a temporary purpose. At length they produced a design impracticable and unadvisable in every sense of the word. In a happy moment, in the eleventh hour, Mr Paxton's design is placed before them: drowning men will catch at a straw.[116]

So much was at stake, both for the Royal Commission and Paxton, as well as for the building profession. Every detail about the building suddenly gained in significance. This, just as much as its novelty, explains why so much print was expended on subjects relating to the building's window-frames, its concrete foundations, its drainage system and so forth. It also explains the Royal Commission's rather paranoid treatment of several freak accidents in the building which included leakage, storm damage to the window panes, and fire, and which were meticulously recorded and investigated on the one hand, but played down to the press on the other.

The aesthetic debate about the building, meanwhile, spilled over into related aspects, such as the way the building was to be painted. Owen Jones's colour scheme of white, yellow and blue, rather than being suitable to the materials used, as many people – such as Cole and Ruskin – now desired, and rather than being appreciated as a scientific demonstration of the use of colour, which was what Jones, in a paper introducing his ideas to the Institute of British Architects, said he wanted, instead magnified what Paxton had done by lightening once more the impression of the iron structure and giving it an ethereal, surreal and also fairy-like quality. This, however, caused another furious debate, resulting in what one observer termed 'the Great Paint Question'.[117]

Come men of England, listen all,
I'll sing you a song about a Hall
That sends Belshazzar's to the wall:
The Glorious Exhibition!
Of Glass and Iron tow'ring high
Like fairy structure in the sky,
To keep the goods and people dry,
While gazing there with rapt'rous eye.
So cramm'd with wealth from ev'ry clime,
Of the ridiculous and sublime,
From Eden's dawn to England's prime
The Glorious Exhibition.

4

SETTING UP SHOP

Despite all the publicity surrounding Paxton's building, it is fair to say that once it, and the site at Hyde Park had been accepted, the opposition to the Exhibition had had its teeth drawn. If anything, from this point on the certainty that the event would take place now began to attract more and more people to the project. The Royal Commission concentrated again on building still further an Exhibition 'movement', using tried and trusted methods as well as some new ones. It also now sought finally to put its intentions regarding the Exhibition into practice. Nevertheless, even at this final stage it did not have things all its own way. The opposition, though it had been largely robbed of its main players – perhaps because of this – still at times launched hysterical and hyperbolic attacks. Led by Sibthorpe, opponents portrayed the event variously as bringing hordes of pickpockets and malingerers to London, raising the threat of plague due to the millions collected there, bringing about moral degeneration and economic collapse or even revolution. The Royal Commission had to be careful not to let any of this develop into hysteria. There were also still several unforeseen practical problems that forced more compromise. Furthermore, the important issue of foreign participation remained to be settled; opposition at home was now replaced by that from abroad. Then at the last moment, and despite continued efforts to promote the event, the Commission itself made another series of public relations errors which almost scuppered the whole project, but which, ironically, turned out to increase its success just as errors earlier in the campaign had ultimately spurred support.

I

With regard to the Exhibition movement, the Royal Commission continued its attempts at consolidating and integrating all those classes of people who supported its project. One of the most significant examples of this was the mayors' banquet at York on

25 October 1850, which was meant as a return compliment from the provinces to Albert and the Lord Mayor of London who had held the meeting in March, and was also intended as another opportunity for strengthening the network of supporters round the country. This time the occasion was given more solemnity and the Exhibition was accorded the significance of a nationally uniting cause by the collection together of maces, state swords and other civic insignia from councils round the country. The importance of the occasion, and of the guests (Albert and members of the Royal Commission), was underlined by the sumptuousness of the meal, which had been designed by the famous chef Alexis Soyer – his first major connection with the Exhibition – and was called 'the hundred-guinea dish', due to its exorbitant total cost per head![1]

The banquet was also significant in other ways. Though it was in some senses merely a continuation of the use of royalty to promote the Exhibition, Albert's trip to York marked an important step in his campaign to give the monarchy some kind of new, more popular role and was seen at the time as highly innovative. Here, after all, was a member of the royal family going out to meet the provinces rather than calling them to London, and here was a prince mingling with commoners in support of a project that aimed, at least in part, to promote national industry. This was something not seen before; it caused a wave of popular sympathy towards Albert and the monarchy and became a source of deep national pride. As the *Morning Chronicle* put it, in days gone by the monarchy only left London to visit regional aristocracy:

> Widely different indeed are the objects and purposes with which the present Prince Consort of England visits the first provincial city of the Empire. He comes to it, not at second-hand from the mansion of some neighbouring landed lord, but direct from the presence of the sovereign herself, prepared to express as from her own royal mouth the interest she feels in the trade and industry of all her people. Prince Albert, in visiting York, becomes its citizen; he takes up his abode with the Lord Mayor, and meets face to face and hand to hand the corporation of that important centre. He comes to them, moreover, with a purpose – a purpose of great moment – in which the humblest among the townspeople are more directly interested than he can be himself. He comes to advance an object that shall assist in spreading peace among the nations of the world – an object that shall promote the friendly intercourse of man and man, on principles which neither difference, rank, nor creed, nor any other source of discord, can effectually injure . . .

Albert's speech at York was also crucial to the Exhibition movement itself. Not only, as already pointed out, did he use his speech to recall Peel's death and point out that the Royal Commission meeting had been his last official act, thus making it almost impossible to oppose the Exhibition, he also now praised Peel as being the embodiment of English qualities. These he now described:

> Warmly attached to his institutions, and revering the bequest left to him by the industry, wisdom, and piety of his forefathers, the Englishman attaches little value to any theoretical scheme. (Cheers.) It will attract his attention only after having been for some time placed before him; it must have been thoroughly investigated and

discussed before he will entertain it. Should it be an empty theory it will fall to the ground during this time of probation. Should it survive this trial it will be on account of the practical qualities contained in it; but its adoption in the end will entirely depend upon its harmonizing with the national feeling, the historic development of the country, and the peculiar nature of her institutions. (Loud cheers.) . . . Taking this view of the character of our country, I was pleased when I saw the plan of the Exhibition of 1851 undergo its ordeal of doubt, discussion, and even opposition; and I hope that I may now gather from the energy and earnestness with which its execution is pursued, that the nation is convinced that it accords with its interests and the position which England has taken in the world. (His Royal Highness resumed his seat amid a vehement burst of applause, which was repeated again and again with the greatest fervour.)[2]

This was not just an attempt by Albert to flatter the English with talk of their practicality and pragmatism but also an olive branch to all the opponents of the Exhibition. Albert was now trying to portray the opposition as useful, something he had actually intended, but also, crucially, something that had now served its purpose and could end. This was a clever tactic. Much of the opposition to the Exhibition – in particular from protectionists – came from conservative circles which, after all, were at heart highly patriotic.

That Albert's new approach was beginning to work was immediately obvious in *The Times*'s reportage of the York banquet, which almost – but not quite – amounted to an apology. Albert's depiction of Peel, it said, was 'a glorious completion of the national homage paid to his memory'. Warming to Albert's description of Peel as a prevaricator and a changer it continued:

The truth is, we are generally both, and nothing is more usual than to find men entrenching themselves with objections on one subject, while on another they are bearing down all opposition and bent only on progress. There is hardly a public man among us who is not guilty of this national inconsistency. Among other results is the very agreeable one, that our countrymen can reconcile themselves to a novelty, when it must be, with very good grace. There has been a strenuous opposition to the site selected for the Exhibition of next year, and we objected to it ourselves so long as the building threatened to be of a permanent character . . . But, unless we are mistaken, the objectors will often be found as ready as anybody else to take a part in the Exhibition and to rejoice in its success. There are risks and drawbacks in all human affairs. We do not expect the event of next year to pass without ill consequence or mischance, but, as it is to be, we desire for it all possible success, and think it the duty of every loyal, patriotic man among us to assist it with his money, his influence, and his talents, to the utmost of his power.[3]

In the wake of this speech, Albert's own standing in Britain began to rise. Previously he was rejected by many for being German – a term which at the time was seen as combining the evils of being foreign with those of the intellectual boffin; now the *Spectator* remarked 'perhaps it was partaking in some degree of a bystander's position, with his philosophical training, that enabled Prince Albert to form a broader estimate of the typical English statesman than a mere Englishman could have done'.[4] Albert was slowly finding a niche in the English heart. The whole thing had been a remarkably positive public relations exercise, both for the Exhibition and for him. Lord John Russell wrote to Queen Victoria to congratulate her on her husband's speech, which, he recorded, had made a 'very great impression'.[5] Albert, meanwhile, left the banquet and excitedly wrote to inform his wife that 'everything at York went off remarkably well – people much pleased, journey quick, my stomach deranged from hurry, nervousness, and M. Soyer'.[6]

Another way in which the Exhibition movement was consolidated at this time regarded the working classes. Despite the dissolution of the Bishop of Oxford's committee, the Royal Commission was still intent on extending the Exhibition's attractions to as many members of the working classes as it could. The decision had been taken, however, that this should not result in any democratic scheme which might endanger the bourgeois thrust of the Exhibition, and the whole matter was given to Alexander Redgrave, an official at the Home Office, to administer. Redgrave soon discovered that any effort on the part of the Royal Commission to trammel the activities of the working classes was unpopular and would be as likely to back-fire as to enhance the number of visitors. As a result, the Royal Commission limited its own activities regarding the working classes to the bare minimum, though in view of worries voiced in the press about huge numbers of marauding northerners and foreigners, and the concerns of certain clerics about the effects on moral health of having thousands of people of both sexes trying to find accommodation at once, it did offer to compile a list of suitable places of accommodation.[7]

Interestingly, the main effort to help working classes visit the Exhibition came from commercial quarters and from the local committees. The railway companies, obviously desiring to profit from what all believed would be vast numbers travelling to London, now offered to put on excursion trains for those travelling to the Exhibition which charged a rate less than the parliamentary fare (an arrangement, stipulated by Act of Parliament in 1844, whereby railways had to run at least one train a day at a rate of no higher than a penny a mile). These, however, were to be restricted to travelling clubs.[8] This obviously opened the way for commercial ventures to organise trips to the Exhibition – an opportunity famously taken up by Thomas Cook.

The local committees, meanwhile, set up their own savings schemes so that people could afford the trip to London and make use of the rail offer. In fact, this development bore remarkable similarities to the simultaneous cooperative and savings societies movements in that it encouraged workers to pool their financial resources rather than destroy them through revolution. It also made sure the Exhibition, when it came, was viewed as a treat. The Royal Commission, recognising perhaps that this amounted to a fulfilment of its aim to encourage workers to value the virtues of property, did step in behind the scenes to encourage local committees to continue supporting this type of savings association and also pressurised the rail companies to reduce their rates still further, even though, as Redgrave noted, the privatised rail system made any coordinated price reduction difficult.[9]

In London, meanwhile, the practical work of setting up the Exhibition now began. The Royal Commission, as a body of inquiry, had no formal power to undertake work and in the hectic period that had just passed no one had thought to deal with the

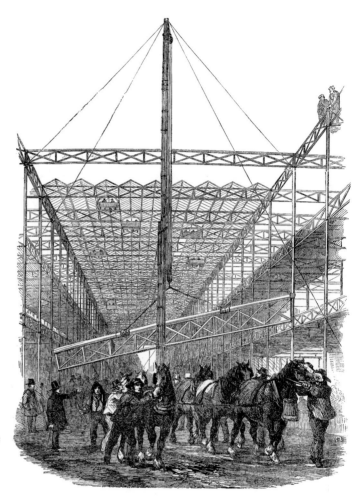

Building the Crystal Palace.
Worker unrest plagued the
construction of the building. The
Royal Commission issued press
statements to the contrary, as the
dispute reflected badly on the
Exhibition's commitment to the
welfare of the working classes.

matter. Time, however, was now running short, if such a vast building was to be built by
the beginning of January 1851, which was when the Commission calculated it would
need to begin work inside. As a consequence, Granville had suggested that 'we may give
them [the contractors] a large amount of moral encouragement to run the risk'. Fox and
Henderson, at some personal hazard, therefore began building the Crystal Palace on 1
August, two weeks before the Royal Commission received its Charter of Incorporation.[10]

A Medal Committee held an international competition to choose designs and displayed
the entries at the Society of Arts – an event which served to quell somewhat the Society's
complaints that it was being sidelined by the Royal Commission.[11] Eventually the
committee chose three medals, one each by Hippolyte Bonnardel of Paris, Leonard Wyon
and G.G. Adams of London. These were then commissioned with Latin inscriptions chosen
by another committee consisting of Gladstone, Macaulay, Lord Lyttleton, Dr Liddell and the
Dean of St Paul's Cathedral, a membership which once again demonstrated the desire to
unite men from a wide selection of bourgeois spheres of action.[12]

Reflecting the Commission's need for cash, as well as its unwillingness to be tarnished with the 'jobbery' label, tenders were sought towards the end of 1850 for companies to provide refreshments for the three spaces available – at each end and in the middle of the building. Reflecting the temperate tenor of the 1850s, the concerns of the opposition and the desire to make the Exhibition an educational rather than a social event, the tender permitted only 'light and moderate refreshments' to be consumed in 'certain prescribed parts of the building', and the Royal Commission stated that 'it would be inconsistent with the nature of the Exhibition to allow the building to assume the character of an hotel, tavern, or dining-rooms'.[13] This rather prim stipulation was not, however, without its opponents. *Punch*, for one, highlighted that it undermined the international spirit of the occasion. 'Foreigners,' it said, 'who never commit any such excesses, are to be punished – and forced to take ginger-beer – because you English, when there is any little party of pleasure, cannot be trusted with anything strong to drink'.[14] Of the tenders that were received – including one offering a large sum of money (£10,000) which turned out to be from a notorious brothel keeper![15] – the one accepted was that of Messrs Schweppes & Co., together with two subcontractors, 'who', as the Royal Commission later recorded triumphantly, 'paid the sum of £5,500 for the privilege'.[16]

In addition to these more mundane arrangements, the Commission also now began to apply some of the techniques gained through the Society of Arts' experience in order to promote the occasion. While the building work was being done, tickets to view it were issued on a restricted basis, in particular to aristocrats and those who had links with the Exhibition – such as members of the Society of Arts, MPs, Lords and other select dignitaries. The Royal Commission underlined the sense of privilege by reminding visitors perpetually of the great favour that was being granted them and making their visits as brief, but as impressive, as possible.[17] This exclusivity was reinforced by Paxton's wooden hoarding – which was later ingeniously converted into the floor of the building! – surrounding the Crystal Palace and preventing all but the cheekiest and most intrepid children from watching what was going on. Even the press were kept out. As *Punch*, commented: 'we presume the newspapers will, each of them, secure one of these inquisitive brats in the character of "Our Reporter", for no one else seems to have an opportunity of knowing what is going on'. Most significantly, perhaps, Queen Victoria paid regular – in the latter stages almost daily – visits to the Exhibition. Once again, all this ensured that viewing the building became a fashionable event long before the Exhibition opened. The papers, in particular the *Morning Chronicle*, which had begun to act almost like a house journal for the Royal Commission, printed a daily list of dignitaries viewing the building, as if it were a court event. The names of visitors read like a register of the aristocratic *beau monde*.[18] By November 1850 visits of gentry to the building were becoming so frequent as to be inconvenient, and a charge was introduced of 5*s* to try and limit the numbers. In January, the Royal Commission decided to stop public visits to the building altogether, largely in order to halt negative press coverage from architectural journals and from the opposition, which persisted in rumours that the building was going to fall down.[19] The wider public demand for tickets was such, however, that Fox and Henderson – much to the chagrin of the Commission – began to issue their own.[20] Even though this was soon stopped, the public continued to mass outside the grounds in order to watch the work.

This theme of exclusivity was extended to the Royal Commission's resolutions on entrance tickets to the Exhibition. Here, the decision was taken to sell season tickets at £3 for men, £2 for women. Only season ticket holders would be allowed in on 1 May. With regard to day tickets, for the two days following the opening ceremony entrance would be £1, it would then be 5s a day until 24 May, whereupon the charge would become 1s a day, except on Fridays and Saturdays, when it would be 2s 6d. Such a structure ensured once again that seeing the Exhibition became associated in people's minds with privilege – with benefits for ticket sales. It also, however, ensured that the Exhibition would draw in the masses, something upon which Lord John Russell in particular insisted. Yet at the same time the minimum entrance price of 1s still ensured the part of the masses that came in belonged to the sector of society which had some sort of income – in other words it supported the Exhibition's aim to appeal to all those with property and unite them in one cause. The sum of 1s prevented any malingerers or trouble-makers entering the building.

Additionally, and reflecting once more the Royal Commission's concern to avoid any accusations of 'jobbery', it was decided that all Commissioners, members of the Executive Committee and exhibitors themselves would pay for entrance. Though this decision was understandable given all the Commission had gone through, it was highly unpopular. The Commission was to face indignant and angry protests throughout 1851 from exhibitors. Eventually a compromise was reached, in that it was decided to let exhibitors in free for two days after the closing ceremony in October.[21] The Royal Commission also interpreted its own rules flexibly during the Exhibition. Nevertheless, it did seem to be a rather ill-advised decision and stirred up a question that was always going to be difficult into a veritable hornets' nest.

Once again it was Paxton who discovered the Royal Commission's weak point. In a letter to Lord John Russell, substantially published in *The Times* on 23 January 1851, Paxton directly attacked the social agenda of the Royal Commission which lay behind the admissions system. The decision to charge exhibitors, he argued, was a tax on the workers who, after all, had made the whole Exhibition possible. If the privileged few wanted exclusivity, then they should still have it but by paying for entrance for the first two weeks. After that, he said, entrance should be free. Moreover, in a collectivist solution which to the twentieth-century observer immediately resonates with socialist overtones, he called for Parliament to vote a grant for the Exhibition to pay for the deficit. It was not just for the foreign visitors that he asked this, he said:

> I ask it for the large body of our own working classes – for those men whose skill, whose industry, will, I doubt not, be triumphantly represented at the forthcoming congress of labour. Thousands of these men – the sinews of the land – are at this hour depriving themselves of many little household comforts to enable them to visit London; and the inevitable cost of such a visit should not be increased by a further tax. Therefore, I ask for the working-men of England a free entry into the structure dedicated to the world's industry – free as the light that pervades it.[22]

This was, then, not just a criticism of the pricing system but also an attempt to change the whole meaning of the Exhibition, to transform it from a festival of the wealth of industry as enjoyed by the bourgeoisie into a celebration of the workers who made that wealth possible.

Though mainstream opinion, as represented by *The Times*,[23] immediately rejected Paxton's solution because it involved the taxpayer, his letter obviously caused much annoyance at the Royal Commission. It prompted the immediate communication from Grey that 'the Prince has been a good deal annoyed by reading your letter in *The Times* of this morning . . . if each Commissioner or member of the Executive Committee should think himself at liberty to enforce his separate views by means of the public press, nothing but confusion would ensue. By the adoption of your plan for the building you have been brought into official connection with the Commissioners; any such communication, therefore, from you, appears to His Royal Highness to be equally objectionable, and likely to produce equal inconvenience'.[24] Granville, meanwhile, immediately began a damage limitation exercise by writing to all the major papers to distance the Royal Commission from Paxton's letter. Revealing the gulf which existed between the Commission and its gardener-architect, he commented to Grey: 'Paxton's head has been turned by the events of the last six months and it is not surprising that they should have had that effect upon a self-educated man'.[25] Paxton's latest attempt to hijack the Royal Commission's agenda using the press was unsuccessful. Nevertheless, it probably encouraged the protests that did come during 1851 regarding admissions prices. It also perhaps encouraged radical working-class objections to the Exhibition. It certainly won Paxton no friends at the Royal Commission.

The notion of the Exhibition as a vast scientific experiment, or stock-taking exercise regarding man's progress, also now began to make itself obvious in the Royal Commission's debates. A Catalogue Committee decided that two catalogues should be produced. Once again, tenders had been called for – as the Commission was worried about being seen to profit if it applied for its own copyright.[26] The best application this time, in terms of the funds it brought the Royal Commission, was from Messrs Spicers and Clowes, a company that would prove to do very well out of the Exhibition and that now offered to pay £3,500 'for the privilege' of publishing the catalogue – the Commission to get a sixth of all profits.[27]

The first catalogue was to be a smaller guide priced at 1s for people coming to the Exhibition. The other, meanwhile, was entitled *The Official Descriptive and Illustrated Catalogue* and was to be much more monumental, costing a tidy £3 3s per volume, and offering 'a record of the most varied and wonderful collection of objects ever beheld, and . . . a book of reference to the philosopher, merchant, and manufacturer'.[28] This blurb revealed not only the growing sense of the Exhibition as an historic event but also the confident belief of mid-Victorians that they had reached the pinnacle of civilisation. Both catalogues, according to their editor, Robert Ellis, Librarian at the House of Parliament, sought to expose the Exhibition to scientific inspection and, in order to secure this, the leading experts of the day – Professors Owen, Royle, Lindley and Liebig, I.K. Brunel, P. Pusey, and H.J. Hope – were asked to annotate its various sections.[29] In order to tell the story of the Exhibition's organisation, an historical introduction was planned and the job of creating it was given to Cole. Albert, however, who by this time knew Cole's weaknesses as well as his strengths, instructed him bluntly that 'accuracy is indeed the first essential in such an introduction . . . there should be a total absence of anything like "puffing". It should be a simple matter of fact statement of the various proceedings connected with the Exhibition, taking care that the dates given should be exact, and supporting the statement by such quotations from public documents as might appear to be necessary for the purpose.'[30]

Another extension of the Exhibition's 'scientific' dimension was the final settling of the number of classes and juries by Playfair. Right from the Buckingham Palace meeting in February 1850 the approximate number of classes had been viewed as thirty. Playfair had gone along with this as to create any more would have made a Council of Chairmen unworkable. In order to stop squabbling among the London local committees about the selection of goods for the Exhibition, Playfair, after discussions at the Board of Trade, had used the thirty provisional classes as the basis of a jury of selection system there.[31]

However, despite the pragmatic roots of this system, by early 1851 it was all being presented as the result of a great scientific exercise. Playfair's report stated that: 'The working of these Committees was closely watched, in order to test the efficiency of the proposed classification, and the admirable manner in which they performed their duties, and the satisfaction with which their labours were received by intending exhibitors, and by the public, proved that, with a few modifications, the classification might safely be adopted.' His system had also been used to classify all incoming goods from abroad: 'In the working out of this measure, it was obvious that a public estimate of its efficiency would be obtained, because if it were not sufficient to meet the wants of exhibitors, numerous representations on the part of the public must inevitably have been made . . . In carrying out these divisions, no practical difficulties have ensued, and hence the general efficiency of the classification may be inferred.'[32] The classification system and the juries, in other words, were now to be viewed as scientifically proven. This scientific segmentation sat rather uneasily beside the original educational and – as it was called at the time – 'philosophical' one discussed by Albert and the Society of Arts.

Playfair also ensured that just as any experiment concluded with the writing-up of results, the juries should produce reports on their sections. This idea first arose not just from intentions of making the Exhibition scientific, but because Playfair had good contacts with continental Europe and knew that governments there almost always produced official reports on exhibitions. He correctly predicted that foreign governments would be sending reporters to the Great Exhibition and at first argued that Britain must produce an analysis, if only to keep up with its continental neighbours. However, the Royal Commission objected to Playfair's suggestion because it seemed to smack of *dirigisme* at a time of free trade and because it had rather nationalist overtones. These objections appeared to clarify Playfair's plans: the jurors' reports were not now to be produced for the purpose of promoting national industry but rather in order to create an authoritative, scientific judgement on the Exhibition, or as Playfair termed it, 'a starting point for the industry of the world'.[33] The authorship of these reports should include foreigners because they would make the reports less biased and even more objective.

Another area in which the new theme of science made itself obvious was in the selection of exhibits. Here, of course, there were several forces at work already. The Buckingham Palace minutes spoke of seeking works which 'although they might not form a manufacture profitable in the general market, would, by the effort necessary for their accomplishment, permanently raise the powers of production, and improve the character of the manufacture itself'. A large part of the task of choosing what went into the Exhibition, however, was devolved to the local committees and to the Foreign Commissioners. But the randomness which underlay this now became valued on scientific grounds as supporting the 'universality' of the Exhibition and its significance as a revelation of God's natural laws. The Society of Arts' experience also dictated the choice of many exhibits – among them what would become known as the 'Lions of the Exhibition'. These were selected for their pulling power on the public. The 'Lions' included, as ever, goods from the royal collections, in this case so many that a whole section was devoted to them in the official catalogue.[34] Others were famous works of art, hence imposing pieces of sculpture such as Kiss's *Amazon* – whose presence at the Exhibition John Scott Russell had been careful to secure while in Berlin in 1849![35] – and Hyram Powers' *Greek Slave*. The Society's principle had also been expanded to works depicting royalty or politicians, highly popular in the days before mass-produced images, and collections of extremely valuable jewellery, including, most famously, the Koh-I-Noor diamond.[36] This also partly explained why Albert was so concerned to secure Russian and Austrian participation in the Exhibition: their displays, he hoped, would consist of objects of the highest wealth and value.

Yet in addition to these influences, science now took its place. Exhibits were organised that, instead of displaying merits of workmanship of design, consisted of collections of things – minerals, gems, types of agricultural produce – in order to show some principle or other. Some exhibits were accepted because they had an educational purpose, such as the display from Manchester that took the viewer through the process of textile production from cotton plant to finished garment, the many models on view and the exhibit from the schools of design.[37] Work was undertaken to ensure that the Exhibition was all-encompassing, in order to strengthen its character as an investigation of God's laws in all their glory. Playfair and his helpers ensured local committees produced an adequate showing. Where they were not capable of generating an exhibit themselves, one would be organised for them, for example J. Forbes Royle, head of the Botanical Department at the East India Company, was employed to produce a display of the animal and vegetable produce of London, which promised otherwise to be deficient in its efforts.[38] The Commission also made efforts to include displays from those parts of the world that could not organise an exhibit themselves: hence Royle was also asked to produce a display of the goods of India, one that ended up being an historical and educational spin on the country's manufactures and culture.[39] In other words, the new emphasis on science had transformed the Exhibition from the spontaneous educational exercise envisaged by the Society of Arts into an affair that involved a high degree of stage-management, and where universality had become one of the criteria jostling for dominance when it came to selection of exhibits.

Yet Royle's involvement in the Indian exhibition highlighted the dangers of this scientific exercise. Here was, after all, someone who not only had an academic interest in the products of the sub-continent, but was also an employee of an organisation set up to exploit that place. Royle's intentions were undoubtedly good: he believed that Indian culture was inefficient, backward and oppressive, and that the export of British industry there and the introduction of Indian raw materials to British consumers would bring wealth to the Indian population as well as to Britain. Nevertheless, the Exhibition's scientific display of the world was organised by a particular group in society – in this case imperialist merchants. The Exhibition's displays from colonial territories served both to introduce British consumers to colonial goods and to inculcate the viewing public with what was said to be a scientific, and therefore reliable, view of the world.

The same situation existed with regard to the Chinese display, for example, though here the academic basis for its selection was less in evidence. The Chinese government, when approached regarding the Exhibition, had cryptically rejected the Western values of education and industrial development at the heart of the Exhibition with the words 'the excellence or inferiority of an art depends upon the talent or incompetence of the person. If men have not the ability to master an art, it is not in the power even of their fathers or elder brothers (to make them), far less sense would there be in the government addressing them publicly on this head'.[40] To the Victorian mind, this rejection seemed tantamount to a denial of a universal truth, and therefore both loathsome and absurd – and the Chinese, as will be discussed later, became the anti-heroes of the Exhibition.

However, in the absence of official Chinese cooperation, a 'Chinese' display was put together by Edgar Bowring. Bowring was an official at the Board of Trade who had stepped in to replace Northcote as Secretary to the Commission due to the latter's illness. He also had strong connections with British merchants based in China through his father John Bowring, who by this point was Governor of Hong Kong. It was these merchants, as well as their counterparts in London, who were contacted by Reid, the head of the Executive Committee (himself an ex-colonial administrator), and who now determined the image of China at the Great Exhibition.[41] Once again, the desire to make the Exhibition universal resulted in the production of an image more in line with British commercial interests than with the state of China itself.

In other white settler colonies – for example southern Africa, Australia, and Canada – the scientific basis of selection was missing almost completely, with the selection of goods being made almost wholly by indigenous merchants and local administrations who wished to advertise their wares in London. These largely consisted of raw materials. If the Exhibition was a scientific picture of the world, then it was one that showed Britain in a particularly favourable light and the rest of the world as an inferior, but certainly lucrative, place.

In spite of the fact that many of the goals discussed previously now appeared to be becoming reality, there were still several important modifications during the process of putting the Exhibition together. The first and possibly most momentous of these was the decision to group the displays according to countries. This arose largely because practicalities demanded it. Sallandrouze, the French Commissioner, who had the benefit of experiencing rather Byzantine French exhibitions but who also hoped to keep the French exhibits together for patriotic reasons, had tried to persuade the Royal Commission of this system early in 1850.[42] At the time, however, this idea was rejected. It would, after all, have negated the Society of Arts' desire to place foreign – in particular French – goods directly next to British goods, and the idealistic internationalist view of the Royal Commission, supported in particular by Albert.[43] Later, Playfair's scientific segmentation with its 'universality' also militated against this. Still, Sallandrouze's comments had provoked worries. Cole, at the Dublin exhibition in July 1850, also noted the alienating effects of a system of show that was too high-brow and observed the difficulties of actually setting up so many classes.[44] The major crisis came, however, when the Executive Committee was actually faced with the job of deciding where things should go in the Crystal Palace.

By the end of 1850, once opposition to the Exhibition seemed largely quelled, the Royal Commission was faced with far more British exhibits than the initial enquiries with the local committees had suggested. Cole had solved this problem by taking the local committee estimates, reducing them in proportion to the space available and asking the local committees to select accordingly. The situation with regard to foreign countries was much more difficult. Here, the problem was one of enormous uncertainty about the extent of participation. In many cases, the distances involved were such that no information could be had about what was being sent until it actually arrived.[45] This might not be until very late in the day in the case of Russia, the United States and many of the colonies.[46] By putting British and colonial exhibits in one half of the building, separated off from each other, and foreign ones in the other, the Executive Committee hoped to limit the disruption caused by this uncertainty.

Another change which came about due to practical considerations was the decision to scrap the idea of putting agricultural implements in a separate area in Hyde Park as had been planned, and instead include them in the main building.[47] Originally, there had been great fears that the United States, in particular, would swamp the Exhibition with agricultural goods – and Paxton's building had itself partly been accepted because of the enormous uncertainty about how large the American contribution would be.[48] These were just some of the indications in 1850 and 1851 of the growing sense of American industrial power in Britain. The wild exaggerations of American participation revealed much about the ignorance, as well as the concerns, in the mid-nineteenth century about the emerging power in the West. The problem had provisionally and rather vaguely been solved by saying that such goods should be placed outside. This would also have come some way towards appeasing the Royal Agricultural Society, which, it was planned, would administer the agricultural section as some recompense for the removal of its own show from Hyde Park. However, when it came to the crunch, no one fancied taking on the Kensington lobby again. Concerns were also soon voiced about the administrative and aesthetic clumsiness of having one section divorced from the others.[49] Most crucially, perhaps, it soon became obvious that the United States' contribution would not be as great as feared.[50] Yet putting the agricultural section inside the building still involved finding an enormous amount of extra space. Fortunately, yet again, the flexibility of Paxton's building saved the day: though the original competition had specified a one-storey building, galleries were now introduced all the way along and room was created for agricultural implements. Part of the reason for asking for high tenders for refreshments facilities, in fact, was to pay for the internal reorganisation that went on in December and January prior to the opening.[51]

All these changes were highly important in terms of the way the Exhibition actually operated. The decision to move over to a national form of representation added a new dimension. The Society of Arts' four sections and Playfair's thirty classes, which represented design education and science, would still be kept. But now they would operate within each country's national display rather than across the whole building. This meant three different systems of layout and three different ways of viewing the Exhibition.

Obviously, the national subdivisions undermined some of the original intentions of the Royal Commission. Indeed, it has to be recognised that it introduced an element of contradiction into the Exhibition. However, it also served to make the event far more accessible to the vast majority of people. The British side of the Exhibition had already cashed in on the power of local rivalries for the purpose of promoting the Exhibition. This was now carried over to the international level: countries were henceforth to some

Inside the Exhibition building. This picture – from the *Illustrated London News* – reveals the contemporary celebration of glass.

extent competing with each other. National governments were perhaps now more likely to make sure their display was adequate, than if it had been subsumed inside some rather ornate philosophical plan. This was, in any case, a contradiction which had been in evidence in the support for the Exhibition in Britain from the start: for many people, the Exhibition would now be able to show Britain's pre-eminence in the world more clearly than ever.

The decision to include galleries in the building, meanwhile, carried in its wake further changes to the layout. Lighter goods were to go upstairs, heavier ones on the ground floor. The galleries themselves could be used for hanging textiles and carpets of outstanding design. This gave the Exhibition a new, three-dimensional flavour and transformed the building into a riot of colour. The use of three dimensions was also extended to the ground floor. Machines using steam power, it was decided, should go on the north side of the building, where pipes would pump in high-pressure steam from outside, while raw materials would go on the south. Works of eminence – particularly of art – were to go near the aisles.[52] This not only increased the aesthetic impact of the Exhibition as visitors walked down the aisles but also impressed them more consistently with the Society of Arts' message that art represented the pinnacle of the human productive chain.

The only hitch in all this was that introducing agricultural goods, stair-wells and refreshment facilities had the net result of reducing ground-space for exhibitors. This was bitterly resented, particularly by Sallandrouze, and caused a wave of protest in Paris, where the reduction of space was viewed as an attempt by the Royal Commission to embarrass the French. Nevertheless, the Royal Commission at least tried to explain the practical reasons for all this. It also pointed out, rather artfully, that much of the change had been Sallandrouze's own idea in the first place.[53]

II

Now that the Exhibition organisers had gone over to a national system of display, and the Royal Commission allowed foreign countries freedom to set out their own goods in order to simplify the job of arrangement, another complicating element became obvious: the displays of foreign countries were quite different in character from those of Britain. While Britain's half of the building was filled via a system of local committees and with only quasi-governmental direction, most foreign countries' sections were organised by state governments. Their displays reflected this fact. Many of them were far more unified and aesthetically pleasing than the British one. This difference was more acute in the French display. In part, the Society of Arts had always intended British goods to be directly compared with French ones. It is no surprise, therefore, that France had been given a quarter of the space available for foreign countries – a fact which also had to do with that country's proximity to Britain and its level of industrialisation. However, the French display, it might be said, as it had been state-organised was always likely to have an unfair advantage in aesthetic terms over its British counterpart, an advantage which was particularly strong given the long experience of exhibitions of the French Ministry of Agriculture and Commerce.

Another consequence of the state-organised nature of foreign sections was the emphasis there on luxury, impressiveness and wealth. The Russian and Austrian displays, in particular, seemed to be produced more in order to demonstrate abroad and at home the power of the imperial state in terms of art and artefacts. This trait was perhaps exaggerated further now that the Exhibition allowed direct comparison between countries and the way was open for governments to begin competing with each other.

The fact that states were given responsibility for displays also allowed many of the traditions that had been built up at continental exhibitions to be brought to London unaltered: for example, the tradition of the state using exhibitions to encourage industry was evidenced by the presence of many goods from state-owned manufacturers in the continental European section. Marketable objects were chosen for exhibition, particularly in the submissions from the German states, where regional exhibitions had always been for commercial reasons and more in order to attract the attention of the market than to satisfy some rather abstract educational ideal. The cross-over between the Great Exhibition and its continental forerunners was all the greater as many of the goods that came across had made themselves known to state organisers at the regional and state exhibitions.

All this meant that the foreign section was not designed to create any true picture of the level of industrial progress abroad as the British section had partly been. Yet there were also other reasons for the divergence of foreign powers from the organisational principle set by the British. With regard to the German states, Austro-Prussian rivalry had prevented any coordinated activity, while the Prussian effort to set up a unified display under the aegis of the *Zollverein* – German customs union – foundered on the opposition of the smaller states, who were worried about appearing to give up any sovereignty at the Exhibition. The result was a fragmented and rather bewildering display under the heading of the *Zollverein* which did no justice to economic development there.[54]

The United States' submission, meanwhile, was probably even less representative. Here, the federal state had washed its hands of any responsibility for the Exhibition – Congress, revealingly, deciding that no money should go to support such a scheme. Things were made worse, however, by the fact that the states themselves could not agree on a central organising body to correspond with the Royal Commission, a forewarning, perhaps, of the Civil War to come. In this situation, American exhibitors were required to face the enormous costs and difficulties of transport across huge distances alone. The only points of cooperation in this situation were a unilateral decision by the President – head of the armed forces – to provide the naval frigate, the *St Lawrence*, to transport goods across the Atlantic, the aid of several intellectual societies – the National Institute for the Promotion of Science and the Arts in Washington and the American Institute in New York[55] – and the financial donation from George Peabody, an American Anglophile millionaire living in London.[56] Nevertheless, the United States' display, given the fear and trepidation with which it had been initially treated by the Royal Commission, turned out, on the face of it, to be surprisingly plain and quite disappointing. Of the original 40,000 sq ft allotted to America, only 12,800 was occupied.[57]

The last reason for the unrepresentative nature of the foreign side of the building can perhaps best be summed up as protectionism. Even in Britain many producers had viewed the Exhibition suspiciously as an event that would allow foreign manufacturers to spy on British production techniques. Ironically, this tendency was all the greater abroad. The British had so much more power of investment and marketing. Moreover,

British economic dominance appeared to rest on cheap mass-produced emulation of expensive artisan goods from abroad. Protectionism had a marked influence in the German states, for example, and many top manufacturers, particularly those who relied on the domestic market, were to be missing from the Exhibition.[58]

Yet it was far more than just a matter of competition: the fact that industry was often far less developed abroad meant that society's whole commitment to industrialisation was smaller. Many people rejected the social values suggested by industrialisation and attacked for these reasons the form of production it necessitated. There was far greater fear on the part of artisans and agricultural producers of what was obviously an industrial project, and much more ignorance about the aims of the Exhibition. Foreign governments themselves, resting as they often did on a patriarchal, artisan economy, were perhaps less committed to the industrial aims of the Royal Commission than was supposed. A notable case, for example was Portugal. Here, Albert was forced to use his familial connection with his cousin, King Ferdinand, to get together a display, as there appeared to be no developed industry and therefore no network of industrialists and local politicians with industrial connections to rely on.[59]

On the one hand, then, the new prominence given to France did, at least, strengthen the Society of Arts' desire to promote design education in Britain. But on the other, the foreign half of the Exhibition contrasted strongly with the British half in that it appeared to consist almost entirely of raw materials and artwork. What industry that was there

Foreign goods coming to London.

seemed, superficially, unimpressive. A new division appeared to have emerged in the Exhibition between the industrial western half of the building and the pre-industrial eastern half. Obviously, this was always going to be the case to an extent because of Britain's industrial lead. Nevertheless, the factors which lay behind the organisation of the foreign exhibits meant that the schism was exaggerated and a picture was produced which, from the point of view of industrial Britain, was remarkably and misleadingly flattering.

The inclusion of foreign countries not only changed the look of the Exhibition, but also the way it functioned. Just as the Royal Commission had wanted to involve the wider public in Britain, and found itself accommodating the latter's demands, so it also had to accept some of the things which its prospective allies abroad required. One example of this was the demand from Prussia and the German states, revealing again the long tradition of exhibitions for the purpose of market-expansion, for labels to be attached to goods showing the prices of articles. This resembled the earlier campaign by Birmingham, which had been resisted in order to prevent the Exhibition becoming 'a bazaar'. This time the Royal Commission again managed to strike a compromise: it agreed with the Prussian Commissioners that labels could be attached saying that a good was exhibited 'for cheapness', and that manufacturers could prepare their own price lists if they wished.[60]

Another, more substantial problem, however, was the Foreign Commissioners' objections to the jury system as worked out by Playfair. This had proposed that juries be kept small for efficiency's sake but had the result that not all foreign countries could be represented on any one jury. Indeed, according to Playfair's plan, foreign countries would only be represented on approximately a third of the total juries – and the potential commercial and political consequences of this situation were enough to cause an angry deputation of Foreign Commissioners to see Granville and Playfair. This resulted in the proposal, emanating from practices at continental exhibitions, that any jury would simply recommend an award first of all. Before this was sent to the Council of Chairmen, however, it had to be agreed to by several other juries in related classes. This meant that by and large a fair decision was much more likely. It also significantly reduced the power of the Royal Commission, and in particular the Society of Arts clique, to determine what was rewarded and what was not. In order to get the decision passed, Granville had had to confront the 'jealousy' of the Executive Committee (in particular Cole and Dilke) towards this new plan.[61]

With such enormous differences between the Great Exhibition and its forerunners on the continent, and also with the strong resistance that existed abroad in protectionist quarters towards what was going on in London, the Royal Commission needed to treat foreign participants with some tact. It was vital to the Society of Arts' scheme that foreign participation be maintained. Many people saw the whole point of the Exhibition as lying in its creation of international connections, particularly relating to the market. The support of many free traders for the Exhibition also lay in the fact that they hoped it would help convince foreign countries of the benefits of following Britain's example.

Yet there was also a political agenda behind the support for foreign participation. Just as the Exhibition's organisers sought stability at home through gathering together the forces that supported industrialisation, integrating them and putting on a display which advertised their way of life, so they also hoped the same thing could be applied abroad.

The Great Exhibition should be an occasion to strengthen the links internationally between people committed to the *status quo* and the principles of industrialisation. This would not just have economic benefits for all concerned, but would also further the cause of moderate liberalism abroad by bolstering all the forces there that sympathised with the aims of the Royal Commission. For this reason, the international connection was viewed as vital by an enormous cross-section of political opinion: from idealistic cosmopolitans like Richard Cobden, for example, to more realistic moderate liberals like Lord John Russell; from the bombastic patriots like Lord Palmerston, who thought all the world would be a better place if the whole of it adopted the British constitution, to more subtle characters like Prince Albert, who knew from first-hand experience the power of the British model of liberalism abroad, and was convinced that by bringing foreigners to London, and by demonstrating the glories which existed in Britain, the forces of political reaction abroad – specifically in the German states   would be diminished.

Thus the Royal Commission, parallel to its efforts to gain allies in the British provinces, had carefully nurtured a network of foreign sympathisers abroad, which in 1850 it formalised under the Foreign Commissioners system.[62] This network was made up of those who had been previous correspondents of the Society of Arts, those who had set up similar organisations to the Society, the organisers of exhibitions on the continent, and government ministers abroad who sympathised with the aims of the Commission. As Commissioners, they were given responsibility for representing the Royal Commission in their home countries and choosing jurors.

Together with the jurors, Foreign Commissioners represented a kind of alliance of moderate liberal political establishment, industrial and intellectual circles which was similar to the Royal Commission and the local committees – with the notable difference that abroad this alliance tended to be far more dominated by state representatives, in particular bureaucrats, in recognition of the political situation there.[63] This difference, however, was overlooked for the most part. British liberals tended to the optimistic belief that once liberalism was in train, it was unstoppable. As far as possible, therefore, Foreign Commissioners were involved in the decisions of the Royal Commission. Jurors, it was repeatedly stressed, would have much say in determining the criteria of awards. Meanwhile, the Society of Arts, continuing to view the Exhibition as a means of building up its own organisation but also recognising the need to nurture the network, offered Foreign Commissioners full use of the Adelphi rooms during the Exhibition and facilitated social integration between British and foreign sympathisers. Later, it made them corresponding members, automatically increasing its membership enormously.[64]

Meanwhile, the political agenda of the Exhibition was also revealed by the plan to open a large number of political and cultural establishments in Britain to foreign visitors. Significantly, this idea stemmed from one of Albert's closest sympathisers on European politics, someone who had worked alongside Albert quietly on all sorts of matters relating to the Exhibition, Christian Carl Josia von Bunsen, the Prussian Ambassador to London.

Both Bunsen and Albert were convinced that educating people in Europe – and particularly in the German states – would bring massive dividends for the moderate liberal cause. Thus anyone coming from abroad to visit the Exhibition would be provided with a ticket that would gain the bearer entrance to a variety of establishments stressing the success and vitality of Britain's liberal system, including the Houses of Parliament, the Royal Mint and Bank of England, various hospitals, prisons and museums, and the Society of Arts.[65] The Exhibition was thus to be an advert not only for an economic system, but also a political one. There is no doubt that Albert had fully considered the potential of the Exhibition in terms of European politics, given that at the same time as organising the Exhibition he had been applying himself assiduously in memoranda to the German question.[66] It was in a sense to be Albert's alternative, educational approach to the same question that Lord Palmerston, the Foreign Secretary, was dealing with less tactfully in his sermons to foreign nations and through gunboat diplomacy as seen in the Don Pacifico affair.

Yet relations between Britain and continental Europe were extremely poor at the beginning of 1851. Britain's parliamentary system and relatively liberal make-up rankled with foreign reactionary powers. Palmerston's hectoring, his official reception at the Foreign Office of the well-known Hungarian nationalist Kossuth, and the insolence with which he had dealt with the Haynau affair – when an Austrian general, reviled in Britain as a cruel reactionary, was attacked by workers while visiting a London brewery – made Britain appear even more revolutionary. For the conservative powers abroad – in particular Prussia, Austria and Russia – participation in the Great Exhibition was to be an extremely sensitive matter. The Royal Commission's flexibility meant, however, that these states managed to find in it enough of profit to themselves to continue participating. Nevertheless, the danger was always there that they would bolt at the first sign of political liberalism.

There were already indications that this might happen at the beginning of April, when foreign secret police reports began to show that notorious revolutionaries were going to use the Exhibition as an excuse to travel to London and agitate among their countrymen there.[67] Russia immediately stopped issuing passports and stepped up its efforts to prevent the middle classes travelling to London; they were obviously seen as the greatest threat to the political *status quo* at home.[68] The government of Naples, another reactionary power, tried to stop its people from having any contact with the Exhibition whatsoever: as the British envoy there reported, 'the idea of the government seems to be that the Exhibition will afford a pretext for the assembling of all the violent Republicans in Europe, and that the Neapolitans by mixing in such society would run great risk of having their minds tainted with revolutionary doctrines . . .'[69] Several days later, King Frederick William IV of Prussia wrote to Albert informing him that he could not let his brother, William, the Prince of Prussia (and future Kaiser) come to London for the opening of the Exhibition on account of the number of revolutionaries who would be present in the city. With his letter, he sent detailed police accounts of those individuals bound for London.[70]

Bristling with sarcasm, but also betraying his political views, Albert wrote back to Frederick William, informing him that there had also been rumours that the wind would blow the building down, prices would rise in London, the black death would return or God would revenge his wrath on the new Babel about to appear in Hyde Park. Nevertheless:

> . . . as far as England was concerned, I can only assure Your Majesty that we have no fear here either of an uprising or an assassination, that certainly very many political refugees from many countries are accommodated here and perhaps also conspire with

each other, but that they in reality behave peaceably, live in great poverty, and probably have already come to the conclusion from their own experience that the English people have nothing in common with their views and that London is perhaps the worst terrain in Europe for their plans to take root.[71]

Albert's confidence had been bolstered by a letter from Lord Normanby in Paris, who pointed out that with the economy now enjoying a boom, revolutionaries would find it difficult to gain supporters in London. More importantly, however, Normanby was also receiving very detailed reports from the French secret police about the activities and identities of European revolutionaries, all of which suggested their weakness rather than their strength. This was an early demonstration of Britain's growing amity with the French government of Louis Napoleon.[72]

Still, the Royal Commission did go as far as to suggest that foreign police be sent over to work with their British counterparts in preventing revolutionary activities in London, an astoundingly progressive concept in the nineteenth century, but also an amazingly generous gesture given the connotations it had for national sovereignty. As a result, some thirty-six police from several foreign states were present during the Exhibition.[73] There were, after all, those in the British establishment, who were less confident than Albert about social harmony. More than anything, however, this was a confidence-building measure by the Royal Commission, designed to head off any opposition to the Exhibition at the reactionary courts.

Even though the Royal Commission had compromised yet again in order to keep foreign countries on board, the generally acrimonious diplomatic situation between liberal Britain and reactionary Europe, and the suspicion showed towards the Exhibition, still made things difficult. Perhaps the most prominent example of this occurred over arrangements for the diplomatic corps to be present at the opening ceremony on 1 May. Granville had arranged with the Doyen of the diplomatic corps, the Belgian representative M. van der Weyer, that all diplomats would be present at the opening, and that van der Weyer would give an address to the Queen on behalf of his colleagues. After their conversation, and without waiting for confirmation from the rest of the corps, Granville had had the event published in the newspapers and then left London.[74] The diplomats of the reactionary governments – in particular Barons Brunnow of Russia and Koller of Austria – now decided to interpret the opening programme as a slight on their dignity, maintaining that no other country should be allowed to speak for them, and led a protest of diplomats against the decision of the Royal Commission. However, in reality, this was obviously an attempt simply to embarrass the Royal Commission, with any luck bring about the end of the Exhibition, and also cause a diplomatic row with Britain, which had been brewing for some time anyway.[75]

The whole affair revealed the naivety of the Royal Commission when it came to dealing with foreign diplomats. While the Commission had learnt much regarding British public opinion, it was still out of its depth when it came to dealing with the wily world of foreign policy. As Granville rather meekly admitted to the Foreign Secretary Lord Palmerston, 'I am ashamed to say that it never struck me as a possibility, particularly after my interview with the Senior Minister, that what was intended as a mark of respect to the representatives of governments who had in almost every instance taken measures to further the objects of the Exhibition, would be declined by them'.[76]

This naivety also, however, allowed Palmerston to carry out something he had been longing to do for quite some time: he gave the Royal Commission – and Albert – a good dressing down for meddling in foreign affairs.

Palmerston and Albert had been at loggerheads over foreign policy for quite some time, particularly regarding reactionary courts, and Albert and Victoria had developed a tendency to bypass the Foreign Secretary which was irritating to Palmerston. Unfortunately for Albert, the Prime Minister, Lord John Russell, on this occasion was forced to concede that Palmerston was the correct channel for any communications with the diplomatic corps and that 'the unlucky deviation from the usual course' had given the edge to Brunnow.[77] Palmerston, meanwhile, masterfully delivered a blow to both Brunnow and Albert by saying that the best way to involve the diplomatic corps in the Exhibition opening would be to have them there as 'spectators' rather than 'actors'.[78] Brunnow would have no further part in determining the success of the event, while Albert's idealistic cosmopolitan notions would be severely reduced and made more in tune with Palmerston's more patriotic approach. Albert bitterly resisted what he felt was a diminution of the Exhibition's internationalism, arguing that the opening was 'not a purely English ceremony for an *English* object, but an international one in which *all nations* have taken an *active part*'.[79] Palmerston, however, held his ground, adding fuel to the fire even by supporting Brunnow's objections that the ceremony would not be normal diplomatic protocol.[80] In the end Albert was forced to give way. The Exhibition opening became more like a British

Punch's fears about foreigners in London. Opponents of the Exhibition feared moral degeneration would be a consequence of so many foreigners in the metropolis. (*Punch*, Volume XX, 1851, p. 174)

event attended by foreigners. This was, perhaps, one of the most important episodes in the ongoing feud between Buckingham Palace and Palmerston.[81]

Despite all the Royal Commission's apparent confidence regarding keeping revolutionaries at bay during the Exhibition, there were also many people in the political establishment in Britain who were worried about the potential dangers of so many people being convened in London. The opposition, of course, continued to warn of the dire consequences for social stability of allowing vast numbers to enter Hyde Park. Richard Mayne, the Commissioner of the Metropolitan Police Force, also pushed for the Royal Commission to expand the Exhibition's police cover and to introduce regulations to limit the number of visitors to the building at any one time.[82] The Royal Commission made certain concessions on this front, allowing for an increased number of police within the building, building a lodge for a permanent police presence at the front of the Exhibition and connecting this with the Commissioner's office – via Buckingham Palace – by telegraph. In addition, as has already been mentioned, guides were appointed to show people from railway stations to the building and a similar system to the foreign police forces was introduced by bringing officers from the provinces (two from each of the twelve major towns) who could help identify known criminals or rabble-rousers.[83] But, when it came to policing outside Hyde Park, the Royal Commission – rather cannily perhaps – played on the fears of others and refused to pay for any extra officers, meaning that the state had to set up extra forces free of charge.[84] As in many other ways, the Exhibition relied upon the state, even if the Royal Commission paraded itself as an independent body.

Another person worried about the potential for public unrest was the Duke of Wellington. Wellington had been coaxed by his high opinion of Albert and the monarchy into supporting the Exhibition; he allowed his name to be used to head the subscription fund and permitted part of Hyde Park barracks to be the site for the Model Houses. He was also extremely popular with the public and would be sentimentally remembered as having mixed among commoners at the Exhibition in what would be his last major public engagement. Nevertheless, Wellington remained far less sanguine than Albert and the Royal Commission about the public. He was, after all, a Conservative rather than a Liberal. He was also someone whose political landscape had been mapped out in an age quite unlike that which now appeared to be dawning – a time when the masses were to be feared by right-thinking politicians and monarchs rather than encouraged and exploited.

In November 1850, as Granville reported to Albert, Wellington took 'a violent crotchet about the dangers of the Exhibition', and, as Commander-in-Chief, demanded that military forces be placed in and around London to forestall any kind of public disorder.[85] As a consequence, in addition to the Life Guards, Foot Guards and Light Dragoons near to Hyde Park, regiments were drawn in from round the country and stationed in and around London during the Exhibition. Afterwards the Royal Commission reported rather smugly that 'from the judicious manner in which the troops were disposed, the public would have been ignorant, but from rumour, that the ordinary force had been augmented even by a single regiment'.[86] However, the military movements in Britain suggest an establishment, if not a government, which was actually somewhat nervous about what was about to take place.

Even the Royal Commission's confidence, however, was not unlimited. Plans for the opening ceremony of the Exhibition were only put together two weeks before it was meant to start, possibly because so many other things – including the participation of several states – still seemed uncertain. When discussions did take place between the Executive Committee and Albert's entourage on 17 April, however, there was no question of having either Albert or Victoria in the building at the same time as thousands of commoners – the season-ticket holders, who were allowed in on 1 May. There was, after all, little tradition of such things. There were reports of revolutionaries in London and Victoria had been attacked violently several months previously. Moreover, there was no real experience in London of how vast crowds would react in such an enclosed space as the Crystal Palace and several people worried that things might get out of control. Thus it was decided that Albert would show Victoria around in a private opening ceremony at 11 a.m. and the public would then be allowed in at 1 p.m.[87]

There was, however, only one problem with this arrangement. Organisers had spent a long time telling the public that it was their project in order to get support and in a sense had encouraged them to believe that Albert, the Royal Commission and the élite that they represented were working in the people's interest. As a result, the public now reacted violently towards being excluded from the opening ceremony. This outrage was all the stronger as their entrance times were having to be put back to allow for a private royal visit.

Once the Executive Committee's decisions reached the press, a national outcry ensued. This seemed to be an example of exactly that type of élitist, self-interested decision-making which the Royal Commission had tried to make the public believe was not part of the Exhibition project. It also ran directly counter to the popular desire for more accountability of government, a desire that the Exhibition project had exploited and, indirectly, encouraged. The situation was perhaps all the more dangerous, given the fact that it was season ticket holders who were being excluded; not the working classes, who were in many ways less of a threat, but rather the middle classes and those with property. These were exactly the people the Exhibition wanted to attract, and also those with most political clout. As the liberal *Daily News* indignantly, but also perceptively concluded;

A more impolitic, a more absurd, or a more ludicrous resolution the Commissioners could not have come to. That a mere knot of individuals, about whom, with the exception of the Queen, the Prince, and one or two ministers, the people of England care not one farthing, should thus, like maggots in a huge Cheshire cheese, enjoy the opening of a vast national exhibition, which in itself, and in its inauguration, is not only a national but a European *fete*, is monstrous. That these gentlemen should enjoy the honours and privileges of a private and premature view is all very well. They may enjoy it in secret and in quiet on the last day of April, and the public will not inquire. But that upon the day which has been clearly announced for the first day of opening, not only the public, but even that *élite* of society, which could afford, and which has paid, its three guineas for season tickets – that they should be excluded, is really impertinence, to use the least offensive word.[88]

The Times also admitted that 'Her Majesty's advisers are leading their Royal mistresses to a course which will be profoundly unpopular and without an adequate motive'.[89] Even

East end of the Crystal Palace. The building was topped by the flags of all nations.

Punch became serious, commenting that 'the Executive Council of the Great Exhibition have just done a very snobbish thing, and they had better undo it as fast as possible . . .'[90]

Yet despite all their anger, the newspapers still underlined their patriotism and loyalty to Albert and Victoria personally. In the same article as its attack on the arrangements, the *Daily News* wrote that 'we have heard it rumoured that this Exhibition was to be made the opportunity of disturbances, and, these disturbances to be raised by foreigners. We never believed one word of such a calumny on the exiles who are among us. But we are certain that if any ill-advised fool durst raise the look of hostility to our Sovereign or our institutions, the sole peril would be for the foolish individual who ventured it in his ignorance'. *Punch* said that while the arrangement was 'a clumsy piece of fencing' meant to protect the Queen, in fact it was 'calculated, we should think to disgust Her Majesty most exceedingly'.

The press was now daring the Royal Commission to show its lack of faith in the public. It was also, however, offering Victoria and Albert the loyalty of liberal Britain. This was pointedly made clear to Albert by Thomas Bazley, one of the token members of the manufacturing community who had been included in the Royal Commission. Pointing out that 'my intercourse with general society enables me to hear sentiments expressed in channels, to which your own exalted position does not permit you to approach,' Bazley informed Albert that 'I hear the most fervent wish expressed, that if

Her Majesty and your Royal Highness could mingle with the throng of expected visitors at the Exhibition on the first day of opening, a degree of satisfaction would be produced, not less gratifying to Her Majesty and your Royal Highness, than to the multitudes who would be honoured by the August presence thus crowning the triumph of your Royal Highness in having originated the Exhibition'.[91]

To their credit, Albert and Victoria themselves always remained entirely practical on the question of appearing at the Crystal Palace, and the initial plans had come about primarily as a result of advice from their staff and past example. With the most crucial sector of support for the Exhibition becoming alienated, however, their advisers were beginning to change their tune. Granville, for one, was now extremely worried about losing the support of the middle classes and swiftly worked out a plan whereby Albert and Victoria could move around the Exhibition building even with the public present. Lord John Russell was now converted, and wrote to Albert, 'I observe that the enemies of the International Exhibition, who are not a few, are taking advantage of the late order to stir up discontent – Unreasonable, and indeed absurd, as this discontent is, it will be as well not to let it grow. The fashionable society in London might be disregarded, but it would be a pity to alienate the manufacturers and the middle classes'.[92]

More importantly, however, Albert had constantly been looking for ways to restructure the monarchy in order to revive it. Given the situation, he no doubt recognised the opportunity which now seemed to have arisen to do just that. The decision was therefore taken by Victoria on 20 April to hold a public opening ceremony, with the attendance of both the Queen and the season-ticket holders.[93] An official announcement appeared in *The Times* several days later (24 April). With just a week to go until opening, the practicalities of a public ceremony were now hurriedly arranged.

Ultimately, however, Albert and Victoria's decision has to be recognised as very brave. The couple were now proposing to go before the masses in a way which no other European monarch would have dared do at the time and which even in Britain seemed full of risks. To many aristocrats abroad and at home it was as if Victoria and Albert were about to perform a death-defying act and inwardly they held their breaths. The decision also marked an important step in the reconstruction and development of the tradition of monarchy in Britain – carrying forward what Albert had achieved at the York banquet of the previous year. Victoria and Albert were now to become modern royals, that is royalty who found support not in the aristocracy but in the new classes which industrialisation had produced.

The public, for its part, reacted ecstatically to the new plans. It was, in fact, remarkable how just a few gestures of solidarity from the monarch sufficed to create feelings of heightened patriotism and devotion. What the reaction revealed was that despite the threats of Chartism, the British public was largely in support of the social *status quo* and simply wanted more political say. Such gestures as this were signs that this would happen. They allowed pent-up political frustrations, which otherwise might have built up into something far more revolutionary, to be released. With a monarch who put her trust in the people, liberals and conservatives could be united, as could aristocracy and commoners. The social solidarity which the opening ceremony now suggested caused a deep wave of last-minute support for the Exhibition. Peel would have been pleased with the outcome, even if it came about by force of necessity rather than design.

I felt a thrill of love and awe,
To mark the different garb of each,
The changing tongue, the various speech
Together blent,
A thrill methinks, like his, who saw
'All people dwelling upon earth,
Praising our God with solemn mirth
And one consent'.

Behold her in her Royal place;
A gentle lady – and the hand
That sways the sceptre of this land,
How frail and weak!
Soft is the voice, and fair the face;
She breathes Amen to prayer and hymn, –
No wonder that her eyes are dim,
And pale her cheek.

The fountain in the basin plays,
The chanting organ echoes clear,
An awful chorus 'tis to hear,
A wondrous song!
Swell, organ, swell your trumpet blast,

March, Queen and Royal pageant, march
By splendid aisle and springing arch
Of this fair Hall!
And see! above the fabric vast,
God's boundless heaven is bending blue,
God's peaceful sun is beaming through,
And shining over all.

'May Day Ode', William Thackeray

5

THE GREAT EXHIBITION EXPERIENCE

The Great Exhibition was the result of a long gestation process, rather like the formation of a political movement. An alliance had been formed consisting of all those groups committed to the principles of property. It included the old aristocratic élites as well as the new industrial sectors. At the wider level it also included the masses who had an interest in maintaining the *status quo* rather than overthrowing it. The pinnacle of this bonding process was the opening ceremony of the Exhibition. Here, the highest secular authority in Britain lent her position to this alliance: this was an important gesture on the part of the state, reconciling it with the new social order that industrialisation had created. The Great Exhibition also received benediction from even higher quarters than Queen Victoria: the speech and prayer of the Archbishop of Canterbury at the opening ceremony fulfilled what had been tending to take place anyway – the presentation of the Exhibition as a religious project revealing God's order and the promotion of industrialisation as a holy quest.

The fact that the Exhibition was the occasion for bringing together all these various groups was reflected in the way it looked. Rather than representing the logical outcome of one group's aims, the Exhibition was the result of a rather arbitrary compromise between many different interests. Its layout and exhibits betrayed this. This created – as will be seen later – the effect that the Exhibition could mean many things to many people and be significant in many different fields of human activity simultaneously. It also meant, however, that it could seem simply awesome or even chaotic. In addition, although the event has to be recognised as a triumph over adversity in the sense that opposition had been strong and no one had tried organising this type of event before, in fact not everything had gone according to plan. The Exhibition still had some important defects.

The opening was not the end of the process of integration. Throughout the summer of 1851 discussions continued to take place – in particular among the juries – refining further the purpose of the Exhibition. All manner of social and official activities facilitated closer contact between and harmony among those involved with the Exhibition; it encouraged links to be forged and bonding through celebration. Most importantly of all, however, the public were now allowed into the Exhibition building and were finally involved in a discussion which had been to this point dominated by a relatively small number. Their reaction was not a foregone conclusion: even at the beginning of May, the forces of protectionism, which had taken some time to match the political mobilisation of the Royal Commission, appeared to be reviving. However, nothing they had to offer could stand up to the overwhelming public acclaim for the event. Much of this was due to the plans of the Royal Commission, and much about the way in which the Exhibition entered the public imagination had been envisaged, if not arranged, prior to its opening. Yet while the Exhibition still remained at the heart of it all, public celebration soon went beyond the control of the Royal Commission. The event ended up being far more popular, and perhaps far more important, than had been expected.

I

Though it had only been decided upon at the last minute, the opening ceremony owed much to the tradition of ceremonials which had been developing in connection with the Exhibition over the last year. At the banquets, decorative symbols and modes of behaviour had been invented or borrowed and then acted out to underline the unity of the Exhibition movement and promote its aims. The opening ceremony carried this technique to new heights by creating a pageant full of details and devices which would not only reflect the desire to unify the aims of all the Exhibition's supporters but also to make these aims popular. Thus, for example, a procession was organised which would physically blend the people involved in the Exhibition into one moving line. The event also resembled other recognisable ceremonies such as the coronation and the state opening of Parliament. There was to be a throne for Victoria provided by the East India Company and placed centrally on a podium. Dignitaries dressed in court dress and official apparel were to surround her – much to the consternation of Royal Commissioner Richard Cobden, who now found himself suddenly taking part in a monarchical piece of theatre and steadfastly refused to wear court dress.[1] The reason for borrowing from established ceremonies had much to do with the speed with which the opening had to be organised and the lack of any other precedent.

The use of aspects from those traditional ceremonies was, however, also a way of showing that the Great Exhibition, while it was still viewed as an independent event organised by the Royal Commission, enjoyed the rank of a state occasion. Lord John Russell, in view of the public debates which had taken place on 'jobbery', was keen to prevent this being taken too far; he made sure that the Queen went to the Crystal Palace not in the coach of state but in the one she used to go to theatre visits.[2] Nevertheless, the implication that this was a state event was there, and the fact that the state ceremonial had been borrowed was underlined by the decision of the Royal Commission to involve the Lord Chamberlain in their meetings to discuss the whole matter.[3]

The investment of the Exhibition with the authority of the state and the direct patronage of Queen Victoria did much to raise its profile and impact. The allusion to the state opening of Parliament, meanwhile, corresponded with the popular way of viewing the Exhibition as a moderate liberal affair. Much rhetoric surrounding the Exhibition had come to speak of it as a 'parliament of industry'. This parliament was now seemingly to be extended to include all nations – appealing to British patriots who wished to show off their institutions to the rest of the world as well as to idealist cosmopolitans. The extension of monarchical ceremonials to include a project as blatantly industrialist as the Great Exhibition allowed the monarchy to metamorphose into a modern institution. The point has been made frequently that the nineteenth century was the time in which new ceremonies were created to accommodate an industrial populace.[4] The Great Exhibition – and in particular its opening – was one of those occasions.

The other main model for the way in which the ceremony was organised was the church service. Though afterwards this seemed almost a natural part of the Great Exhibition, in fact the religious blessing of what was obviously an industrial and materialist project seemed a surprising innovation and at first the Archbishop of Canterbury resisted any use of religion at the opening ceremony.[5] Its occurrence, however, is easy to explain. Since Albert's speech at the Mansion House the previous year, the Exhibition had been ever more presented as revealing the logic of God's universe. As a result, it had drawn increasing support from religious circles and this had been recognised in the rhetoric and speeches used. Albert even raised the religious significance of the Exhibition to a central position by giving it the motto 'the earth is the Lord's, and the fulness thereof; the world, and they that dwell therein'.

There was also a personal aspect to this decision to ensure the ceremony had a religious component. While Albert did not appear to be dogmatic in religious matters, he did demonstrate a rather holistic sense that reality – even the new industrial reality – was of God's making, and had chosen the same motto for the inscription over the entrance of the new Royal Exchange buildings in 1838. He also demonstrated a tendency to promote cooperation between Christian faiths and had taken a prominent part in the meetings of the Society for the Propagation of the Gospel in Foreign Parts, an organisation that included several different religious groupings. Such integrative thoughts fitted neatly alongside the aims of the Exhibition organisers, and as the Tract Society appreciatively noted concerning Albert's motto, 'it attributes nothing to any individual; it proclaims no national or municipal greatness; it breathes no flattery to monarch, merchant, class, or kingdom: – it is simply a devout recognition of Almighty God, "from whom, and by whom, and for whom are all things . . .".'[6]

In addition, however, shortly before the Exhibition a sentiment made itself known in various quarters which to present observers seems rather incredible: namely, the fear that something as enormous and unprecedented as the Great Exhibition needed a religious blessing of some sort. There had been no event before the Great Exhibition where countries had worked together (apparently) harmoniously to produce something of this order. This in itself seemed to lend credence to the claims of internationalist idealists that a new era of world peace was dawning. The Exhibition also presented Victorian Britain, and indeed the world, with a picture of the enormous technological changes that had taken place in the early nineteenth century and seemed to promise even greater ones in the future. The sense of expectation and awe arising from these facts, coupled with the dire warnings of the Exhibition's opponents, produced a public awareness of the historical significance of what was about to take place: hence, for example, Thomas Hardy would later call 1851 'a precipice in time'.[7] This bubbled over, however, into an almost millennialist fear of what was about to take place. The press carried many articles of this persuasion just prior to the opening of the Exhibition. The *Morning Chronicle* in its Easter issue pointed to the various pietists warning of

> . . . a natural and proper retribution for any great scheme of secular unity. A bulky pamphlet before us works to shreds the examples of Babel, the treasure cities of Pharaoh, the House of Dagon, the riches shown by Hezekiah to the Babylonian ambassadors, and other instances of inauspicious hospitality and pride before a fall. Some have canvassed, with a sinister leaning, the peculiar construction of the building; others have talked of fire; to some delicate apprehenders a large accumulation of respectable foreign gentlemen dispersed throughout the hotels and lodgings of the metropolis has suggested a fear of the black fever or the sweating sickness; some appetites are craving with . . . famine, while a considerable number of intelligent persons firmly believe in the existence of a conspiracy on the part of all the revolutionists and Socialists in Europe to seize our metropolis and destroy our constitution.[8]

In this atmosphere, people turned to religious quarters for reassurance. Even a paper such as the *Manchester Guardian*, which prided itself on its enlightened views, took up the theme of the *Chronicle* and pointed out that:

> . . . pride . . . goes before a fall. There was a wise superstition among the ancients that a man who was eminently successful was tempting the immortal gods, and would be overtaken by some dire misfortune, unless he averted the doom by sacrifice and self-abasement. Such a feeling comes wholesomely to check the exultation of a people over the ceremony of the 1st of May. The Christian view of it was expressed in the general desire for some form of religious service, and its celebration accordingly by the Primate of the English Church.[9]

It was as a result of all these influences that Albert personally wrote to the Archbishop of Canterbury on 22 April, informing him that 'we felt anxious that the blessing of Almighty God should be invoked upon the undertaking in a short prayer'.[10]

One factor influenced the opening ceremony that had not been planned by the Royal Commission: the weather. After weeks of rain, wind and storms, which had done so much to embarrass the organisers of the Exhibition, 1 May turned out to resemble the first day of spring. There was sun, a light breeze and the promise of summer. Underlining the extent to which the Exhibition had in many respects become an official event, the day was declared a national holiday and Parliament delayed its meetings until 6 p.m. Many were reminded of an older tradition of May Day holidays in London and as the *Daily News* put it on the morning of the opening, 'Today our true-born Queen, seated on her dais, amid all that is rich and rare in the Crystal Palace, will blend the prestige of regal state and modern intellectual power with these simple holiday reminiscences of our olden time'.

Many people began arriving in Hyde Park as early as 6 a.m. The officials, and some of the Royal Commissioners began converging on the Crystal Palace by 7 a.m. Gradually, the streets from Buckingham Palace, along the route which the royal party would travel, were packed with onlookers, many of them at windows, on roof-tops and in the trees.

Hyde Park on 1 May. The crowds stretched from the park back to Leicester Square. This picture shows royal carriages passing from Constitution Hill into the park.

London was covered with flags – from windows, church towers, in Hyde Park, on the model frigate, the *Prince of Wales*, which had been built as a naval exhibit in the Serpentine river, and around the Exhibition building itself. In the park, crowds quickly formed during the morning until some 300,000 people were gathered.

At the Crystal Palace, doors at the western, eastern and southern sides of the building opened to the 30,000 season-ticket holders at 9 a.m. Some seats were reserved for dignitaries and those connected with the Royal Commission and the exhibitors, but for the most part people were asked to assemble along the main passages on the ground floor and in the galleries, women at the front and men standing behind. Most people arrived early, hoping to secure a position with a good view. At 11.30 a.m., the Royal Commissioners, the Executive Committee and Foreign Commissioners assembled in front of the throne, on the south side of the transept, either in court or evening dress – a stipulation which was flexible enough to suit foreign customs (as well as those of the likes of Cobden). Opposite them, in the north of the transept, stood state officials, foreign ambassadors and ministers, ministers of the British government and the Archbishop of Canterbury, all in formal dress.

At around the same time as they were taking their positions, Queen Victoria, Albert and the royal party, which amounted to nine coach loads, left Buckingham Palace, turned left up Constitution Hill, then crossed into Hyde Park and along Rotten Row. At 12 p.m. precisely, Queen Victoria and Albert entered the Crystal Palace from the north side of the building and walked through the Coalbrookdale gates which spanned the transept and formed one of the central exhibits (and are still to be found in Hyde Park

Queen Victoria's entry into the Crystal Palace.

today). As they did so, a military band outside struck up 'Rule Britannia', fanfares announced the entrance of the Queen, men in the Palace and park took off their hats and a lone sapper on top of the transept, who had been attracting much attention in Hyde Park, raised the royal standard.

The royal party dressed and acted as if it were a state occasion. The Queen was in pink watered silk brocaded with silver and wore a tiara formed out of diamonds and feathers. She also had on the ribands of the Order of the Garter. Prince Albert wore a field marshal's uniform. With them was the Prince of Wales in full highland dress. The Princess Royal – demonstrating the strengths of home industry – wore a white satin slip with two skirts of Nottingham lace and a head-dress formed of roses. As the group moved towards the podium, the national anthem was played under the direction of Sir George Smart, the organist of the Queen's Chapel Royal, with the massed choirs of the Chapel Royal, St Paul's Cathedral, Westminster Abbey, St George's Windsor, pupils of the Royal Academy of Music, the chorus of the Sacred Harmonic Society and many others, and accompanied by two organs played by the organists of St Paul's and Westminster Abbey. The opening ceremony made use for the first time of strange but atmospheric acoustics of the Crystal Palace and the quadraphonic effects of having organs – which were exhibits themselves – placed in each of its recesses. The only possible comparison was to the atmosphere in a cathedral.

As Victoria rose to the throne, Albert walked round to the south side of the podium, joined the Royal Commissioners and led them to the foot of the stairs. The scene looked just like that of the opening of Parliament – though now the whole world seemed to be gathered in front of Victoria, its artefacts as well as its representatives. This was an image which was entirely flattering to Britain as well as to its monarchy. The reduction of foreign representatives to the level of subjects of Victoria was emphasised by the fact they were now not able to speak or respond in the ceremony. As the Doyen of the diplomatic corps later described it, they were 'mute as fish . . . thoroughly ashamed of what they had done'.[11]

Albert now gave a speech which recounted the history of the way the Exhibition had been set up. The speech was long and dry. However, it was more the symbolic act of giving the speech that was important: Victoria was being invested as the patron of the Exhibition. The state and the Exhibition were fused. As if to underline the point, Albert presented Victoria with a copy of the official catalogue. Albert's speech also acted almost like a church sermon: it even ended with the words 'it is our heartfelt prayer that this undertaking, which has for its end the promotion of all branches of human industry and the strengthening of the bonds of peace and friendship among all nations of the earth, may, by the blessing of Divine Providence, conduce to the welfare of your Majesty's people, and be long remembered among the brightest circumstances of your Majesty's peaceful and happy reign'.[12]

Taking up the religious theme, the Archbishop of Canterbury now led the congregation in prayer. Once this was done, the Crystal Palace was filled with the sound of the 'Hallelujah Chorus' from Handel's *Messiah*, led by Sir Henry Bishop, Professor of Music at Oxford, and making use of the two organs and massed choirs. The choice of music was significant: the oratorio, as a religious piece which could be played in secular surroundings, was entirely suited to what had just taken place. The effect of this rousing chorus within the Crystal Palace can only be imagined. For an instant, under the sunny skies shining through the roof, God must have appeared to be on the Royal Commission's side. It is revealing to note that years later the Crystal Palace would be the permanent home of the triennial Handel festival; an attempt, perhaps, to perpetuate the glories of 1 May 1851.[13]

Once the chorus was over, a procession was formed which made its way around the building. At the symbolic level, Victoria was being shown her Exhibition. She was moving directly in front of many thousands of subjects in a way that was quite unprecedented. The procession was also, however, a highly vivid demonstration of the unity of state and Exhibition, as well as a final mark of royal approval for the project. It was led by heralds, who were followed by Fox, Paxton and Henderson, the superintendents of the building works, the various committees of the Royal Commission, the Executive Committee, Commissioners and Foreign Commissioners, foreign ambassadors, cabinet ministers, the Bishop of London and the Archbishop of Canterbury, the White Wands (Treasurer and Comptroller of the Royal Household). Then followed the royal party, which included, in addition to Albert and Victoria, the Princess Royal, the Prince of Wales, the Prince of Prussia (later Kaiser William I of Germany), the Duchess of Kent, Prince Henry of the Netherlands, the Princess of Prussia, Prince Frederick William of Prussia (later Kaiser Frederick William III), Princess Mary of Cambridge, Prince Edward of Saxe-Weimar and the Duke of Cambridge. They were followed by a number of royal functionaries whose names now appear archaic, but whose presence marked the alliance which had been formed between the old and the new order: they included Gold Stick in Waiting, the Master of the Horse, the Groom of

The procession viewing the Exhibition. The procession was the embodiment of the new alliance that supported the Exhibition – aristocracy, politicians, the arts, industry and science.

the Stole, the Captain of the Gentlemen at Arms, the Captain of the Yeomen of the Guard, Master of the Buckhounds, Lord of the Bedchamber to Prince Albert, and so on. As the procession made its way round the Crystal Palace, a military band struck up a march and five organs placed in different parts of the building were played by organists from the churches of St Luke's in Old Street, St Sepulchre, the Temple and from the cathedrals of Notre Dame and Winchester. Once more this added to the rather ethereal atmosphere of the occasion.

When the Queen had returned to the podium, she declared the Exhibition open. This was immediately followed by fanfares inside the building, and outside by the firing of guns on the north bank of the Serpentine. The Coldstream Guards and Fusilier Guards struck up the national anthem once more and, as they did so, covers were taken off some of the most impressive exhibits and the fountains began to work. Some of the latter had been filled with eau de cologne and the air began to fill with its scent. As the royal party left, the barriers were taken away inside the building, the doors were opened and the Exhibition began.[14] Once the Queen and Prince Albert reached Buckingham Palace, they appeared with the royal group on the balcony.

While the opening ceremony was very much a piece of theatre organised by the Royal Commission to fulfil a particular function, much that happened was also spontaneous. For a start, there was not really enough space around Hyde Park to cater for such numbers as arrived on the day. Before the ceremony, as early as 8 a.m., enormous traffic jams had formed from the centre of London to the Exhibition, consisting predominantly of horse-drawn coaches and cabs belonging to the privileged who had seats in the Crystal Palace. Many, therefore, had to get out and walk with the masses who were going to Hyde Park. Ironically, this seemed to support the liberal aspirations of the Exhibition. As *Punch* gleefully put it, 'the proudest equipage of the peer was obliged to fall in behind the humblest fly or the ugliest Hansom; there being no privileged order, but the order of arrival'.[15] The *Daily News* noted that 'such of the ticket holders as had not got carriages, or had not had the prudence to engage a cab or fly overnight, had, if they came from a suburban district, to walk for miles . . . Many of the male visitors left their carriages and separated from their parties, leaving the ladies to follow leisurely, while the elder dowagers deferred their visit till the afternoon in expectation of a crush, which, however, did not take place'.[16]

In Hyde Park festivities autonomous of the Royal Commission were taking place. People were celebrating all around the Crystal Palace. A gigantic marquee had been erected. Balloon trips were organised. In general, people were enjoying the day's holiday, and the livelier show outside the Exhibition building formed a useful informal counterweight to what was going on inside. Macaulay, for one, noted that the people in the park were far more interesting exhibits than those housed in the Crystal Palace.[17]

The crowds that gathered in the Crystal Palace early were forced to sit or stand for several hours before the ceremony began. This gave time for observing prior arrangements and allowed a sort of camaraderie to develop among the crowd. The *Daily News* explained that as large sections of London society were there *en masse*:

> . . . few were without friends or companions, and a kind of morning *conversazione* was established. Here a speculative squire, who had occupied one of the lady's seats on the chance of holding it throughout the celebration, deaf to hints and insinuations, and the sarcasms of the fair expectants, was to the consolation of the bystanders induced to give way to the eloquence of a policeman. There a cathedral choir attended by wardens with wands, and including the whole body from the organist in his doctor's robes and the veteran basses, down to the urchin treble just entered on his noviciate, wandered about without knowing how to get to their places of performance.[18]

The spectacle of dignitaries and politicians arriving to take their places in the crowd was entertainment in itself. The arrival of the popular Duke of Wellington, who was celebrating his eighty-second birthday that day, sent a wave of rapture round the building. Moreover, the wait allowed those present to study the building and absorb its unfamiliar ambience.

Some of the spontaneity derived from the fact that there had been so little time to organise things. Henry Cole recorded that no one had thought to reserve seats for the Royal Commissioners. The police did not know the nave from the gallery. No barriers had been put up around the transept, meaning that sappers had to be used to keep the crowd from pushing forward towards the throne.[19] Not all the ceremony worked: in particular Albert's speech was almost certainly too long. The effects of the music during the procession were chaotic. Even the most loyal accounts of the opening found it hard to be positive about its effects – Queen Victoria herself cryptically recording that 'the organs were but little heard'.[20] There was also some confusion about the wearing of hats during the religious part of the ceremony. As the *Daily News* explained, 'it was from

The transept from Kensington
Road.

ignorance of the religious part of the day's proceedings – no programmes being posted
or distributed, and the voice of the Archbishop being inaudible, except towards the close
of what seemed to those at a distance rather a long prayer, when indistinct tones of
devotion were heard'.[21]

Still, even at the time these details were overlooked in the general festival atmosphere.
It was indicative of the generally uncritical mood that one visitor, a Chinese man,
probably from the visiting junk anchored in the Thames, who had come adorned as a
mandarin, was shown to the transept where foreign representatives were collected and
was treated as an official of China. During the 'Hallelujah Chorus' he caused excitement,
but no fear, when he approached the throne and bowed before Victoria. 'This live
importation from the Celestial Empire,' the *Examiner* recorded:

> managed to render himself extremely conspicuous, and one could not help admiring
> his perfect composure and nonchalance of manner. He talked with nobody, yet he
> seemed perfectly at home, and on the most friendly terms with all. A most amusing
> advantage was taken of his appearance, for, when the procession was formed, the

diplomatic body had no Chinese representative, and our stray Celestial friend was quietly impounded and made to march in the rear of the ambassadors. He submitted to this arrangement with the same calm indifference which marked the whole course of his proceedings . . . His behaviour throughout was that of 'a citizen of the world' . . .[22]

This was a surprising, but soon fabled, addition to the artificial picture of China presented by the Exhibition!

Not everyone was impressed by the opening ceremony. *John Bull*, representing a constituency of protectionists, Tories and staunch Anglicans, reacted strongly against the use of sacred and parliamentary ceremonies for the Exhibition. This, it said, was another obvious attempt on the part of free traders to hijack the trappings of state and it warned them 'not to try the patience of the English people too hard, lest they provoke to animosity and disgust those who are at present disposed to treat a questionable undertaking with forbearance'.[23] When *The Times*, meanwhile, compared the opening effusively to 'a second more glorious inauguration of the Sovereign', *John Bull*'s reaction was sharp. It almost feared, it said, 'to follow up the sentiment to its legitimate consequences. For what does this profane suggestion really amount to, but that the solemn consecration of the Queen in the temple of the King of Kings was less glorious, than her "inauguration" in the temple of Mammon.'[24]

For most shades of opinion, however, the opening ceremony was an enormous success, acting as a powerful advert for the Exhibition and further encouraging the alliance that supported it. Aristocratic and conservative interests in Britain breathed an enormous sigh of relief that revolution had not broken out and, sensing that the monarchy's position had been strengthened by the opening ceremony rather than destroyed, suddenly began to warm to the whole concept. This was betrayed in the congratulation Queen Victoria received the evening of the opening from her mother, the Duchess of Kent, which stated that 'I felt so nervous and anxious yesterday and this morning and *now*, I feel very happy and *pleased. Ich habe einen schweren Angst, aber ein leichtes Herz!*'[25] [I have a heavy fear but a light heart.] It was also obvious in other messages Victoria received, such as that from Lady Lyttelton, which admitted that 'I own I was not without anxiety – and was visited by many fears and doubts – the result has been, thank God, so delightful, as to do much more than dispel them.'[26] *John Bull*, which had feared politically for the monarchy, likewise stated that 'it is with the utmost thankfulness that we record the happy termination of the opening of the "Crystal Palace", by Her Majesty, without any untoward occurrence to mar the amusement of the day. For this all, whatever view they may take of the Exhibition itself, one cannot but feel deeply grateful to HIM, Whose gracious Providence watches over this nation and over our beloved Queen.' It was even generous enough now to concede that 'viewing the "World's Fair" merely as a fair, as an amusement, albeit of an intellectual kind, it has undoubtedly thus far proved successful; and for the sake of the holiday folks we are right glad of it'.[27]

Such relief was not restricted to the aristocracy and conservatives, however. The unprecedented nature of the Exhibition, together with protectionist warnings, had produced such a general jangling of nerves that even Lord John Russell, in his congratulations to the Queen, admitted that of all the things he could mention, 'the general conduct of the multitudes assembled, the loyalty and the content which so

The first view of the
Exhibition after entering. At
the centre of the transept is
Osler's Crystal Fountain
surrounded by sculptures.

generally appeared were perhaps the most gratifying to a politician.'[28] *Punch*,
meanwhile, sensing that Sibthorpe's argument had been smashed to pieces, celebrated
with a poem entitled 'The Lament of the Member for Lincoln'.[29]

Liberal observers found much to admire in the demonstration by the monarchy of its
support for industry and the common man. As the *Morning Chronicle* put it, 'as the first
conception of the scheme now completed came forth from Buckingham Palace . . . so it
was in keeping and in harmony with the whole idea and the whole execution of it, that
the last finishing touch should have been given by Royalty – that Queen Victoria should
have opened in person the Great Parliament of Labour'. This was important
terminology: the similarities between the opening of Parliament and of the Exhibition
also chimed with the feelings of a wide swathe of liberals. The inclusion of foreign
countries in this ceremony, meanwhile, flattered their belief in the global inevitability of

The transept looking south. At the far end are the main entrance doors.

liberalisation and the universal applicability of British institutions. The *Morning Chronicle* continued by pointing out that the Crystal Palace was 'a Parliament truly, in which, though all are silent, all are eloquent members. A congress as well as a Parliament, with its representatives of all climes and zones – torrid and icy; of all the great divisions of the globe . . . one vast brotherhood, obeying the eternal and immutable law which makes labour necessary to the due development and due evolution of human existence'.[30]

For most liberals and Whigs, and many conservatives too, it was a deep source of national pride that Victoria and Albert were able to walk before the population and be so adored – in contrast to the polarised situation on the continent and in particular to the German states, where political reaction was presently reaching its zenith. As *Punch* – which once again was moved to solemnity – said: 'It was a magnificent lesson for foreigners – and especially for the Prussian princes, who cannot stir abroad without an armed escort – to see how securely and confidently a young female Sovereign and her family could walk in the closest possible contact, near enough to be touched by almost everyone, with five-and-twenty thousand people, selected from no class, and requiring only the sum of forty-two shillings as a qualification for the nearest proximity with royalty.'[31] To have this kind of impact on foreigners had been, of course Albert's intention. King Leopold of Belgium, Albert's uncle and mentor, and a fellow advocate of moderate liberalism on the continent, wrote to Victoria that 'I am glad that foreigners saw for once, that to the highest authority in the state even a great and free country like England may show real and great respect'.[32]

Taken as a whole the ceremony also produced an attractive effect – though it was difficult to put one's finger on what it was. *The Times*, for example, previously sceptical towards the Exhibition, began its report by saying 'the edifice, the treasures of nature and art collected therein, the assemblage, and the solemnity of the occasion, all conspired to suggest something even more than sense could scan or imagination attain. There were many there who were familiar with magnificent spectacles; who had seen coronations, fetes, and solemnities; but they had not seen anything to compare with this'. This display created, it said, 'an effect so grand and yet so natural, that it hardly seemed to be put together by design, or to be the work of human artificers'.[33]

Once again, the Exhibition appeared to be the focus of some religious significance, and *The Times* was not alone in comparing the whole to a cathedral. Many others spoke of the 'fairy-like' quality of the building, the magical effect created – which in part seemed to be due to the glass roof and the new sensation of being in a transparent building. For others, the ceremony transformed what had previously been millennialist fears about the Exhibition into positive sensations of its historical importance. The *Daily News* spoke of the music which 'swelled out in harmony like the noise of many waters heard in some apocalyptic vision, making the hearts of the hearers vibrate like the glass of the edifice that inclosed them'.[34] The *Morning Chronicle* was moved to write that 'the Exhibition in Hyde Park will form an era at once in the national and in the industrial annals of the world. It will attract, probably, the greatest human assemblage ever collected together upon one small spot of the earth's surface, and it will determine the exact degree up to which, in the middle of the 19th century, the skill and ingenuity of man have arrived.'[35]

As a whole, the impact of the opening was enormous both in terms of consolidating the base of support for the Exhibition and also in terms of advertisement. Most of the newspapers on 1 and 2 May were given over almost completely to the events in Hyde Park. Many – *The Times* included – produced special supplements devoted to the subject. Doubtless, some of the hyperbole involved stemmed from a need to prove the success of the Exhibition in the face of an opposition which had not gone away, but which, rather, seemed to be regrouping. Recently, the protectionist movement had stolen some of the Royal Commission's clothes and adopted the tactic of holding banquets. One of these, held on 3 May at Drury Lane theatre, was strategically timed to destroy the Exhibition festivities. Behind the scenes, while dealing with the opening, Lord John Russell was feverishly working at holding together the fragile alliance which supported his government. The protectionists seemed seriously in danger of getting the upper hand, to the extent that Russell did not dare seek a new election but preferred to cling on in the hopes that then, as he put it, 'some junction might be practicable'.[36] In this situation, the Exhibition's supporters were almost obliged to enthuse about the opening. But the excitement the event caused went far beyond support for free trade, which in any case was played down by the Royal Commission, for fear of splitting its supporters. Rather the euphoria seemed to be the result of the fact that for the first time in decades a genuine unity seemed to have been produced between the ruling classes and the various interests produced by industrialisation.

One final result of all this is worth mentioning. More than anything, the opening of the Exhibition represented a personal triumph for Albert. Having spent years fighting for a role in British politics, and looking rather superfluous to requirements in comparison with his wife's constitutional role, Albert now appeared to have created a success of his own. The press had increasingly identified Albert as the source of the Exhibition idea – encouraged by the Royal Commission for its own mercenary reasons – and it now laid the success of the opening at his feet. *Punch* was just one of many newspapers that noted that Albert, 'by the idea of this Exhibition, has given to the Royal Consortship a new glory, or, rather, has rendered for ever illustrious, in his own case, a position too often vibrating between the mischievous and the insignificant. Prince Albert has done a grand service to humanity, and earned imperishable fame for himself by an idea, the greatness of which, instead of becoming less, will appear still greater as it recedes from us'.[37] Albert's success also, it might be suspected, sorted out one or two issues within the royal marriage. This, perhaps, lay at the root of Queen Victoria's letter to Lady Lyttelton, which stated that:

> To see this great conception of my beloved Husband's great and good mind, which is always labouring for the good of others – to see this *great* thought and work crowned with triumphant success, in spite of difficulties and opposition of every imaginable kind and sort – and of every effort which jealousy and calumny could resort to cause its failure – has been an immense happiness to us both – but to *me* the glory of *his* name united with the glory of my dear country who shone more than she has ever done on that great day – is a source of pride, happiness and thankfulness, which none but a wife's heart can comprehend.[38]

II

The way the Exhibition actually looked can only be explained in terms of the history of the process of organisation that had preceded it. Rather than being the result of one, overarching idea, the Exhibition was the product of the fusion of the various groups' aims, the financial vulnerability of the Royal Commission and its need to attract visitors, the need to devolve control over the event in order to maintain support for it and questions of practicality. Indeed, the Exhibition's success owed much to the fact that there was, in the end, something there for almost everyone. Yet the attempt to harmonise so many voices also led to some serious weaknesses.

Coming to the Exhibition from the Prince of Wales' Gate on Kensington Road, visitors passed through the two park lodges, which housed the police, and towards the main entrance with the arched transept towering above it. With the sun invariably behind them, visitors would be faced with a mesmerising reflection of the sky, over 100 ft high. Stretching away from them on either side, 1851 ft long – a figure which for obvious

The Indian section. At the centre is the ornately carved ivory chair.

reasons became folklore[39] – was probably the longest building most had ever seen. Passing through the doors, on through a set of turnstiles built specially for the Exhibition by the Bramah company, round the umbrella stands and through a set of park gates by Cottam and Hallen, which formed the first exhibit and perhaps symbolically marked an entrance into a new landscape, then on past the stalls selling catalogues on either side, they were confronted with the first full aspect of the Exhibition which was enormously impressive.

Almost everywhere flowers and palm trees were planted, making a point of the daylight and giving the whole view a cool and exotic feel. The height of the building, and its sense of altered reality, was underlined by the presence of one of the full-grown Hyde Park elms towards the far end of the transept and by the blue and white of the colour scheme. At the very centre of the building, where the transept was crossed by the main avenue, Osler's Crystal Fountain, some 27 ft high, entirely made of coloured glass and forming a celebration of glass manufacture to counterpoint Paxton's, played with the sense of light and sound. Another fountain echoed this further on at the intersection of the transept and a second, lesser passage. Around and about, imposing and artistic works of sculpture were placed and colourful displays of silks and other textiles were hung.

The transept was used to form a frame of reference for the visitor. For one thing, the statuary chosen immediately imprinted the stamp of royal patronage and state approval on the Exhibition. Directly at the front and in the centre, facing incoming crowds, was a statue of Queen Victoria. Further back, behind the Crystal Fountain, were statues of Albert and Victoria on horseback. The transept was also used to impress the visitor with the importance of artistic design. Previous discussions about the layout had resulted in the more artistic produce being moved towards the aisles to give them prominence. The transept was, in effect, the most important aisle and the building's arch had almost accidentally magnified its pre-eminence as a forum. Cutting across the north–south arrangement of machines, industrial produce and raw materials, therefore, the transept created an aesthetic frame of reference which ran from the centre of the building outwards. This fact, as well as the dramatic impact they generated, explained why the Exhibition on the left began with the exquisite works of India – including an ornately carved ivory chair and much embroidery – and just behind them Class 30 of the British exhibits; on the right, the newly arrived faced the exotic and mystical works of China, Tunis and Turkey. Around and about, meanwhile, partly included in the Exhibition and partly there for ornament, sculpture was displayed, including John Bell's *Eagle Slayer*, Foley's *Youth at the Stream*, Engel's *Amazons and the Argonauts*, and the Coalbrookdale Company's reworking of Bell's *Andromeda*. Much of this was pure white and with the plants it created a rather strange ethereal effect.

In addition to these principles of arrangement, however, other considerations were obvious here. The religious aspect of the Exhibition was recognised by a group of three sculptures representing *God's Victory over Satan* by Lough. Patriotic and liberal supporters

John Hampden, a seventeenth-century figure of significance to liberals in Britain.

were appealed to by statues of Lord Falkland and the parliamentary opponent of Charles I, John Hampden. A statue of *Victory* by the Prussian sculptor Rauch underscored the competitive nature of the Exhibition but also seemed to translate the pageantry of war across to industry, a theme which was repeated throughout the building.

Popularity was immediately courted, meanwhile, by the Koh-I-Noor diamond, which was positioned at the start of the eastern part of the main aisle. This diamond, which weighed 186.5 carats, was in a metal cage over 6 ft high and locked to the floor. Surrounded by other jewels, it was lit by gas-light from below. It had a long, mythical history but had come into Queen Victoria's possession after British forces invaded Lahore. It therefore represented at once incalculable wealth, mystery, monarchical power and the strength of the British Empire. One popular publication noted it was one of only three diamonds in the world of such value but that it was actually badly cut. The reason for this was 'it is said that it was done by an Italian lapidary; and when it was found in what an unworkmanlike manner he had cut it, he was immediately executed'.[40] Such urban myths ensured that the wondering and the morbidly curious made the diamond their first port of call.

Also housed next to the transept were the offices of the juries and the Executive Committee, which were immediately on the right and left of the turnstiles. At the far end, where Victoria had entered for the opening, a refreshment court allowed visitors to sit and absorb the atmosphere. Tucked away next to them on the right, two lecture theatres underlined the educational importance of the Exhibition.

If visitors moved forward to the Crystal Fountain and turned left, they looked down the western branch of the main avenue, in other words down the centre of the British and colonial side of the building. This was a view that stretched almost 900 ft to the western entrance and was made to seem longer and higher by the colour scheme of the inside of the building. The aisle was 72 ft wide and 72 ft high and the first floor galleries opened on to it on either side 20 ft up. From the galleries, the emblems and flags of British localities were displayed in the tradition begun at the mayors' banquets. From the roof, above the galleries, hung carpets and textiles of all shades and colours. This maximised the use of space, cut down the glare of sunlight, and gave the Exhibition a heraldic look. On the ground floor, counters jutted out into the avenue and, every few steps, passages led off to either side into the different displays. Four fountains marked major intersections and echoed the effect of the transept. The most prominent were the 'Acis and Galatea' fountain by Thomas, the sculptor of ornaments for the Houses of Parliament, and Seeley's fountain. In the centre of the avenue, stretching into the distance, more celebrated exhibits were gathered.

The fact that this was the main avenue meant that the exhibits placed there occupied a special place. Again the attempt was made not only to use the space to attract the visitor, but also to emphasise the Exhibition's system of priorities. Where the transept had focused on art, however, the main avenue betrayed the wider discussion which had gone on between the Exhibition's supporters. Here, science, commerce, education, art were all honoured and their union promoted. Other groups of supporters were flattered by being allotted a space in this area too. The displays in the main avenue also often acted as marker points, indicating a display which might lead off on either side. Quite often, what was on the main avenue would represent the culmination of that side display.

As the visitor walked westward from the transept, therefore, the first major displays he or she saw were two so-called trophies, one belonging to Messrs Keith and

The main avenue looking west from the transept. At the centre is one of the trophies designed by the Saxon architect Gottfried Semper; they were considered works of art in themselves.

Shoobridge, the London silk manufacturers, the other devoted to Canadian timber. These were displays of goods piled high, based on the shows of war booty in former times – a tradition which had been taken up in Napoleonic French exhibitions[41] and found its way into the Crystal Palace. Trophies were to be found repeatedly down both the main aisles. Here industrialists, rather than soldiers, were the new national heroes. The silk trophy celebrated one of the few examples of intricate luxury textile design to be manufactured in Britain – with a nod in the direction of the metropolis. The timber one highlighted the wealth of Britain's foreign possessions in terms of raw materials – an image of the colonies which would be repeated again and again. It also marked the Canadian display which led off to the left. This had around 220 exhibitors and concentrated largely on raw materials. There were many ores and minerals on show, including specimens of gold, one of which weighed a quarter of a pound, and from New Brunswick a display of various agrarian products. The only developed artefacts were a fire-engine from Montreal and a piano constructed to resist huge temperature changes.

Further down the main aisle, there were several exhibits of a Gothic and medieval character, including a replica of a fourteenth-century statue of Edward III's wife, Philippa of Hainault, executed by George Gilbert Scott and various other ecclesiastical objects. These objects marked a court to the left filled with medieval replicas, soon to become one of the most famous parts of the Exhibition. The Victorian craze for Gothic and medieval design represented a symptom of the crisis which industrialisation had caused in the world of design. Historical styles were just one solution put forward to what was generally perceived as a need for more attention to design. At this point, despite buildings like the Houses of Parliament, Gothic and medieval styles had not reached the popular position they would later achieve. Yet the interest had already generated an unusual British strength in Gothic design and the medieval court represented a pragmatic attempt to show this off in one unitary display. Here the works of Pugin, Crace, and Myers and Hardmann were collected. Though much of it consisted of replicas of religious artefacts, some also demonstrated the attempt to apply Gothic design to industrial goods. Crace, for example, had produced a Gothic cabinet which dominated the court. At the front, near the main avenue, John Chubb had produced locks and keys in Gothic style. The exhibits in the main avenue represented a tribute by the Exhibition to the attempts made by Gothic designers to reunite design and industry. Also in the main avenue was a Gothic altar produced using Jordan's Patent Carving Mechanism. This allowed ancient carvings to be reproduced almost perfectly – symbolising the aesthetic possibilities of mechanisation.[42]

It was also another demonstration of the importance of religion at the Exhibition. This was emphasised again further along the main avenue (past Thomas's fountain) by the Harriet Ross Monumental Irish Cross, which towered 16 ft high and was covered in ornate carvings from the Old and New Testament. Apart from being one of the few exhibits to be celebrated *and* produced by a woman – a subject to be discussed below – this cross, with the other Gothic pieces behind it and the Jordan altar in front, made the building seem more like a cathedral than ever. Many other exhibits supported this. Their selection was the result of the increasing importance religion had gained during the discussions about the Exhibition. Now, however, they served to underline the message that the Exhibition's aims were God's aims.

The stone cross was a statement of support for skilled craftsmanship. It also demonstrated another facet of the Exhibition – its tendency to monumentalism and excess: as Robert Hunt's popular guide to the Exhibition pointed out, this exhibit was 'said to be the largest piece of ornamental furniture ever made'.[43] Size and excess were one way of celebrating the powers of the present industrial age in relation to those of the past. They also proved to be a crowd puller. All over the Exhibition, objects were to be found which were there because of their size.

Further west, a 'chemical trophy' extended the form of symbolic celebration to science. Displays of cutlery by Joseph Rodgers and Sons, one of the most respected Sheffield manufacturers, indicated the presence of the hardware department on the left-hand side and, once again, gave prominence to a British sector of production which was exceptionally successful because of its craftsmanship rather than its cheapness. Here, once more using excess as a way of celebrating design, was Rodgers' famous penknife with eighty blades.

A 'rustic summer house' produced by the Coalbrookdale Company followed this. Some 20 ft wide and 30 ft high, the structure was made of bronzed wrought iron and demonstrated the advanced techniques of metalworking developed by the company, at a time when British know-how in the area was second to none. It also represented an attempt to show off the application of art to industry: at its centre, Bell's *Eagle Slayer* was reproduced, shooting his arrow into the ornate roof. Beyond this, two exhibits followed

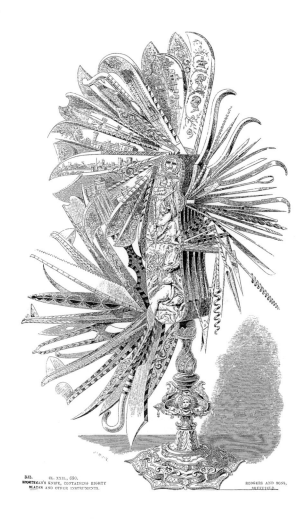

Rodgers and Sons. The penknife with eighty blades.

3.15. CL. XXII., 690.
SPORTSMAN'S KNIFE, CONTAINING EIGHTY BLADES AND OTHER INSTRUMENTS.

RODGERS AND SONS, SHEFFIELD.

which celebrated and encouraged a closer connection of science with industry: first, a complete set of light-house lenses, which, as was pointed out in one guide, 'proved the advantages of the study of abstract science, the arrangement of the glass prisms being determined by the nicest inductive examination and mathematical calculation of the laws regulating the reflexion and refraction of light'.[44] Second came Lord Rosse's gigantic telescope, measuring 20 ft long and with the largest refractor ever made.

A little further along, past another trophy – this time devoted to furs, skins and feathers – architects and engineers received their share of the plaudits with a terracotta model of St Nicholas's church in Hamburg and models of the Dnieper bridge, Stephenson's Britannia bridge over the Menai Straits, Brunel's Chepstow bridge over the Wye, the new fortified breakwater at Plymouth and the harbour on the Isle of Wight.

All of these were either recent constructions or were about to be completed. Such models served to inform a curious public about recent works they had perhaps heard about. They were also meant to impress visitors with the latest marvels of the industrial age. At the very end, before the umbrella stands, was a gigantic model of the docks of

The main avenue from the western end. At the centre is the dome of the Coalbrookdale summer-house. Also clearly visible are the lighthouse lenses, Rosse's telescope and Seeley's fountain.

Liverpool. This was a concession to the city authorities there: accompanied by facts and figures about the city, it was more an advert for the port than anything else. Pragmatically, however, the Royal Commission had accepted it as the price to pay for continued support in Liverpool. In all, therefore, the selection of goods down the main avenue could only be explained as the result of the effort to include and integrate all the various pockets of support for the Exhibition.

At the western entrance to the main avenue was another set of ticket offices and catalogue booths. Just outside were articles placed there because of their enormous size and weight. On the left were examples of mining and stone. One block of coal from Coed Talon mine weighed in at 16 tons. Another showed the coal strata. Yet another, from Tipton, Staffordshire, was 18 ft in circumference. These demonstrated all at once British strength in the predominant form of fuel of the time, the use of science to mining and a will to educate. According to the *Morning Chronicle*, the piece of Tipton coal was probably the largest object ever to come out of a mine.[45] Great public interest had been attracted in December 1850 when one attempt to raise the block had resulted in the chains and gearing breaking. As if to underline the gigantism and glorify the power of industry, the chains used to lift the coal were also shown. On the right of the western entrance were goods relating to machinery, produce and transport, including huge anchors, lifeboats and enormous examples of earthenware pots.

As the visitors turned back inside the building, the south-to-north principle of arrangement at ground level reflecting the order of the productive process now became more obvious. Along the extreme south wall was Class 1, comprising mining and mineral products. Throughout this the educative aims of the Exhibition, as well as the desire to apply artistic design to the question at hand, was in evidence. Working models demonstrated the mining process and the way in which coal was sorted. There were many show-case arrangements of stone and ores – those of gems were a particular attraction. James Tennant, a mineralogist from the Strand, showed four cases of minerals 'for educational, scientific and ornamental purposes'.[46] New materials were celebrated, including cement, which had only been really become commonly used in the 1830s in Britain and was now worked into a bust of Shakespeare. There was even a display by Harris of Manchester of different types of manure (though the *Official Catalogue* did note this had been 'deodorised'[47]).

Class 1 stretched towards the transept and as it did so concerned itself increasingly with metal ores and metallurgy. At the end, visitors entered into the sculpture court, which demonstrated the artistic use of stone. On its left, closer to the main avenue, was the medieval court, where the artistic uses of metal were displayed. Thus the north–south productive arrangement blended with the east–west aesthetic one. In the sculpture court, showing the Executive Committee's canny decision to include other organisations in the Exhibition, was a display of statues entered for the Art Union prize competition.

Parallel to the south wall, but closer to the main avenue, and thus one step up the productive chain, were agricultural implements (Class 9). Here, some of the big British agricultural machine-producers were to be found, including Ransome and May, Hornsby and Son and Garrett. Steam-driven ploughs, drilling and threshing machines demonstrated the contribution industrialisation had made to farming – and countered implicitly any idea of the two sectors being opposed to each other. Also here were John Milton's beehives, which symbolised the work ethic being promoted by the Exhibition and even drew directly on the Exhibition's aims for inspiration by showing one hive shaped like a city house containing four different families of bees 'thus demonstrating that a very considerable number of bees from various queens will work together in perfect harmony'.[48]

Milton's beehives. Bees were considered fascinating because of their commitment to labour. Industry was a virtue much prized at the Exhibition.

Nasmyth's steam hammer.   The Jacquard loom.

A further step up the productive chain – textiles, furniture and hardware – was shown along the main avenue itself. Here, from the transept back to the western end, the regional nature of British production at the mid-century and the efforts of the Executive Committee to harness local patriotism were demonstrated by the large collections of Birmingham hardware, London furniture, Sheffield cutlery, Yorkshire woollens and worsteds, and Dundee jute. Immediately on the other side of the main avenue, meanwhile, less localised products were shown. Moving from the transept outwards, the visitor encountered paper, furniture, leather and cotton goods. This meant that on either side of the main avenue at its western end, fabrics predominated: the goods of Manchester uneasily surrounded the model of the Liverpool docks.

Finally, north of these goods, placed there because of the noise and the need to connect with the steam-power generated from outside in the boiler-house, were the machines. This began with the machinery at rest and the carriages court because they were not dependent on steam-power. The machinery at rest showed vividly how technological advances had brought the capabilities of machine tools to new heights. Nasmyth's steam hammer was here; it could produce iron bars and girders of a size not before known but was famous for also being able to operate so delicately as to only crack an egg-shell. The steam press used to build Stevenson's Britannia bridge was here. So, too, was the crane Fox and Henderson had used to build the Crystal Palace – the first of many objects which pointed to the building itself as one of the main exhibits demonstrating the feats of industry. Within this section there were also models of older steam engines – for example William Murdoch's engine for road travel of 1785. Such exhibits provided another educational dimension. The carriages court belonged closer to the avenue as the goods exhibited there were more consumables than machines proper. They were also not just feats of engineering, but prized for their design and aesthetic appearance too. Like a present day motor show, many of the most sought after and fashionable makes were to be found here.

In between these sections and those further north was a stretch of railway, 530 ft long, with locomotives and carriages parked on it. Both gauges were shown – the 7 ft one that Brunel had favoured on his Great Western Railway and the 4 ft 8 in one which had been the legal norm in Britain since 1846. Power and speed was represented by Great Western Railway's locomotive produced at Swindon, an engine in production since 1847 with 1,000 horse power and capable of speeds up to 60 mph. Here was also an example of South Eastern Railway's London to Paris locomotives, the *Folkstone*.

The railway section formed a barrier between the acceptable face of machinery and its more dirty reality – the machinery in motion. It was also a natural link between the more familiar machines in the carriages court and machinery at rest, and those behind, which often concerned only manufacturers. These, ranged along the north side of the building, showed the impressive scale of mechanisation in textile production. The sight and sound of so many working looms was astounding for many visitors. This area tended once more towards educative displays such as that by Platt & Sons, one of several big Manchester companies, which took viewers through all the stages of textile production from raw cotton to the finished article. Design had its place in the shape of the several powered versions of a Jacquard loom – a loom developed in France and

The *Folkstone*.

known for its ability to produce complicated woven patterns. Further towards the transept, precision crept in as the display's main virtue once more, with the machine-tools display of Whitworth & Company and Fairbairn & Sons. The revolution caused by mechanisation in newspaper production was given its slot further along, with Herbert Ingram's vertical press, on which *The Times* was printed, and the working press of the *Illustrated London News*. Attention was also focused on the Exhibition again by Cowper's press on which the Exhibition catalogues were printed, and the coin press on which Exhibition medals were stamped.

Because lighter goods had been put upstairs, the virtues of design being promoted by the Exhibition were if anything more concentrated and obvious there. The commercial benefits of artistic design were demonstrated by the exemplary pottery – near the aesthetic heart of the transept on the north side – of Herbert Minton, Wedgwood and others. Close behind was glassware, including another display by Osler and two chandeliers – one in Gothic and one in the Alhambra style.

Moving west, the emphasis moved to Class 7, which displayed goods relating to civil engineering, architecture and building. The possibilities of new building techniques and materials were demonstrated by many models. Here, the Exhibition made a bow in the direction of the conscience of the middle classes – but still celebrated the new capacities of the industrial age – by including a display by the Metropolitan Association for Improving the Dwellings of the Industrious Classes of model dwellings

Albert's model houses. The houses were meant to be affordable and decent; they were constructed using new building materials, such as hollow bricks, and were intended to provide hygienic conditions. After the Exhibition they were moved to Kennington Park, where they still stand.

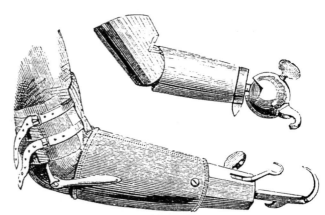

Major Little's artificial hand. The crowd-pulling, grisly nature of such exhibits masked their importance as new applications of technology to medicine.

Major Little's Artificial Hand.

for artisans. The use of new materials, it was suggested, could resolve the lack of decent housing among the lower classes. Industry, in other words, could clear up its own mess. This was the logic that also lay behind the full-scale Model Houses displayed outside the Exhibition building in the Kensington Barracks yard. Revealingly, poverty was not identified as the result of industrialisation, but rather as something that had been around for centuries. The confident display of solutions produced by industrialisation to what were seen as perennial problems was one of the characteristics of the exhibits in the Crystal Palace. Also in Class 7 was a model of an emigrants' house, made of 'galvanised tinned iron, corrugated', and a 'model of a house, and plans for purifying towns, destroying putrescence, affording economical means of removing manures (inoffensively) by rail; and precluding the necessity of cleansing drains, &c'.[49] Still in Class 7, tucked away in the far western corner, were models of alternative buildings for the Great Exhibition.

Alongside Class 7, overlooking the main avenue, was Class 10, which had precision as its theme. It was devoted to philosophical (i.e. scientific), musical, horological and surgical instruments. This included blades and scalpels, but also new medical technology like an 'artificial leech', which could painlessly suck blood from the infected patient, a stomach pump 'with several useful adaptations', an 'inhaler, for opium and other medicines', a false nose, and Major Little's spectacular artificial arm. Class 10 also contained many clocks, which demonstrated once more the achievements of precision tool-making, as well as often taking on highly artistic forms. Precision was also the theme of the many philosophical instruments which were displayed, including many weather-recording devices.

Class 10 also, however, gave space to the latest innovations, in particular the power of electricity. Ranged here were electric telegraphs, which showed the public the machine that was currently revolutionising communications in Britain and the world; in 1851 the first telegraph cable was laid between Paris and London. Here also were several examples of electric clocks, including one by Charles Shepherd of London, which could operate several different faces simultaneously and would soon change the look of railway stations everywhere. The Exhibition building itself made use of this technology, and once more underlined its own position as an exhibit, by placing an electric clock in the centre of the transept's arch. The latest progress in the battle to create reliable electric lighting was displayed by working arc lamps. (The filament bulb would not come in until the 1880s.) So, too, was the increasing attention being paid by scientists and inventors to the building of electric motors.

The emphasis on precision and design also explains the presence of musical instruments in this department. Just as much of the sculpture had been displayed in order to show technique and new use of materials, the display of musical instruments had nothing to do with artistic qualities of sound and everything to do with techniques of production, design and use of material. There were pianos here that had two or even four keyboards, that could be raised or lowered in pitch by moving the sound board, or that could transpose to different keys. There were others that were ornately designed, such as one by Collard & Collard of Cheapside in mottled oak and gold inlay in the Louis Quinze style. There was a 'Harp Ventura' – named after its inventor – that was played like a guitar but sounded like a harp, and a 'newly-invented euphonic serpent'. At the head of the display at the end of the western nave, was the gigantic Willis's Organ, which had over 4,500 pipes, the smallest being ⅜ in long, the largest 32 ft.

The same considerations also explained why photography was to be found here, tucked away in the far end of the nave with the scientific exhibits, rather than towards the centre of the building with the other aesthetic goods. Photography was still seen as a scientific curiosity rather than a technique containing artistic possibilities. In Hunt's popular catalogue of the Exhibition these were called 'sun-drawn pictures', and the reader was informed flatly that 'the truthfulness of these pictures shows how valuable an adjunct to the artist is the scientific application of the fact that some salts of silver blacken in the sunshine'.[50]

Perhaps because it was placed so far away from the entrance and was not downstairs, where more serious classification systems reigned, this section also showed a stronger tendency to use the crowd-pulling techniques of the fairground. The medical display demonstrated a strong fascination with the gruesome – for example, the collection of glass eyes, the collection of surgical arms or the 'patent fulcrum and chair for extracting teeth'. It also had other artefacts which, while demonstrating the extent of precision, were also rather disturbing. For example Count Dunin's mechanical man, composed of 7,000 steel plates, could be expanded or contracted 'from the size of the Apollo Belvedere to that of a colossal statue'. Among the clocks were curiosities, such as the one which functioned though dangled in a glass globe full of silver and gold fish, or the one which took thirty-four years to complete. The philosophical instruments, meanwhile, tended to range from the imaginative to the entertaining; for example, there were working models of the globe, showing the ebb and flood of the tides, but also 'phantasmagoria lanterns', which projected gradually changing images rather like the diorama shows that, as will be seen, were so popular outside the Exhibition. At the very end of the nave innovative devices culminated in aerial machines, which included one by William Sadd of Wandsworth that consisted of 'two revolving wheels for propelling, and a rudder at each end to steer the machine; and two floats to raise or lower it without the aid of ballast. The whole is sustained by two cylindrical balloons, placed horizontally'.[51]

At the end of the western nave, round the back of Willis's Organ, was Class 8, devoted to naval and military engineering. Here were many different models of ships and naval equipment. There was also, however, a display of Ordnance Survey maps, which had been in production since 1805 and sought to cover the whole country at a scale of 1 inch to 1 mile. The latest completed work – Lancashire and Yorkshire maps – was on display, underlining the value of science to cartography and as a consequence once more implicitly suggesting the power man now had over nature. Such positivist messages abounded in the Crystal Palace. Other exhibits in Class 8 pointed to innovation, such as Hugh Bell's 'Model of a Submarine Boat'. Still others stressed design, including the collections of guns and swords found here, which smacked more of craftsmanship than military importance. A big display of swords by Wilkinson & Sons of London showed one blade encrusted with 104 precious jewels. It also showed all the swords used by the British army, but they were arranged to illustrate all the various stages of production and, therefore, according to educational principles. Any more blatantly militarist show would have alienated the large body of pacifist liberal opinion which existed at the mid-century. One type of exhibit that did seem to predominate here was ship's furniture and equipment which was designed to float. The popularity of this area of design work owed much to the fact that long-haul oceanic travel was just opening up to the wider public, in particular as a consequence of steam ships. The overwhelming confidence in technology, which would later be expressed in rhetoric – and lethargy – surrounding ships like *Titanic*, had not yet developed. Shipwreck was still viewed as a real danger.

Up the southern gallery, towards the transept, the lighter and more ornate products of industry were to be found. On the right, near the exterior wall, were samples of animal

Scottish vegetable produce. Such collections gave the Exhibition the air of a museum.

and vegetable substances. This section was surprisingly small, in contrast to the huge space given over to industrial machinery on the ground floor, and made the British half of the building seem far more machine-orientated than the eastern half. This was the result, however, of the arrangement with the Royal Agricultural Society.[52] There was a rather formal Scottish vegetable display here, inadvertently almost making that part of the country look like another colony devoted to raw materials. Then came foodstuffs. Once more, new techniques of production were shown, for example, honey produced in the jar or champagne produced in England from rhubarb stalk. So, too, were new techniques of preserving food. Condensed milk was displayed. Different sorts of food were shown canned, which, as the *Official Catalogue* pointed out, was a new way of keeping it fresh on long sea voyages and while in hot countries. Fairground techniques were used again to hammer the point home with a specimen of mutton left on Fury Beach after the Arctic mission of 1824 was shipwrecked there, found by Sir John Ross in 1833 and still in perfect condition. There were also three cans of mutton and vegetables produced in 1813 by Donkin, Hall & Gamble of Bermondsey, who had pioneered this French-invented method in Britain. Even the liberal aspirations of most of the Exhibition's supporters found expression here in the display of 'specimens of free-labour produce, loaf-sugar, coffee, rice, &c. as distinguished from the slave-labour produce of Cuba, Carolina, Brazil, &c'.[53] At one of the central junctions was to be found a display of produce from Fortnum & Mason. Samples of tobacco from Lambert & Butler were also on show. Finally, just at the transept, the increasingly scientific treatment of food preservation crossed over into Class 2, which contained chemicals.

On the left side of the southern gallery, along the main avenue, the more aesthetically pleasing goods were arranged. This included Class 23, where ornate metalwork and jewellery were placed and which, as even the normally factual *Catalogue* stated, contained 'objects of great attractiveness to almost every individual'.[54] Here were, for example, exhibits by Garrard & Company, jewellers to the Queen, and a large display of over 100 jewelled objects by Hunt & Roskell of New Bond Street. Directly under the daylight, the many jewels and shining gold could be seen to best effect. These goods were some of the most heavily designed and valuable of the Exhibition. Heading the display were – rather predictably – exhibits shown by Queen Victoria. Many trinkets reflected the royal patronage of the Exhibition by depicting miniatures and images of Albert and Victoria. In this section a silver display by Hancock of London depicted Queen Elizabeth entering Kenilworth Castle. This was a recurrent theme, partly because of the aesthetic interest in historical styles but also since Victoria's reign, with its commercial glory, immediately recalled Elizabeth's. However, much of the display in Class 23 revolved around demonstrating new techniques, such as electro-plating. Here was also a collection of articles submitted for the Goldsmiths's Prize – another example of the Exhibition incorporating important events in the London society calendar.

An exhibit which it is important to point out here is the so-called Exhibition Vase by William Beattie. Standing 4 ft high, and again in Elizabethan style, this showed figures of Newton, Bacon, Shakespeare and Watt on each corner – representing Astronomy, Philosophy, Poetry and Mechanics – and Prince Albert offering the palm of victory to Industry. This was another attempt to physically represent, and thereby cement, the links that had led to the Exhibition. It was this same effort to weld together all these bourgeois interests that later produced the design of the Albert Memorial.[55]

Left: Shield presented by the Prince of Prussia to Victoria and Albert. The Prince (and future Kaiser) was at the opening ceremony. The shield was placed at the opening to the eastern half and represented monarchy and British foreign sympathies. *Right*: Hyram Powers' *Greek Slave*. Acclaimed by many as one of the outstanding works of art at the Exhibition, the statue was also a political comment.

One thing which was noticeable in Class 23, though it could also be seen in many other sections, was the eclectic style of the exhibits. Rapid industrialisation had meant that no one style had yet come to dominate. Rather, a range of styles jostled for popularity. These included not only Gothic and Elizabethan, but also other historical styles such as rococo, Renaissance and classical, all of which owed much to the educational movement and an increasing interest in the past. There were also other aesthetic solutions to industrialisation, such as naturalism, exoticism, and geometric art.[56] These stemmed from, respectively, the growing interest in science and botany, and popular romanticism embodied by Wordsworth; colonial expansion; and the influence of industrial production itself with its endlessly repeated activities.

Next to the transept, finally, were the most intricate and colourful goods: lace, embroidery, silk and velvet. Many of the silks and embroideries showed designs of Victoria and Albert. An Axminster carpet destined for Windsor Castle hung on display. Here also was a 'state bed' by Faudel & Phillips of Newgate, covered with embroidered spreads 'from original designs and selections from the decorations by Raffaelle, in the Vatican, and copies of the *Aurora* of Guido Reni and *Night* by Thorwaldsen'.[57]

Back on the ground floor, this time heading eastwards down the main avenue from the transept, similar considerations to those influencing the western side of the avenue governed what the Royal Commission decided to include in the Exhibition. After Bell's *Andromeda* and the Koh-I-Noor came a shield presented to the Prince of Wales by the

Prince of Prussia, marking both royalty and its foreign connections. Then came large wine jars and mosaics in the Spanish and Portuguese sections. Next an 18-ft high zinc statue of Queen Victoria made by the Vieille Montagne Company announced the entrance to the French exhibition and was both an impressive stamp of monarchical power on the Exhibition and a demonstration of Franco-British collaboration, heralding perhaps a new era of internationalism. Various famous works of sculpture followed – *St Michael and the Dragon*, the *Dancing Fawn*, the *Death of the Stag* – leading to one of the most famous works at the Exhibition of all, Kiss's *Amazon*, which, due to its size and dramatic quality, dominated at the centre of the *Zollverein*'s display. The *Amazon*, shown partly as a demonstration of the renowned Berlin school of sculpture and partly as an example Prussian zinc casting, was followed by the colossal Bavarian lion, which, as Hunt's exhibition guide pointed out, was 'in every way striking, as a work of art, and is no less so as an example of metal casting'.[58] At the very end of the main avenue, heralding the United States' section, was Hiram Power's *Greek Slave*, a statue that belonged in the pantheon of aesthetic exhibits but that also had political overtones. The *Greek Slave* was depicted being sold to the Turks. Behind her was a Christian cross. The statue immediately appealed to liberals and Christians.

By and large, the displays from foreign countries were ranged across the main avenue, from north to south. Where countries were too small to stretch the distance, they were confined to one side or the other. Thus, again moving from the transept, the displays from Turkey (including Egypt, Greece and Turkey itself), Spain, Portugal, Tuscany, Rome and Sardinia were to be found on the north side and those of China, Brazil and Tunis on the south. These countries had not managed to present an enormous display and what had been sent was more of an aesthetic character than an industrial one – hence it was close to the transept. After these came Switzerland on the south side. The Swiss display was fronted on the main avenue by a collection of top quality Swiss watches and clocks. Behind, however, was a substantial display of textiles, demonstrating that this country at least had a more industrial production base.

After Switzerland came France. This was by far the largest foreign display: it ranged across the building from north to south, and also – in the north – back behind the Italian and Turkish displays to the transept. This layout symbolically suggested France's importance in industrial and aesthetic terms. Perhaps because of its experience in staging exhibitions, France had the most efficient and focused section of all. To the south, two mini-courts concentrated visitors' minds first on the luxury goods for which it was famous: clothing, silks and shawls, jewellery, bronzes and furniture. A little further along, spanning the main avenue, was another larger court which also showed fashionable goods, together with the machines that created them, and behind this, on the south, was a court devoted to furniture. Above, hanging from, and on, the galleries were larger textile goods – at the front, silks from Lyons, behind, woollen and lace goods from Paris, and cottons from Mulhouse. Machinery was placed towards the north wall, as it was in the British half, and included the equipment used for chemical production. Back towards the transept, meanwhile, a special court had been created to display the prestigious manufactures of the Sèvres china factory and Gobelins and Beauvais tapestry production.

One characteristic that immediately caught the eye in the French display – in particular in comparison with the British contribution – was its overwhelming emphasis on quality of design rather than cheapness of production. As the *Official Catalogue*

The Gobelins Room – the heart of French aesthetic prowess.

commented regarding the French exhibits, 'wherever these admit of the introduction of a design, even in the commonest articles, there the peculiar and graceful indications of artistic feeling, which render the patterns produced popular, even among those who may not be able to recognise the cause of their harmony, are manifest'.[59] Many French goods – for example the bedsteads – could be directly compared with their British counterparts and found to be far more ornate. It was revealing that in the French exhibition photography – Daguerreotypes on silver and Talbotypes on paper – was to be seen used for artistic purposes, whereas the British still showed it as a scientific curiosity. In such ways, the French display fulfilled the duties allotted it by the Royal Commission: British manufacturers were being brought face to face with France's strength in artistic design. They were also being shown that art sold well. Consumers, meanwhile, were being made aware, here and elsewhere, of the benefits of artistic design.

The fact that French industry had had to focus on quality of design rather than cheapness of production also meant there was a strong emphasis on technology. The inclusion of machinery for applying chemistry to textile production was superior to anything similar to be found in the British half of the Exhibition. There were also many instruments either of a highly precise nature – such as Froment's theolodite – or which represented important innovations – such as Froment's improved turbine, which was capable of turning 200 revolutions per minute and which was exploring a technology that would one day lead to the jet engine. As the British had all but cornered the market in industrial machinery, French goods tended to exploit areas where machinery could be useful in everyday life, hence the various examples of calculating machines, including a machine for reckoning workmen's wages.

Yet against expectations, for perceptive observers there was also strong evidence in the French display of industrialisation taking place on the British model. This included specimens of mixed woollen goods to rival Yorkshire manufactures, machines that could mass produce nails or pens, and hard-wearing kitchen earthenware. Mostly, however, these goods were overwhelmed by the exotica around them. And, for the moment at least, Britain appeared to be able to produce cheap goods better than France. As the *Official Catalogue* concluded, 'the excellence and abundance of the objects of minute art would appear to indicate a high state of refinement; but their perfection forms, however, an observable contrast to the state of articles of a more ordinary character, and extensive demand'.[60]

After France came Belgium. This section was probably the most like Britain's in terms of its transverse principle of organisation, which perhaps had much to do with the fact that Belgium was the one country whose economy resembled Britain's. It was also sizeable, showing the advanced industrial state of Belgium's production. In the far south of the display were raw materials and agricultural products – sugar, soap, sugar beet, flour and seeds. On the south side of the main avenue were cloths and textiles and, a particular Belgian strength, lace, which hung from the galleries on the northern side. On the north of the main avenue was furniture, behind which were musical instruments and domestic appliances. Finally, once more at the far northern wall, was heavy

The main avenue looking east.

machinery. The near-identical layout to Britain's meant that – unlike France – it was Belgium's similarity to the western half of the display which struck observers. In a kind of inlet into the Belgian display was that of the Netherlands – demonstrating its relatively lowly state of industrial production.

Like Belgium's, which it followed, the Austrian section straddled the main avenue, marking the country's rank as a major economic player. For many British observers, who were used to press reports of Austria as a backward state, the size of the Austrian section came as a surprise. However, unlike Belgium, Austria did not show any mechanical capacity to speak of – most of Austria's display consisted of either agricultural, artisan or artistic produce. On the one hand, this meant that the display was highly decorative. As the *Catalogue* pointed out, it 'must be acknowledged to have added a large share to the attractions of the foreign side of the building'.[61] On the other, it necessitated a sharp deviation from the transverse scheme followed up until now.

Though the omission of Austrian machinery was due in part to protectionist suspicion, the sudden disruption to the Exhibition's scheme simply underlined Austria's nature as a non-industrial state and it was made worse by the decision to place agricultural goods in the north where previously machinery had lain. Still, at least for the purposes of the Exhibition, the Austrian display was of value. Within the sphere of artisan production, it showed remarkable strengths, such as the impressive Leistler rooms, filled with furniture by this Viennese furniture maker. Here was to be found a Gothic bookcase of incredible detail which was a present from the Austrian Emperor to Queen Victoria. The large collection of cutlery and hardware – as the *Catalogue* remarked – rivalled Sheffield's and was worthy of note. There were also examples of map production and printing that received much attention by being placed near the main avenue. These, however, were produced by the Imperial Court and Government Printing Office and the Imperial Military Geographical Institute in Vienna: the state involvement in industry was given unfortunate prominence.

The *Zollverein's* display, which came after Austria's, was perhaps the most confusing and deceptive of all the foreign sections. At first sight, it did not look impressive. Protectionism had kept away many important industrialists, in particular machine manufacturers. The section in the north where machinery would have been had been half given over to the eastern refreshment court. Some important German states, notably Bavaria, Württemberg and Saxony, had insisted for commercial and political reasons on arranging their goods separately from those of Prussia's customs union. The German states which did not belong to the *Zollverein* chose also to stay apart. The whole process of deciding who would be in and who would not lasted so long that in the end space had to be found wherever it was available: the *Zollverein* ended up not just next to Austria, but eastwards behind Russia and the United States, and a large portion upstairs in the galleries. As a result, its display did not appear designed to convince visitors of national economic strength. It did not fit into the Royal Commission's transverse scheme, nor, for that matter, into any other recognisable one.

Nevertheless, in the midst of all these shortcomings were important merits. Added together, the space allotted to the German states was impressive, easily outstripping the United States in magnitude and rivalling France. Possibly as a result of the commercial nature of German exhibitions prior to 1851, the southern half of the display was stuffed full of marketable textiles, leaving little room for agriculture. The

The main avenue from the eastern end. In the foreground is the United States' section, with Powers' *Greek Slave* and Goodyear's inflatable rubber boats.

tradition of state-led industrialisation resulted in the best work from the Prussian government's iron and zinc foundries and porcelain works being shown. The work of Saxony's Royal Porcelain factory at Meissen was indisputably fine. There was also a strong showing by smaller-scale producers, with an emphasis on quality rather than quantity: one of the most popular exhibits belonged in this category – the stuffed animals of Plouquet of Württemberg that acted out famous stories and emulated humans. Musical instruments and clocks were a noticeable strength and this supported a marked emphasis on precision and technology. Displays of telegraphs by Siemens and Halske – by then used on all Prussian railways – were shown, revealing the advanced state of communications in the country. There were also chemical preparations for textiles, fine lenses, and machines for more complex tasks such as evaporation and creating newspaper type. One of the most celebrated Prussian exhibits was a set of scales. In addition to all this, the sculpture – especially that of the successful Berlin and Munich schools – was prominent.

After the German states came Russia. In some ways, the Russian display was like a more extreme version of Austria's. There was an almost complete absence of mechanised produce, leaving the far northern part of the building, elsewhere used for machinery, conveniently free for the rest of the eastern refreshment courts. Instead, raw materials formed a large part of the display. The traditional use of art to demonstrate wealth and power was here carried to the international level in an exhibition of gigantic works of valuable malachite and jasper and priceless jewellery. What industrial produce did appear, for example pieces of iron casting, was also of a colossal scale, as if size were a substitute for complexity. However, almost all these objects were produced by the state, from the Imperial copper works of Bogoslovsky and Perm, the Alexandrovsky cannon foundry and the metal works of Artinsk, Barnaoulsk, and Koushvinsk, to name but a few. State power was quite obviously the watchword of the Russian display.

Finally, at the far eastern end of the nave, topped by an enormous eagle hanging from the ceiling, was the United States' display. The first impression to strike visitors arriving here – especially after the Russian department – was its emptiness. The long distances involved in travelling to Britain, the generally self-sufficient home economy, and the lack of state coordination had all taken their toll. The poor impression was not helped by what looked like an effort to space things out to cover the floor available. The next feature that struck the visitor, however, was the relative simplicity and modesty of the goods shown. Once more, this display had no heavy machinery to speak of – and instead the space had been used to give Fox and Henderson room to show off their workshops and yet again attract attention to the Crystal Palace. The US machinery which was there seemed to be of a simple construction and much of it was related to agriculture. Compared with the foreign sections preceding, there seemed to be a veritable dearth of artistic design. The simplicity seemed to correspond to a national economy devoted to decentralised cultivation of the land and egalitarian principles rather than the excesses of luxurious urban life. No wonder that Queen Victoria left the American section thinking it 'certainly not very interesting'.[62]

However, for more astute observers there was much of interest. For prophets of growing American power – and their number was increasing – the vast mineral wealth of the north American continent was apparent, in particular in coal. A gigantic tea-service made completely of Californian gold drew attention to what was taking place in that part of the world. Just as significantly, however, what appeared at first rather puny and simple examples of machine building revealed themselves to be early examples of equipment designed for personal labour-saving – candle and brick-making machines, sewing machines, type-writers and mechanised harvesters. This was a use for machinery that Britain in particular had not really exploited but which in America, where land was cheap and labour expensive, had been developed more fully. Several of the plain exhibits also turned out to be demonstrations of the growing use of the 'American system' of interchangeable parts. Colt's revolvers, developed since the Mexican wars of the 1830s, showed this. So did Robbins & Lawrence, who exhibited lathe-made rifles with interchangeable fixtures. The virtues of goods designed for personal labour-saving and interchangeability, however, sat rather uncomfortably in an exhibition devoted to British mass production and French art. Meanwhile, telegraphs, new signalling technology for trains and high-speed newspaper presses, while perhaps inglorious, showed that America's great distances would not impede urban life for much longer. Ingenuity was demonstrated by the large display of India rubber ware from Charles Goodyear and the locks of Day and Newell. There was also a surprising demonstration of the developing interest in photography for entertainment purposes in Whitehouse's Daguerreotypes of the Niagara Falls and Langenheim's 'photographic magic lantern slides'.[63]

Goodyear's rubber boat and pontoons.

Moving away from the strictly nation by nation theme, the galleries of the eastern half of the Crystal Palace were simply given over to the lighter goods, with no identifiable order other than the vague attempt to match the geographic layout below. Along the northern wall, however, hung the 'stained glass of all nations'. This gallery, stretching the whole length of the foreign half, made use of the light and formed a dramatic route back to the transept. Its presence in the display was another example of the revival of Gothic art. It also encouraged a more religious interpretation of the Exhibition.

These, then, were some of the characteristics of the Exhibition visitors encountered as they moved from section to section. Yet there are also some more general comments to be made about the layout. First, so far we have been looking at the Exhibition in the abstract – as if it opened on 1 May in a complete state and remained untouched until 15 October. This, however, was not so. Work on the exhibits was nowhere near complete by 1 May. Even the preface to the main official catalogue admitted that many British exhibits were not in place and consequently none of the labels could be attached until the Exhibition was already open. One observer recorded on 6 May that 'the sound of the saw and the hammer salutes the visitor from every side, and I think not less than five hundred carpenters and other artisans are busy in the building today'.[64] Many of the foreign countries could not get their exhibits there on time, with the result that throughout the summer the Exhibition was being added to and changing. Many Russian goods arrived late due to the winter. A large number of additions from France, Italy, Portugal, the United States and the *Zollverein* arrived during June and August, partly because they were seasonal goods, partly because industrialists there were waking up late to the Exhibition's importance. India's main consignment of packages arrived only in mid-May. Those from Hong Kong arrived in August. French and American goods were still turning up the week before the Exhibition closed![65] On the one hand, these changes made the sense of overall layout even more imperceptible. On the other, the Exhibition kept attracting renewed interest as novelties arrived.

Though the point has been made that the Exhibition's layout gave priority to works of an artistic bent by placing them in the transept and main avenues, it should be noted that this meant art *as applied to industry*. Few of the objects were there solely for aesthetic reasons but rather to show how new techniques, materials or machinery could be used to produce art or, conversely, how art could be used to improve industrial goods. Hence George Baxter's artistic prints, prized for the mechanical method of reproduction, were to be found in the fine arts court, the Gothic altar in the main avenue was there because it had been machine produced by Jordan's patent mechanism, and much of the statuary demonstrated new techniques of colouration or new materials. This stemmed from the integrative aims of the Exhibition organisers. However, because art seemed so prominent, and because Class 30 was labelled 'Fine Arts,' observers and historians mistook the Exhibition for an art gallery and perhaps unfairly criticised its artwork as deficient in aesthetic terms.

While the artistic design of goods revealed the eclecticism typical of high Victorian design, it often did so in an exaggerated form. The Buckingham House minutes had indicated that this was what was desired by the Royal Commission. The rather more specific criteria sent out to foreign countries had mentioned 'increased usefulness, improved forms and arrangements, superior quality or workmanship . . . beauty of design in form, or colour, or both with reference to utility'.[66] In many instances, however, the desire to show off craftsmanship led to rather ludicrous results, for example industrial machinery built incongruously in the Egyptian style, the Emperor of Russia's patently over ornamented vase by Garrard, decanters that were almost impossible to pick up and furniture that was completely unsuitable for use. This tendency was not restricted to artistic design, however: pianos built for four players showed that technical ability could also be driven to unreasonable extremes. Such exaggeration was neither representative of Victorian produce in general, nor of the aims of the Royal Commission. The latter, as will be seen, accepted such objects, saw them as a way of provoking interest in aesthetic design and, through the juries' reports and elsewhere, argued for more balanced design.

However, exaggeration sat ill at ease alongside the Exhibition's attempt to sell itself as a 'snap-shot' or stocktaking of life at the mid-century. The Exhibition's many attempts to provide complete arrangements of goods – be it of metal ores, swords, or tobacco – demonstrated the desire to create an objective, scientific view of production. So, too, did the exhibits that seemed to create an experiment out of the Exhibition itself. The contradiction between exaggeration and objectivity went back to the differing aims of those who had supported the Exhibition, and the fact these aims had not been fully absorbed into one overarching rationale. Small wonder that observers and historians have had difficulty deciphering what was representative and what was not.

Other general characteristics of the Exhibition are worth mentioning. There was, for example, an obvious tendency to show objects that were either sentimental or told a story. There was a profusion of exhibits that had an obvious erotic aspect to them. This jars with the common perception of Victorians as prudish. In the French section it was driven to extremes, in the statue of Clesinger's *Drunken Faun*, and the juries complained that the artist had 'allowed his imagination to be perverted and degraded to the service of a low sensuality'.[67] Playfair also recounted that the erotica was so prominent that shortly before the opening ceremony most of the bishops handed in a letter calling for it to be covered up if they were to take part. Playfair rather acidly suggested to Prince Albert that bishops' robes ought to be used. In the end, strategic fig-leaves were

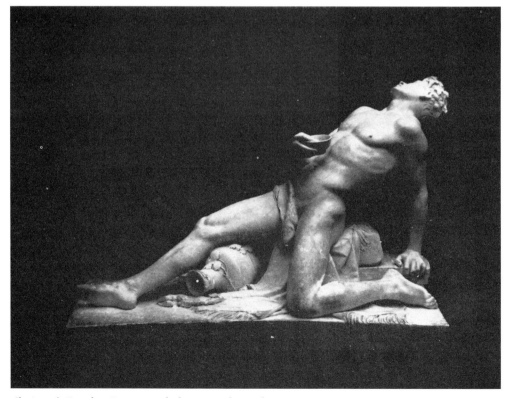

Clesinger's *Drunken Faun*, a work that caused moral outrage.

temporarily introduced, and some of the most prominent exhibits were drawn back into the alcoves.[68] Nevertheless, these exhibits were kept on view.

There were also displays that simply constituted fairground-like curios. Some of these, it has to be said, did have serious purposes in mind, such as the 'air-exhausted coffin', which tackled the issue of body transportation in an age of sea-travel, or the 'emigrants' mattress', which reflected the real concerns about the welfare of migrants. Others, however, were simply there for entertainment. There was, for example an alarm bedstead: the catalogue explained that at a given time 'the sleeper, without any jerk or the least personal danger, is placed in the middle of the room; where at the option of the possessor a cold bath can be placed'.[69] From the Channel Islands came 'a pair of scissors and a knife, so diminutive in size that the two do not weigh a grain'.[70] Sentimental, erotic and humorous exhibits, though used later to ridicule Victorians, were in fact given a position in the Exhibition in order to make it more popular and on the basis of past experience.

In conclusion, then, there were many influences at work on the way the Exhibition looked. The fusion of aims of the Exhibition's supporters, the pre- and misconceptions of exhibitors, the concerns of foreign countries, practical difficulties and considerations, and the effort to make the Exhibition attractive all contributed in various ways. In general, the aim to promote the unity of art, science and industry was the most obvious principle of arrangement. But many others made considerable inroads into this overarching rationale. On the one hand, this was a strength. The Exhibition accommodated the demands and interests of so many groups that for a time almost everyone seemed to be talking about it. On the other, the coexistence of so many aims and ideas produced confusion, both at the time and later, about the meaning of the Exhibition.

However, even though there was a profusion of aims and motifs presented by the Exhibition, it is also important to point out its limits. For one thing, the Exhibition still reflected the fact that its supporters came predominantly from those groups who supported industrialisation, capitalism, moderate political change and property. The interests of the working classes were not strongly represented or defended. Labour-saving devices were unabashedly displayed. Others were shown which would result in worse working conditions rather than better. Where the issue was addressed, this came from the philanthropic position that the working classes would be better off if they behaved like the bourgeoisie: Prince Albert's Model Houses were produced of cheap materials in order that they become affordable and the working classes become property owners. There was also a firm belief that poverty could be eradicated by greater industrialisation and the exploitation of new materials.

In a similar way the Exhibition excluded any native voice from the colonies: the displays that were shown came almost exclusively from colonisers interested in making their goods known to the European market. Attached to the display of Colt's pistols, for example, was a notice giving an excerpt from a Select Committee Report of the US Senate pointing out that 'on the Texan frontier, and on the several routes to California, the Indian Tribes are renewing their murderous warfare, and a general Indian war is likely to ensue, unless bodies of mounted men, efficiently equipped for such service, are employed against them . . . A few bold men, well skilled in the use of these weapons, can, under such circumstances, encounter and scatter almost any number of savages.'[71]

Finally, the Exhibition reflected very much a conservative view of gender relations. Occasionally, exhibits from women were shown that matched the talent of men, such as Harriet Ross's Stone Cross. In general, however, prominent exhibits by women simply reflected traditional activities, such as a carpet produced by 150 London women for Queen Victoria, shawls and veils by women of the Shetlands or the coverings of Faudel and Phillips's state bed. Such omissions reveal that, no matter how complex or universal its system of layout, the Great Exhibition was still an advert for a particular way of life.

III

While the opening of the Exhibition was enormously successful, this was arguably still just a temporary and rather superficial show of support. It was really only during the months after the first visitors arrived that the Exhibition established its roots in the minds of the public. It was at this time that the bonds and aims shared by a small group of people around the Royal Commission were further consolidated and then also exported to a wider public. During this period, the Royal Commission continued binding together its supporters through its decisions regarding juries and the catalogues. Meanwhile, the enormous numbers of visitors, the festivities and the coverage the Exhibition received in literature, ensured its permanent success.

Almost as soon as the Exhibition had begun, the first meeting of the Council of Chairmen of the Juries took place on 5 May in order to discuss what merits would be rewarded at the Exhibition and how the prize system ought to operate. Though Playfair had originally intended this body to be elected by the juries themselves, the Royal Commission in fact appointed the members in conjunction with the Foreign Commissioners in April.[72] This ensured that, while there was representation of foreign views, the agenda of the Council was securely that of the Royal Commission. Until this point, instructions regarding what was to be awarded by prizes had remained vague, in order to allow local committees and Foreign Commissioners leeway in deciding what to show and to prevent any dissent creeping in at an early stage. Now, however, a discussion took place which, while it took account of foreign and local committee demands, saw the priorities of the Royal Commission dominate.

In order to keep all supporters happy, the Royal Commission had decided at an earlier point that while it did not want to restrict the Council's decisions, prizes ought not to denote order of merit but rather excellence in different qualities. Manchester producers of cheap goods would have nothing to fear from being placed next to Parisian luxuries. There would also be three medals in each class.

Yet the Council immediately ran into difficulties over these two conditions. As the medals had been designed in three sizes, people would immediately assume they denoted order of merit. Moreover, while beauty might be more important than utility in one class, it might not be in another, and confusion might arise. Instead, the Council suggested reducing the number of medals to two – a Prize Medal, which would be awarded by the jury of a class, and a Council or Great Medal which would be awarded by the Council of Chairmen on the nomination of the jury.[73] This new system was accepted by the Royal Commission and the third medal was dropped, instead being used as a commemorative medal for jurors. The Council also suggested that the Prize Medal be awarded for an aspect of workmanship, 'utility, beauty, cheapness, adaptation to

Outside the western end, a column of Cornish granite. The Exhibition venerated scale of production.

particular markets and other elements of merit being taken into consideration according to the nature of the object'. The Council Medal, meanwhile, should be for 'some important novelty of invention or application, either in material, or processes of manufacture, or originality combined with great beauty of design; but that it should not be conferred for excellence of production or workmanship alone, however eminent'.[74] In other words, while competition and any possibility of national or regional friction was reduced, the new system definitely placed an emphasis on aspects of design rather than workmanship. The Council Medal, by definition, had more kudos attached to it than the Prize Medal. The Royal Commission heightened this distinction by stating that the Council Medal 'will only be given for very pre-eminent and indisputable merit,' and that the number of those receiving it would be much smaller than for the Prize Medal.[75]

These decisions demonstrated the fact that those in support of education in industry, the reformers based around the Society of Arts, had retained the upper hand. This assertiveness caused some friction: the report of the Chairman of the Council – Viscount Canning, son of the Prime Minister – reveals it did not go down well with foreign jurors. 'Many of these,' he stated, 'had taken part in the national exhibitions of France and Germany; and to them the distinctive character of the two medals, and the avoidance of all recognition of degrees of merit between the recipients of prizes, were novel principles, and at variance with their experience.'[76] However, in the detailed list interpreting the criteria of award for each of the thirty classes, the Royal Commission did still make an effort to accommodate as many interests as possible.[77] In fact, the virtues outlined stood almost as a list of ideals shared by this international pro-industrial body of men. Ultimately, as it became obvious that foreign manufacturers in fact benefited from this emphasis on design, the two-tier system and the decisions of the juries gained supporters abroad. And despite some minor problems regarding claims for a Council Medal which had to be turned down,[78] the fact that there was not a competition over medals but that they were simply marks of excellence, reduced the amount of dissent among all involved.

The Royal Commission had earlier decided to have a system of 30 juries with 270 jurors made up equally of British and foreign members. Efforts had been made to ensure foreign confidence by arranging for cross-jury consultation. In April, rather than entangle itself in quarrels, the Royal Commission simply called a meeting of Foreign Commissioners and asked them to divide the total number of jurors among themselves and nominate candidates to sit on the juries. In Britain, local committees were asked to list people known for their expertise in the products of each region. The Royal Commission chose the requisite number of jurors from these lists.

When they began meeting on 12 May, therefore, the people selected represented an important body of expertise in Britain and Europe. They were highly influential people – in particular abroad, where they were often top-ranking civil servants, academics industrialists, scientists and artists. They were also figures who, while committed to industrialisation, were supportive of the political establishment. They were known to represent expertise in their particular locality and therefore commanded more respect. This was particularly the case in Britain where the consultation exercise had created the sheen of democratic input. Ultimately, however, the Royal Commission had still had a hand in determining the juries' membership. And guiding the juries' day-to-day activities was Playfair, with a team of deputies including Stafford Northcote, Ibbetson

The stained glass gallery. This gallery added to the cathedral-like atmosphere of the building.

and Lloyd. Once again the jury system was a compromise between the aims of the Royal Commission and the desire to tie in as much support as possible.

The juries' activities lasted six weeks and the awards were made known on 16 July. The task had been enormous – some 17,000 exhibitors and over 1 million exhibits were inspected. In the end, 170 Council Medals and 2,918 Prize Medals were awarded – demonstrating the special value placed on design. The awards of the Great Exhibition are important not just because the whole jury system and the discussions relating to it brought together one of the most influential classes of society internationally and forced it to agree on a set of values. They also allowed the Royal Commission's aims to be spelt out to a wider audience: while Britain came top of the awards list with 78 Council Medals and 1,302 Prize Medals, France was not that far behind with 54 Council Medals and 619 Prize Medals. While this result could satisfy British patriots, France's considerable strength was made obvious. It was also much more marked when the fact was considered that France had just 1,710 exhibitors in comparison with Britain's 6,861: the ratio of Council Medals was three times greater per exhibitor in France than in Britain. Even France's ratio of Prize Medals was almost twice as great as Britain's.

While France had the benefit of experience, and Britain the disadvantage of a decentralised system of selection of goods, this was still a resounding victory for French produce, particularly with regard to design. A look across the thirty classes also revealed that Britain's Council Medal winnings were concentrated on machinery and hardly at all on the upper echelons of production, while those of France were spread quite evenly from raw materials to fine arts and included some surprising strengths, for example in chemical treatment of raw materials. According to these statistics, the weaknesses of British production were there for all to see.[79] As Asa Briggs concluded, 'the greater the design element, the more likely it was that Britain would not win a major award.'[80]

The distribution of medals also showed that while over-indulgent and entertaining exhibits might be popularly prized at the time or focused on later in order to ridicule the Exhibition, they did not feature in the juries' list of what was to be praised. Goods that were picked out by the *Art Journal*, a popular illustrated guide to the Exhibition, and seized on by many as representing contemporary taste or by Nikolaus Pevsner in his acerbic look at the artefacts in the Crystal Palace, were not in fact rewarded at the Exhibition.[81] While, for the reasons outlined, over-decoration was a feature of the artefacts displayed at the Exhibition, the juries decisions in fact promoted simplicity of design, and artistic ornament suitable to the use and shape of the artefact.

The award of medals also sent out a strong message about industrialisation globally. Britain and France between them took the lion's share of medals. Most other countries did not win one Council Medal – suggesting that while their workmanship was of an order to gain Prize Medals, they had not developed academic, scientific and artistic knowledge. This created an image of power in Britain and France. Elsewhere, it suggested emulation of these two countries would bring advances.

Two other points are worth noting. First, the United States received few Council Medals, given the space it occupied at the Exhibition. This, however, was possibly down to the different criteria of design shown in its section and the fact they were not appreciated fully by the juries. Second, the Prussian *Zollverein* similarly had few Council Medals, but many Prize Medals. The suggestion here was that its produce was imitative rather than innovative – something that would soon change, if it was ever true at all – but that for the moment sent soothing signals to British manufacturers.

It was during the summer months of 1851 that the *Official Descriptive and Illustrated Catalogue* was produced. As has already been mentioned, the Commission had given the tender for this to Clowes and Spicers, and it had been hoped that it would be on sale by 1 May. However, with so many exhibits late in arriving, and exhibitors not sending back the forms on which they were meant to describe their displays, the decision was taken to publish the *Catalogue* at the end of the Exhibition, rather than at the beginning. The introduction to the *Catalogue* made a great issue of this, saying that 'at a great deal of loss to themselves', the Royal Commission had decided to wait, in order to make the work 'a lasting memorial of the splendid collection of which it professes to be the exponent'. In fact, the Royal Commission had recognised in March 1850 that the only way the *Official Catalogue* would ever be profitable was as an authoritative record rather than a guide to the Exhibition. For that reason, a smaller official catalogue was produced on 1 May. Nevertheless, the delay did allow the main *Official Catalogue* to be much more extensive. It was certainly one of the most impressive feats connected with the Great Exhibition. Totalling 1,724 pages, involving 22 writers and researchers, taking an estimated 11,500 days' work to print,[82] the *Catalogue* was so vast that reportedly no one foundry was able to supply all the type needed.[83] When it appeared towards the middle of October, the work's size, the fact that it consisted at bottom of compiled descriptions from all exhibitors, the strong emphasis given by Ellis to the 'philosophical' – or scientific – methodology of the work, the historical and statistical research on each subject, all seemed to support its authoritative status.

The *Times* welcomed the volumes as 'a very valuable addition to the stock of useful practical knowledge. Independently of the extraordinary undertaking which they are intended to commemorate, they form a collection of facts connected with the industrial progress of the civilized world which cannot fail of producing important results for the future.' The *Observer* said it was 'one of the most interesting manuals of general information in the English language'. The *Morning Herald* proclaimed it 'without a parallel or a precedent in the annals of our literature . . . Every branch of science, art, and industry is here fully and efficiently represented. The most striking and remarkable features, and the whole scope and significance of the Exhibition, are here embodied, divested of all the promptings of partiality and all the infirmities of judgment . . . the work will thus have an enduring interest in the mass of valuable information of almost every description which it contains.' The *Athenaeum*, previously rather cool towards the Royal Commission, pronounced that 'The work is without a precedent in the annals of literature . . . It . . . contains a body of annotations which express the condition of human knowledge and the state of the world's industry in 1851: – and is a document of the utmost importance, as a summary report of this vast international "stock-taking", which no great library – nor any gentlemen's library, of those who aim at the collection of literary standards – can hereafter be without. It is not the work of a day, a month, or a year: it is for all time.'[84]

However, it is important to recognise that the *Catalogue* did have an ideological slant. The exercise of tying together all these exhibits in one whole itself stemmed from the idea that everything conformed to scientific laws and that these laws were God's. Crucially, commerce was also covered by this, as Ellis explicitly pointed out in his introduction when he said that 'an attempt has here been made to convert the changing and inaccurate conventional terms of trade into precise and enduring expressions of science'. The *Catalogue* therefore exported the ideology of the Exhibition while priding itself on its objectivity. In the same way as the juries' decisions, the *Catalogue* also expounded the values of the Society of Arts regarding the need for artistic and scientific input into industry. The four sections and thirty classes of the Exhibition were used as its structure. The commentary supported this perspective. Subtly embedded within the text were comments supporting the message given out by the juries' awards.

The *Catalogue* also bonded the Exhibition's supporters more practically. By including the name and addresses of exhibitors, it recorded all those who had supported the Royal Commission's aims and allowed people to see who conformed to the standards it set. The *Journal of Design*, which had been produced by Cole in order to educate the public about companies producing industrial goods with aesthetic merits, stopped printing at the end of 1851. One of the reasons its editorial board gave was that 'whereas it was difficult in 1849 to ascertain the names of a hundred manufacturers who were positive advocates of industrial art education, the *Illustrated Catalogue* of the Great Exhibition is now a Domesday-Book which records the names of thousands of them'.[85]

Throughout the summer, the momentum of integration of the Exhibition's supporters in Britain and abroad was kept up via a plethora of social activities. On 3 May, the Royal Academy held a celebration banquet in honour of Prince Albert and the Exhibition arranged by its President, the Royal Commissioner Charles Eastlake. This allowed Albert

The Birmingham Fete. Such events helped form solid connections between the Exhibition's promoters in London, the provinces and abroad.

to close the gap that existed between the worlds of art as applied to industry – as embodied in the Society of Arts – and pure art – as represented by the Academy. Albert's speech encouraged the Academy to look leniently on industrial art as displayed at the Exhibition, pointing out that heavy criticism would only kill off any hope of reuniting artists and industrialists.[86] The Middle Temple opened its doors to members of the French bar and held a banquet in their honour; a privilege not given since the days of Elizabeth.[87] The Society of Arts, which had allowed juries and the Council of Chairmen use of its rooms, opened up its reading rooms to Foreign Commissioners.[88] Lloyd's opened its Merchants' Room to foreigners.[89] Balls were held at Buckingham Palace in honour of the royal guests who came to the Exhibition – one on 7 May for the Prince of Prussia and another on 13 June, which was a masked ball set in the period of Charles II.[90] An open-air fete was organised by Lord Ashburton at Richmond in honour of the Exhibition.[91] On 19 June, some 300 jurors, Foreign Commissioners and Royal Commissioners went to Birmingham, where a fete was held lasting from 7 a.m. until 1 a.m. next day: Birmingham had been converted to the Exhibition not least because of the success of many of its manufacturers, and foreign and British dignitaries were taken on excursions to celebrity companies such as Osler's, Chance Brothers (makers of the Crystal Palace glass), Fox and Henderson, and so on. In the evening, a concert was given in honour of the guests. The music included Handel's ubiquitous *Messiah*.[92]

Perhaps most dramatically, the Royal Commission, Executive Committee, Lord Mayor and Aldermen of the City of London were all invited by Louis Napoleon and the city of Paris for a week-long fete in their honour in August. This included a banquet at the Hôtel de Ville, a reception hosted by Napoleon at St Cloud, a fete at the British Embassy, a review at the Champs de Mars, and a performance at the Theatre Français, including a ballet entitled *Crystal Palace*. It also allowed the opportunity for inspecting France's art and technical education system, in particular the Conservatoire des Arts et Métiers, and contributed to the later movement for state-run design education. A large part of the group lost its luggage on the way, meaning that the British guests spent a few days appearing either dishevelled or in newly acquired Parisian garb. Nevertheless, the occasion was light-hearted and Lord Granville, who represented Albert, surprised and charmed his hosts with his near-native French.[93]

Such events helped build up the cohesiveness of the Exhibition's supporters. They also helped backing for the event grow at this late stage: the facts that most of these functions were restricted to the upper echelons and that they were copiously reported in the press meant that the agenda was being set for the wider public. Queen Victoria herself set the pace in this regard. Once the official opening was out of the way, she began to visit the Crystal Palace almost every other day – causing mayhem for the police, who on some occasions had to ask visitors to move round the building on the left-hand side only – but doing wonders for the public's attitude to the Exhibition.[94] When Victoria was not there, foreign royalty or other aristocrats were quick to fill her shoes. Victoria's purchases at the Exhibition also helped focus the public's minds on particular types of exhibit: the *Catalogue* devoted a whole section to what she called her 'achats', usually made via Mrs Wentworth Dilke.[95] In this way, royal patronage helped boost not only ticket sales but also the commercial value of the Exhibition.

The Paris Fete. The Exhibition was a useful support for President Napoleon's modernising government in France. It was also a major step forward in Anglo-French relations, possibly helping bring about the alliance of the Crimean War.

The first Shilling Day, showing the masses rushing to the main Kensington Road entrance. In the background are the Bramah turnstiles invented for the Exhibition.

The consolidation of links was not restricted to Commissioners, jurors and exhibitors, however. There was also a political level to this process. The visit of the Prince of Prussia to London – itself a demonstration of support for liberal projects – was the occasion for Albert and Victoria to arrange the betrothal of their eldest daughter Vicky to the future German Kaiser.[96] The Prussian Minister of Trade, von der Heydt, was able while in London to negotiate a navigation treaty with Britain, facilitating closer economic connections between the two countries and also strongly promoting the position of modernisers at home, where Prussia was currently locked in battle with Austria for the commercial control of Germany.[97] Throughout the summer of 1851 the festivities connected with the Exhibition allowed closer Anglo-French connections to be created, strengthening Napoleon's hand as a moderate liberaliser with the British government and the opposition in France. In addition to these notable examples, countless other politicians, civil servants and people of influence gathered in London throughout these months, getting to know each other, thereby strengthening their position at home.

It was, however, the Exhibition's entry into the public mind which was the most important development during these months. That it was successful in achieving popular success was obvious from the statistics of the Royal Commission. On 26 May, the first shilling day, the numbers of people going in seemed little different from those in the first weeks of May. Those who had been worried by the prospect of numbers never seen before gathering in one building, and by the dire warnings of the protectionist press, now breathed a sigh of relief and ridiculed their own lack of faith. *Punch*, for example, reported that:

> On reaching the doors of the Exhibition, we found massive barriers intended to contain the multitude; but the multitude consisted of so few that they could scarcely contain themselves, for they kept bursting with laughter at the ponderous preparations for resisting their expected violence . . . The high-paying portion of the public go to look at each other, and to be looked at, while the shilling visitors go to gain instruction from what they see; and the result is, they are far better behaved than the well-dressed promenaders who push each other about, and stare each other out of countenance on the days of the high price of admission.[98]

The entrance statistics showed that on the first shilling day; the season ticket holders stayed away in droves. So, however, did the masses: but when the day was reported to have passed off smoothly, the numbers of visitors began to rise steadily from 25,000 on the first day to 51,000 by mid-week. By mid-June the daily number of visitors was approximately 63,000, a figure which would remain more or less constant throughout the summer until the last week in October when over 100,000 people were going in each day![99] These numbers were made up of people who paid at the door rather than by season-ticket holders. The raised prices at the weekends always produced a sharp drop in admissions. All this meant that the majority of the 6 million visitors to the Exhibition belonged to the ordinary working and middle classes. Moreover, statistics for the takings from tickets showed that the Exhibition's financial success was due overwhelmingly to this class of people.[100]

Many of the reasons why the Exhibition managed to capture the popular mind have already been highlighted. The Royal Commission had taken care not to alienate the public and had utilised salesmanship techniques derived from past experience. Local committees had built up a solid base of travel clubs and saving schemes, which brought thousands of people from round the country. All the press coverage, both good and bad, had ensured the Exhibition was the subject of curiosity. Certainly, the fact that the vast majority of the public remained excluded from it for nigh on four weeks, while the press reported glowingly the experiences of the privileged few, was also important. It was also crucial that 1851 saw the beginning of an economic boom in Britain which would last for several years, and which brought many people much more disposable income than previously. But there were also other explanations.

From the building itself to many of its contents, there were so many exhibits that had not been widely seen before and that attracted curiosity. Foreign goods were not as familiar as today and the Exhibition provided an artificial means of travelling the globe, in a similar way to the diorama shows so popular at the time.[101] The Exhibition offered cultural diversity and geographic scope during a period when people's lives were still highly localised, and without the excesses of later times. Art exhibitions were still mainly exclusive affairs: though the Great Exhibition now mingled it with science and industry, the social privilege attached to art, and curiosity about hitherto unseen works drew in crowds. The contemporary popularity of education as a means of self-improvement also contributed to the number of visitors to the Exhibition. A total of 35,540 schoolchildren visited the Crystal Palace, mainly from schools round London. On several days, up to

12 parties with some 1,300 children could be touring the building. Towards September the number of such parties increased, with almost 3,000 pupils in the building on 18 September. (One can only imagine the noise.) In addition, there were many guided tours for college students, cultural and literary societies, and other educational groups.[102] People of responsibility, many of them associated with the local committees, led groups round, demonstrating their own connection with the event.

The Exhibition was also, however, a pleasant experience. Many people came to be entertained rather than instructed. This was something the Royal Commission had expected and encouraged by arranging goods in an attractive way and by including works which were curious, grisly, or simply amusing. Certain exhibits soon gained star-attraction status, the so-called 'Lions' of the Exhibition – for example the Koh-I-Noor diamond, the Medieval Court, the Crystal Fountain, which served as a meeting point for many visitors, the stuffed animals of Württemberg, and the statues of the *Greek Slave*, *Amazon*, *Bavarian Lions* and *St Michael and the Dragon*, and the Coalbrookdale Dome.[103]

While the refreshment courts were not allowed to serve alcohol – a stipulation that owed something to pressure from temperance groups, but also to worries about social disturbance – they were still part of the day's entertainment for many people: the statistics of Schweppes & Company show that over 1 million bottles of soda water, lemonade and ginger beer were drunk, almost 1 million bath buns and 870,000 plain buns were consumed, and 37 tons of salt were used up. The food on offer included savoury cakes, pies and patties, Banbury cakes, Victoria biscuits, school cakes, potted meat and jellies.[104] Jelly, which had previously been a food for the rich, was the most popular: the amount consumed caused a 100 per cent rise in the price of animal skins.[105] For many, the Exhibition would be combined with a picnic in Hyde Park – the free water which the Royal Commission provided being all that was consumed in the building.

An estimated 1 million visitors to the Exhibition came from London itself, nearly half the city's population.[106] For the other millions, however, London was an additional attraction. Most stayed between three days and a week in the metropolis.[107] St Paul's, Westminster, the Tower of London, the various famous churches, palaces and parks were all on the itinerary. So were the theatres – Her Majesty's, Drury Lane, the Lyceum, the Adelphi and St James's – Madame Tussaud's, London Zoo and the British Museum. New buildings no doubt attracted much attention: the Marble Arch, moved to its position at Hyde Park in 1851; the new Westminster Palace; Brunel's recently built tunnel under the Thames. More modern, less high-brow, entertainment could be found at the cycloramas, cosmoramas, dioramas and panoramas – all attempts to use illustrations, or illustrated slides to emulate motion, all precursors of cinema. In the evening, there were balls and orchestras at Willis's Rooms and King Street, and the famous Vauxhall, Cremorne and Surrey gardens were all still open (though the Vauxhall gardens were becoming seedier, and would soon be closed) and held dancing, open-air music, and other variety entertainment. Often in less salubrious surroundings, there was cabaret theatre: music halls were just beginning, including one in Lambeth which even admitted women.[108]

London also supported the Exhibition more directly. Many institutions greatly increased their accessibility during the Exhibition. The British Museum opened five days instead of three per week, and both it and the National Gallery postponed their traditional summer vacation. Kew Gardens was opened five days a week instead of two, while St Paul's abolished the much-debated entrance fee to its ground floor. Sir John

Osler's Crystal Fountain. The fountain was a celebration of glass production. Standing at the centre of the transept, it formed the fulcrum of the Exhibition and became a popular meeting-point. When the Crystal Palace was moved to Sydenham, the fountain went with it.

Cremorne Gardens, one of London's famous – by this time infamous – evening entertainments.

Soane's Museum abolished entry charges four days of the week, while the Societies of the Temple allowed free access to the Middle Temple Hall during the Exhibition. This all extended the attraction of a trip to the Exhibition. It was also a measure of the influence of the Exhibition's liberal aims. Some aristocrats, either out of solidarity with Albert or in order to exploit the social unity the Exhibition exuded, opened their residences to visitors' tours. This included Duke of Northumberland's Syon House and Northumberland House, the Earl of Ellesmere's Bridgwater Gallery, and Lord Ward's collection.[109]

Events – such as the Royal Hippodrome opposite Kensington Gardens, where 14,000 spectators could watch chariot races and tournaments, or the Imperial Chinese Junk moored close by on the Thames – simply attempted to latch on to the large numbers expected at the Exhibition. Many others did the same but drew people in by echoing the Exhibition's themes: the dioramas showed images of foreign countries, the artefacts of which could be found in the Crystal Palace. James Wyld, the cartographer and Geographer Royal, whose maps and atlases could be found in the Great Exhibition, erected a 'Monster Globe' in Leicester Square, ironically, the site that Albert had originally suggested for the Exhibition. It was a domed building, modelled on the Pantheon in Rome, and housed an enormous globe 60 ft in diameter. On the inside was a map of the world, cast in relief from plaster of Paris, to a scale of one inch to ten miles. It was so popular that it remained open until 1861.

Perhaps the most famous attempt to tap the Exhibition's pulling-power, and certainly the most flamboyant, was that of Alexis Soyer at Gore House, opposite the Exhibition, where the Albert Hall now stands. Soyer, the Reform Club chef, had a reputation for his ambitious culinary efforts and his eccentricities. He had already connected himself with the Exhibition via the York banquet, and now proposed a 'Gastronomic Symposium of All Nations'. According to its programme this would cater for 'universal humanity'. Its motto was that 'cosmopolitan customs should demand cosmopolitan cooking'. Together with the cartoonist George Augustus Sala, Soyer converted Gore House, the home vacated by the bankrupted society hostess Lady Blessington, into a fantastical grotto devoted to internationalism, fairytale landscapes, and wild visual extravaganzas. The entrance staircase began the show with a gigantic mural incorporating all manner of important and famous people from Britain and abroad, as well as diverse, and often extinct, flora and fauna. Pitt, Brougham, Wellington, Disraeli, Dickens, Thackeray, Mark Lemon Guizot, Napoleon, Thiers and others were interspersed with 'hippogriffs, griffins, giraffes, scorpions, mice, elephants, mastodons, dragons, and every other possible mount'.[110] Sala's satirical comment was mixed with the Exhibition's universalism. Inside its exoticism was echoed by rooms entitled the Alcove of Camellias, the Blessington Temple of the Muses, the Shower of Gems. Outside was the 'Monster Pavilion of All Nations', a banqueting hall modelled on the medieval castles of the Rhine, with the insignia of numerous countries, where some 1,500 could be fed at any one time. Dignitaries ate inside: the visitor's book recorded Disraeli, Wellington, Fox and

Wyld's 'Monster Globe'. The globe in Leicester Square underlined the universalist theme of the Exhibition.

The Metropolitan Sanitary Association Dinner *chez* Soyer.

Henderson as well as American Congressmen. The food outside was cheaper. Here, functions could be held, such as a dinner for 'the Literati of All Nations', which included 300 foreign writers, journalists and artists, and one for the Metropolitan Sanitary Association. Entertainments took place in the grounds, such as balloon ascents, fortune-telling and concerts, including one by the fashionable Ethiopian Serenaders.[111]

London shops – a perennial attraction – also exploited the Exhibition theme. In expectation of foreign hordes, signs were quickly put up in different languages, some using rather unreliable grammar. Flysheets and small booklets were prepared which could be given to passers-by, and which drew often tenuous connections between a particular shop and the Exhibition. Some shops produced gratis small guides to London in which, predictably, their premises figured highly. Many outlets made a point of stocking goods that were on display in the Exhibition. Such businesses, as well as exhibitors, made themselves known through adverts in the main newspapers. The Royal Commission, aware of the publicity gained via profit even while determined to prevent the Exhibition becoming a commercial venture, allowed the *Catalogue* to carry adverts in the back for exhibitors, their agents, and many London shops. The connection of the Exhibition with commerce had a pay-back in terms of visitors' numbers: many people began to view it in terms of an ideal homes exhibition and were drawn to articles of utility rather than the fine arts sections.[112]

At a time when passports were not required for entry to Britain, it was difficult to ascertain exactly how many foreigners came to the Exhibition. One thing is for sure, the numbers did not amount to the biblical proportions prophesied by protectionists. The costs of coming to Britain, and especially of accommodation in London, were high. Travel, particularly from outside Western Europe, was slow and often uncomfortable. In the three years prior to the Exhibition there had only been an annual average of around 21,500 foreigners coming to Britain, a figure explaining much regarding British insularity. Still, during the six months the Exhibition was open over 58,000 foreigners arrived in the country. The largest number – 27,000 – came from France. The German states sent 12,000, the United States 5,000, Belgium 3,800, Holland 2,900 and Russia 850.[113] For many, Britain, as the most industrialised nation, represented an 'Eldorado of Technology'.[114] The pulling-power of the Exhibition rested here less on anything the Royal Commission did and more on years of British industrial pre-eminence. Few people could afford to come for the entertainment value of the Exhibition. Most were interested in it in a more practical sense.

The apparently small numbers of foreigners hide their qualitative importance: these were mostly royalty, politicians and civil servants in charge of running national economies; or else they were merchants, industrialists and land-owners, interested in utilising or buying things shown, or in inspecting the international market. Some of the visitors from France, Belgium and the German states were technical drawers, artisans, small-scale producers, but also academics, given government grants in return for producing detailed reports on what they saw. Clerics and educationalists also figured highly, demonstrating the value placed on the Exhibition as a didactic event.[115]

Though the Royal Commission did not have the capacity to organise international travel, arrangements had been made – ground-breaking for the time – between the British South Eastern Railway Company and the Northern Railway Company across the Channel in France to offer a coordinated tidal service. Paris was now just 11 hours away, rather than two days, and Marseille 46 hours rather than up to a week. Once arrived, foreign visitors could enjoy everything available in London, and had automatic access to a range of institutions as organised by Bunsen and Prince Albert.[116] Foreign Commissioners looked after arrivals from their own countries, giving them information and finding them accommodation. Many people incorporated their visit with a trip round the country, often to look at British manufacturing centres and cities. For large numbers, the experience of international travel was special in itself. The difference between industrial Britain and predominantly rural home meant that coming to London and seeing the Exhibition was often like travelling forward in time.

Another way in which the Exhibition achieved popularity was through the vast amount of material that was printed on the subject. For one thing, there was an unprecedented amount of newspaper reportage. The royal nature of the opening ensured that this was prime news. So, too, did the constant stream of dignitaries visiting the Crystal Palace.

The Royal Commission, with its history of poor press relations and a membership including aristocrats, at first wanted the press to be excluded from the Exhibition. Cole, however, recognised that the press would be absolutely vital to creating public debate on design, as well as to profits, and single-handedly forced an about-turn.[117] As a consequence, the press were allowed in unrestricted, and the artists of the *Illustrated London News*, which provided a large readership with images in an age when they were harder to come by than today, were allowed in free. Much newsprint was devoted to the Exhibition throughout the summer. Many papers devoted long editorials to what was in the building and what it meant. Serialised tours were written for those who could not go. Mini-guides were produced for those that could. Fashion magazines, for example the illustrated *Lady's Newspaper*, highlighted purchasable goods on show. Foreign newspapers emulated the British example, though often devoting long commentaries to how the national produce was faring in London and inspections of Britain's way of life and political system.

Much press coverage took the form of expert commentary on the Exhibition. Trades journals like the *Builder* and the *Architect* inspected and weighed up relevant artefacts. The *Journal of Design*, which was Cole's publication, meticulously discussed the aesthetic merits and demerits of goods, and even included real samples of textiles at the Exhibition for readers to make a better judgment. Reports produced by European visitors highlighting exhibits of particular value found their way into commercial journals abroad.

There were countless guides published to help visitors find their way round London and the Exhibition – a fact which *Punch* decided to send up with its own spoof *Punchinello's Panorama of London in 1851*, and its *Comic Guide to the Exhibition – Showing How to See Everything That Is in London As Well As a Great Deal That is Not*, which swore not to rely on the 'worn-out phraseology of the musty records of pedantic bygone chroniclers, nor the flippancy and truth-trying particulars of modern Historians . . . but our witty selves.' Many guides were in foreign languages and were full of all manner of comment on British life and institutions.[118] Several encyclopaedias were published at the time of the Exhibition, most notably that by Charles Knight, while alternative catalogues, like that by Robert Hunt, Professor of Mechanical Science at the government School of Mines, supported those of the Royal Commission.

The fact that the Exhibition promoted itself as an educational event spawned many works, in particular for children. *Fireside Facts from the Great Exhibition*, for example, was intended to be read to children and contained details about each section of the Exhibition. The aim of the work was 'not only to convey in an amusing manner a mass of information, but to cultivate in the reader the powers of observation, comparison, induction, and memory, by the exercise of which the mind is trained to investigate and acquire knowledge for itself' and 'to observe a far more important principle by applying such knowledge in the cultivation of faith in the providence of God'.[119] Foreign children were not immune to being lectured on the Great Exhibition: a remarkably similar approach to *Fireside Facts* was taken by F.G. Wieck's *Die Wunder des Glaspalastes*, which explained in laudatory and educational tones the contents of the Crystal Palace. Such works ensured a vast number of children were brought up believing in the importance of the Great Exhibition. They also represented the start of a tradition in educational literature of focusing on the Exhibition for didactic purposes.

In addition to these more formal published works, there were hundreds, probably thousands, of poems, songs, and pieces of music devoted to the Exhibition. (Some examples are included at the start of each chapter.) There were many 'hymns' and 'odes' – including several by the king of Victorian popular poetry, Martin Tupper – and at least one cantata, using excerpts from the scriptures which appeared to support the

Exhibition's aims. Much of this represented an attempt to replicate London social life at home. There were 'glees' – songs written for many parts, which had first been performed at music halls and cabarets. Dance music was published reworked for the piano, such as 'England's Merry Polka for 1851', 'Anelli's Quadrille des Nations', the 'Grand Quadrille of All Nations As Performed at Jullien's Concerts' and 'Labitzky's Great Quadrille of All Nations', which had been performed in front of Prince Albert at the Grand National Concert series, and which was of symphonic proportions. There was also instrumental music, such as the 'Grand March of All Nations'. Such sheet music and poetry was cheaply produced, often accompanied by illustrations, and served to make the Exhibition a familiar subject in many homes. Most was celebratory. Victorian newspapers, always liable to break into rhyme, carried hundreds of poems about the Great Exhibition and even disseminated music.

Much poetry and music focused on a particular aspect of the Exhibition or reflected the public experience of it. Some songs, resourcefully, managed to turn the classification scheme, the awards given, and the catalogue to comic account. Songs like F.C. Perry's 'The Exhibition Lodging House' and G. Linley's 'A Country Girl's Account of the Exhibition' explored the possibilities arising from different groups coming into contact with each other. The theme of Linley's song – country naivety in the big bad metropolis – was most famously explored in book form: Henry Mayhew and George Cruikshank's *1851: or the Adventures of Mr and Mrs Sandboys and Family, who came up to London to 'Enjoy Themselves,' and to see the Great Exhibition*. While such works were generally humorous, they also revealed the depth of division and prejudice still in existence in a country divided by industrialisation. Many works demonstrated the success of the Royal Commission in achieving a particular interpretation of the Great Exhibition: for example, the number of hymns reflects the religious way in which the Exhibition was viewed. The plethora of songs devoted to Queen Victoria's glory as demonstrated by the Exhibition was noticeable.

Out of such songs and poetry, myths and folklore regarding the Exhibition developed. People like Paxton and Prince Albert were deified. The Royal Commission was sent up. The Crystal Palace and the riches it contained were depicted often in fairytale terms, and the multitude of poems about the building reveal just how it captured the public imagination. There were also works about events connected with the Exhibition. One example of this was F.C. Perry's song 'The Humours of a Parliamentary Visit to the National Exhibition', satirising a visit of MPs which actually took place and first sung in Vauxhall Gardens. Another was Sutherland Edwards' poem-book *An Authentic Account of the Chinese Commission, Which Was Sent to Report on the Great Exhibition; Wherein the Opinion of China is Shown As Not Corresponding At All with Our Own*. This lampooned what it saw as the Chinese government's backward response to the Exhibition. Newspaper reports and other works referred to the Cornishwoman who walked all the way to the Exhibition and to the attempts to pick Bramah's lock (eventually achieved – to British dismay – by an American after 51 hours) and so on. All of this helped to bring the Exhibition to a wider audience, though in a way which was simplified but probably indelible.[120] It showed that, often unintentionally, the Exhibition was a photogenic subject.

Illustrated music and poetry fly-sheets were another part of an enormous amount of memorabilia produced in connection with the Exhibition. There were notelets, invitations, visiting cards, calendars and diaries which bore images of the Crystal Palace and views of Hyde Park.[121] There were all manner of cups, plates, picture books, framed prints, table-cloths, miniatures of exhibits, cardboard models, pop-up books, paper peep-shows and so on inspired by the Exhibition.[122] The sheer volume of memorabilia demonstrates the success of the Royal Commission in making the Exhibition popular. Yet it also itself helped make it a familiar, if often cartoon-like, concept for the masses.

The popular success of the Exhibition took many people by surprise. And because of the extent of previous opposition, hardly anyone had thought about what would happen to the Crystal Palace at the end of the Exhibition. The assumption had been it would be removed and reused somewhere else. Neither had any plans been drawn up regarding what was to be done with the enormous profit the event was now set to make. By the end of July, the financial success of the Exhibition, at least, seemed secure. It soon also became obvious, both from the visitors' numbers as well as from the press and elsewhere, that the public had been more than won round. With the types of figures arriving at the Exhibition by early October it seemed unthinkable that the building should go. Because of this, voices began to call for the building to be kept up.

Paxton, ever a man sensitive to popular demands, printed a booklet calling for surplus funds to be used to convert the building into a winter garden: prime among his reasons was that 'it would enable the many to have what the few always have when possible, namely, rare shrubs, plants'. It also could serve as an educational centre, being used for rare botanical species and the display of sculpture.[123] Colonel Reid suggested relocating the Cirencester Agricultural College to the Crystal Palace, which, he said, should be moved to Kensington Gardens.[124] Cole, under the pseudonym 'Denarius', called for Parliament to change its mind and allow the Crystal Palace a reprieve from its 'sentence'. He suggested various uses for the building, all as ever 'self-supporting', including as a venue for London societies' lectures, for a gallery, and for sculpture exhibitions.[125] Albert, however, was of a different opinion. As will be seen, his plans for the Exhibition's surplus were far grander, and demanded far more space: it was here that he first mentioned using the funds to buy 50 acres of land across the road in South Kensington. Albert rather abruptly dismissed the Royal Commission's connection with the Crystal Palace as 'incidental'.[126] The Prince was still wary of doing anything which might be seen as 'breaking faith with the public,' as Victoria put it.[127] However, the Royal Commission's history of poor relations with Paxton, and its own embarrassment regarding the building, possibly also played a part in Albert's decision.

For the moment, however, the issue of what was to happen remained unresolved. The Royal Commission had agreed with the Commissioner of Woods and Forests to close the building before the end of October. No firm date had been set, however, and it was only decided in mid-August that the final day on which the Exhibition would be open to the public would be Saturday 11 October.[128] This time the Royal Commission's tactic of improvisation meant that there was no public ceremony: instead, however, an impromptu rendition was given of 'God Save the Queen', followed by the public stamping on the floor and applauding for over half an hour. Visitors could not be expelled from the building until 7 p.m.[129] Outside, bells were rung for hours into the night. On the following Monday and Tuesday exhibitors were allowed to take in their families free of charge as a concession for having to pay throughout the summer. On 15 October the closing ceremony took place. This time the public was excluded: jury members, Royal, Foreign and local Commissioners, and members of the Society of Arts were allowed in. At 12 p.m. Prince Albert entered without Victoria. Lord Canning read out the jury reports and the names of those who had won medals. (The names were printed in the *London Gazette* on 17 October.) The ceremony concluded with the Bishop of London praying that all may be 'led to acknowledge Thy power, wisdom, and goodness, in the achievements of man's industry and skill; and may depart to their several homes to "speak in their own tongues the wonderful works of God".' Finally, the Lord's prayer was read.[130]

I visited the Crystal Palace,
And there I saw a crowd as great
As ever gathered round a gallows;
A mob is just what I do hate.
Thought I, – This multitude immense
Seems full of happiness and glee;
Yes, but in two or three years hence
I wonder where or how they'll be! . . .

We may learn something good, 'tis true,
By mixing with each foreign nation;
But we shall catch their vices too.
It may be that fraternisation
With those from whom we stood aloof
Before, will foster peace and union;
But – here a Clown with hobnailed hoof
Trod right upon my favourite bunion.

6

❧

REACTIONS TO THE EXHIBITION

It is only when it is recognised that the Exhibition took place for a purpose, and was not a gigantic but pointless exercise, that the reactions to it begin to make sense. Though a motley set of interests had supported it, they were all bound by a commitment to furthering industrialisation in a way that would not harm the ruling and property-owning classes, nor the cultivated pursuits of art and science. In other words, there was an alliance of interests committed to a modernist agenda of capitalism, commercial liberalisation, moderate political change, the accommodation of manufacturing interests, education and reform. The Exhibition celebrated and advertised certain values and a way of life based on industrialisation and progress – values that are much more widely accepted today than they were then.

Though mid-nineteenth-century Britain was relatively highly industrialised, many aspects of life still reflected a pre-industrial age. Industrialisation was faced by stiff resistance in the political establishment as well as in many people's minds. Because of this, the Exhibition's modernist agenda was a provocative message. The reactions of many to the event depended on their position regarding industrialisation and the values connected with it. And what was true of Britain was possibly even more true in Europe and north America. There, industrialisation had not yet changed society to the extent it had in Britain. The outcome of the battle between the forces of modernism and pre-industrial ideas and institutions seemed less certain. As a result the contest was loaded with more significance than in Britain, and the Exhibition's theme more consciously recognised.

Part of the alliance that had promoted the Exhibition was committed to internationalism. The Exhibition was the first occasion – excluding wars – when peoples of different countries were substantially brought together. The novelty of this caused a deep reaction, invoking much mutual comment about 'foreigners', and greater familiarity with details of other lands. As the Exhibition was largely produced by a Western, pro-industrial alliance, however, the global image arising out of this new awareness was one skewed in the favour of the West. At the same time, the British commentary on other countries, and the comparisons that were made, served to underline national differences and raised self-awareness: paradoxically, one reaction to the internationalist Great Exhibition was the attention focused on national deficiencies in relation to other countries, and the boost given to national rivalries.

The fact that an alliance of interests had organised the Great Exhibition meant that the practical results of the event were not as unified as they might have been. A considerable part of the commentary on the Exhibition reflects not just its scale and variety, but also its lack of cohesion, its ambivalence, confusion and its excess. However, in the final analysis the event was enormously popular. The modernist agenda appeared to be particularly attractive to those with a moderate amount of disposable income, in other words to the new classes created by industry. The Exhibition seemed to have united all but a few determined opponents.

I

As the number of those who had supported the Exhibition grew, the objectives that the event was supposed to serve expanded in scope. The original intention of improving the aesthetic design of industrial goods had become linked to many other aims: the improvement of technological know-how; the glorification of industry and mass production; the promotion of free trade; the extension of British markets; the strengthening of the monarchy and all property-owning classes in the face of social unrest; philanthropy; education; and reform. Such aims stemmed from different parts of a broad alliance of pro-industrial groups. Together they constituted what can only be described as a modernist agenda.

The number of people who sympathised with this agenda was very large and, though difficult to quantify, there was a generally positive response to the Exhibition across a broad spectrum of public opinion. The promotion of industrialisation and the values supporting it was widely lauded. The children's book *Fireside Facts*, for example, pointed out that '"industry" has made many a fairy scene, and her secret is, – Work! work! work!'[1] Free traders recognised the Exhibition as 'the highest homage to the principles of commercial freedom'.[2] Philanthropists saw it as the first in a series of 'Labour Demonstrations, in which the history of the earth's industry will be practically written by the very *élite* of her toilers'.[3] Liberals thought it 'a notable illustration of the Law of Progress'.[4] Cosmopolitans and idealists spoke of 'this great reunion, this meeting of the children of the long separated sons of Adam'.[5] Many religious people saw the Exhibition as 'a sort of peaceful contest,' demonstrating 'oneness, brotherhood, – the same nature, the same faculties, the same Father'.[6] So much praise from so many quarters all at once created a sense of solidarity among the Exhibition's supporters. Prior to 1851, there had been worrying chasms between, for example, free traders and the landed aristocracy, the monarchy and the new middle classes, or the Church and industry. The Exhibition now represented a bridge between all these interests. And it was important to keep asserting its value in order to help underpin this new pro-industrial, modernist allegiance.

The Exhibition had presented itself as 'an experiment' – a '"taking stock" of the world's inventive ingenuity and manipulative skill,' as *The Times* called it.[7] This notion had arisen from discussions about the classification system, and from the involvement of statisticians and scientists. Soon, however, it became one of the most popular ways of viewing the Exhibition as the event's supporters realised it could furnish evidence that their values and objectives were the best in the face of what was still strong opposition. The popularity of 'facts' among Victorian reformers and liberals owes much to their need to assert themselves and their position in the face of what was commonly seen as 'prejudice'.[8] There was also the more practical need to map out the world in an age of new means of communications and production. It was no accident that at about the same time as the Exhibition was held statistical books like G.R. Porter's *The Progress of the Nation*, and Charles Knight's *Cyclopaedia* were being printed, and the first national census was undertaken. A large part of the positive reaction to the Exhibition in Britain was in this mould of belief in the empirical: people viewed it as 'proof' of one cause or another. The *Catalogue* encouraged this by talking of itself as 'a guide,' and 'a book of reference to the philosopher, merchant, and manufacturer'.[9]

Punch, quick as ever, satirised this in an article entitled 'the Morals of the Great Exhibition'. It wrote that 'all sorts of morals grow out of it, or are tacked on to it. You overhear them in the Crystal Palace; you pick them up in the Park; they obtrude themselves upon you in leading articles; they oust the weather in casual street-encounters; they beguile the pauses of a quadrille, and set conversation a-going in the railway carriage'. Examples of such morals were:

The Free Trader's Moral: 'A wonderful sight: Illustrates admirably the inter-dependence of nation and nation, and proves, to demonstration that the principles of Free Trade are those of nature and common sense'.
The British Manufacturer's Moral: 'By Jove, we must look sharp – or these foreigners will be cutting us out!'
The Foreign ditto ditto:
'Sacré!'
'Potztausend!'
'Carajo!'
'Corpo di Bacco!'
'Mashallah! (&c &c) After all, these Englishmen have some notions of their own beyond machinery and penknives!'[10]

One of the outcomes of the Exhibition was the strengthened resolve and confidence of each strand of the modernist alliance based on evidence provided there.

The idea of the Exhibition as a record of the state of human progress encouraged many to view it as a mirror, a lens or a glass show-case revealing mid-Victorian Britain and its position in the world. Again, the *Catalogue*, with its commentary on the exhibits as representing the world at large, gave the lead. The Exhibition also encouraged this reflexive interpretation by including models of the Crystal Palace or the electric clocks actually used in the building among the exhibits. Throughout its organisation, there had been exhibitions of building plans, medals, colour-schemes. Observers, in other words, were being encouraged to look at themselves. It was this, just as much as the novelty of the building material, that caused the metaphor of the mirror to constantly recur in poetry and creative literature on the Exhibition. Thomas Shuckard's 'Ode to the

Exhibition', for example, spoke of a dome of iron and glass, 'That centuries as they pass/May see man's first united home'. Another poem, 'The Glass-Berg', toasted 'The queen! And all whose wit and wealth/Are in the Berg displayed'.[11] *Punch* called the Exhibition a 'glass bazaar' and a 'shop of glass'.[12]

One result of this was a critical sense of self-awareness. In part, this had been intended by the Exhibition's organisers and to some extent stage-managed. Those of a reformist tendency – Cole and the Society of Arts – wanted to bring the state of things to people's attention, in order that through such education they might do something about the situation regarding in particular art and science *vis-à-vis* industry. The *Catalogue* was written partly as an authoritative comment on the strengths and weaknesses of what was displayed. Cole's *Journal of Design* offered a commentary, which ran simultaneously to the Exhibition, pointing out the aesthetic merits and defects of exhibits. It was also in this vein that Prince Albert suggested a series of lectures at the Society of Arts, which would then be published, allowing expert opinions on the display to be disseminated.[13] At the beginning of these lectures, Prince Albert's ally at Cambridge University, William Whewell, exhorted readers to think reflectively on the Exhibition. 'This kind of criticism,' listeners and readers were told, 'appears to be the natural and proper sequel to such a great burst of production and exhibition as we have had to witness; – to discover what the laws of operative power are, after having had so great a manifestation of what they do'.

One or two of the lecturers admitted the weaknesses of the Exhibition as a reflective device for viewing the world: Henry de la Beche, for example, noted that the collections of coal and minerals were 'defective', as many samples had been sent because of their value and beauty rather than their representative nature. Jacob Bell, speaking on pharmaceuticals, recognised that many French and German manufacturers stayed away for fear of competition. Most speakers, however, commented on the need for artistic and scientific education in industry as revealed by the Exhibition. Lyon Playfair expressed this most clearly. Commenting on the increasing importance of chemical production he concluded that:

> . . . a rapid transition is taking place in industry; that the raw materials, formerly our capital advantage over other nations, is gradually being equalized in price, and made available to all by the improvements in locomotion; and that industry must in future be supported, not by a competition of local advantages, but by a competition of intellect. All European nations, except England, have recognised this fact; their thinking men have proclaimed it; their governments have adopted it as a principle of state; and every town has got its schools, in which are taught the scientific principles involved in manufactures, while each metropolis rejoices in an industrial university, teaching how to use the alphabet of science in reading manufactures aright. Were there any effects observed in the Exhibition from this intellectual training of their industrial populations? The official reserve, necessarily imposed upon me as the Commissioner appointed to aid the juries, need exist no longer, and from my personal conviction, I answer without qualification, in the affirmative. The result of the Exhibition was one that England may well be startled at. Wherever – and that implies in almost every manufacture – science or art was involved as an element of progress, we saw, as an inevitable law, that the nation which most cultivated them was in the

ascendant. Our manufacturers were justly astonished at seeing most of the foreign countries rapidly approaching and sometimes excelling us in manufactures, our own by hereditary and traditional right

For the reformers connected with the Royal Commission, the image produced by the Exhibition of British manufactures in relation to the world was worrying. They had begun the enterprise with the premise that British manufacturers must be educated; the Exhibition simply fuelled their demands.

However, for most of the other British observers of the Exhibition, especially those with a stake in the new industrial order, the image reflected in the Crystal Palace of mid-century Britain was highly flattering. British manufacturers seemed to be faced by no immediate foreign competitors: even Cole commented in the *Lectures* that 'I have seen no satisfactory proofs of our industry being beaten in perfectly neutral markets, or at present any signs of its being likely to be'.[14] Jurors awarded most medals to Britain. Britain took up half of the building, while foreign countries appeared to have difficulty completing their display. Machinery was more evident in the British display than in that of any other country; elsewhere, raw materials and art-work appeared more prevalent.

This not only demonstrated Britain's technological lead, but also the liberal notion that a parliamentary system like Britain's allowed more profitable methods of production than a despotic one like Russia's. The aesthetic strengths of Russia or India, for example, were explained away by Whewell on the grounds 'that in those countries the arts are mainly exercised to gratify the tastes of the few; with us, to supply the wants of the many'. The Exhibition suggested, meanwhile, that industrialisation and technology could sort out social evils such as poverty, disease or housing. The improvements science and industry had made to people's lives were made obvious from the displays of telegraphy and maps, down to the gas-cookers and prototype refrigerators on display.

Obviously, the image the Exhibition presented of the world was hardly objective. Important perspectives were not included – in particular those of the working classes living in poverty in Britain and indigenous populations of the southern hemisphere. In the organisation of the Exhibition, the Royal Commission kept the upper hand. Half the jurymen were British and those who were not were often of a pro-British or at least pro-industrial background.[15] The displays from many parts of the world were arranged by colonists, rather than natives. Practical aspects meant that many countries could not represent themselves fully. Protectionism kept many important competitors to British manufacturers away. The mirror the Exhibition held up to British modernists was therefore distorted in their favour.

It was almost impossible to stand back from that image and recognise it as an exaggerated one. Many Victorians felt in need of facts in order to push for their rights in the face of anti-industrial opposition. And in any case, while the Exhibition was flattering, it was probably not completely without truth: the British were, indisputably, the most industrialised and productive, the wealthiest, and the most technologically advanced nation.[16] Nevertheless, there were some British observers who openly expressed the view that the Exhibition was less than objective. The reasons for their awareness almost always point back to the event's modernist message. Charles Dickens, for example, was notably ambivalent about the Exhibition. In the journal he edited, *Household Words*, one article, 'Three May-Days in London,' praised the technological achievements of the Crystal Palace, saying it was better than the palace created by Aladdin's slaves of the lamp. The Exhibition was valued for its educational impact, 'that practical education which may teach men to comprehend rightly the past and the present'. Its emphasis on industrial production was praised as being anti-feudal: Dickens wrote that one could see in the Exhibition 'the determination to assert the dignity of labour; to manifest to those who hold that the world is made for the few, that throughout the habitable globe there are the same agencies at work which have given the mechanic of the nineteenth century a greater command of the comforts of life than was possessed by the feudal lord of the sixteenth'.[17] In another article, 'The Private History of the Palace of Glass',[18] Dickens recounted the history of the Exhibition building in almost fairytale terms. Elsewhere, he praised the effects of the Exhibition's internationalism, remarking that 'altogether I think that a little peace, and a little good-will, and a little brotherhood among nations will result from the foreign invasion'.[19] The timidity and prejudice of those who feared London would be awash with radicals and foreigners was ridiculed in 'The Metropolitan Protectives'.[20]

Like other liberals, Dickens valued the Exhibition as proof of liberalism's value. This even tended to make him adopt liberalism's Anglo-centric, proto-imperial way of thinking. In 'The Great Exhibition and the Little One,' for example, Dickens

Punch's views on China. (*Punch*, Volume XX, 'Almanack for 1851)

systematically compared sections of the Crystal Palace with neighbouring displays of Chinese work at Hyde Park Corner and on the *Keyshing* – the aforementioned junk in the Thames. Chinese life and culture was ruthlessly lampooned for its 'backwardness', oppressiveness, and unenlightened character. Dickens compared, for example, the anchors outside the Crystal Palace with the junk:

> As a bamboo palanquin is, beside a railway-train, so is an English or American ship, beside this ridiculous abortion. Aboard of which, the sailors decline to enter until 'a considerable amount of tin-foil, silvered paper, and joss stick', has been purchased for their worship. Where they make offerings of tea, sweet-cake, and pork, to the compass, on the voyage, to induce it to be true and faithful. Where the best that seamanship can do for the ship is to paint two immense eyes on her bows, in order that she may see her way, (do the Chinese do this to their blind?) and to hang out bits of red rag in stormy weather to mollify the wrath of the ocean. Where the crew live in china closets, wearing crape petticoats and wooden clogs. Where the cabin is fitted up with every sort of small scented object that is utterly irreconcilable with water or motion.[21]

Dickens sympathised with the Society of Arts' concern to improve British educational standards relative to those abroad. The focus on foreign – in particular German – systems of education and the comparatively undeveloped British system in 'Mr Bendigo Buster on Our National Defences Against Education' was remarkably similar in tone to Playfair's lecture at the Society of Arts.[22] Meanwhile, Dickens seemed unable to resist neither the sight of the public enjoying the Exhibition, nor the occasion for commenting on British life – the subject of another article, 'A Pilgrimage to the Great Exhibition from Abroad', which was probably one of the most evocative published descriptions of the experience of foreigners arriving in Britain.[23]

Yet despite all this, Dickens obviously remained queasy about many aspects of the Exhibition, something which was more obvious in his private correspondence and his fiction than in *Household Words*. A major cause of this unease was his experience the previous year in the Royal Commission's Working Classes Committee. It was Dickens who moved the vote to dissolve the committee once it became obvious the Royal Commission did not wish direct contact with the working classes. Lovett, the Chartist committee member, recorded the 'dudgeon' felt by the group at what it regarded as 'aristocratic prejudice'.[24] Though little is recorded of Dickens' thoughts on this affair, recent biographers have recognised that it was a formative experience, not just in terms of Dickens' attitude towards the Exhibition, but in terms of his awareness of the self-centred nature of mid-Victorian society and its failure to deal with the issue of the working classes.

Dickens was in a difficult position. At a personal level, he had good relations with the Duke of Devonshire, who had possibly inveigled him into the committee and who in 1851 became the patron of Dickens' Guild of Art and Literature. Devonshire was also patron of Paxton and related to Granville. Politically, Dickens was still a liberal, as opposed to a revolutionary, and supported the aims of the Royal Commission. Professionally, he depended upon the educated middle classes as his audience – the same people who were presently admiring the Crystal Palace. All this prevented him openly criticising the Great Exhibition.

However, the impact of the Great Exhibition on Dickens' thinking is obvious. He completed the biographical *David Copperfield* in 1850. In 1851 he began dealing more directly with social issues in *Bleak House* – a title contrasting possibly intentionally with the Crystal Palace and reminiscent of Prince Albert's Lodging House. *Bleak House* portrayed the worlds of law and fashion as self-obsessed and stagnant, oblivious to poverty and disease – a criticism, perhaps, of the Commission and the droves in Hyde Park. In *Hard Times*, published in 1854, Dickens tackled social issues again, painting an alternative image of industrialisation, and also launching an attack on dry educationalism as the solution to poverty.

The articles in *Household Words*, while superficially positive, in fact contained many oblique criticisms of the Exhibition: the Royal Commission was portrayed as stiff and self-defeating. In 'The Wonders of 1851' it was accused of having cheated the public over the building competition (Dickens talked of 'a certain government office' headed by a Mr Trappem). 'The Private History of the Palace of Glass' was fairytale-like to an almost exaggerated degree – possibly sending up the official history of the Royal Commission. While he praised the Crystal Palace as a technological feat, Dickens also irreverently described how it could be '"brought home" to Hyde Park ready-made, and put up like a bed-stead', and noted that 'if for nothing else, this tremendous pile of transparency is astounding – for its cheapness. It is actually less costly than an agricultural barn or an Irish cabin!' One article, 'The Wind and the Rain,' focused on the weather, explaining that 'our readers are already so occupied with the wonders and beauties of the Great Exhibition, and already read so much about them, that we purposely avoid the subject.'[25] Behind the scenes, Dickens was also making changes to the journal's staff, bringing in the more biting social criticism of Henry Morley and George Sala.

Dickens' conscience had distanced him from the Exhibition, and in his letters he admitted to 'an instinctive feeling against the Exhibition of a faint, inexplicable sort'.[26] As the event dominated life in London, his first response was to escape from it to the coast and to Paris. He described to a friend how 'a perfect storm of letters of introduction rising in all quarters of the earth and bursting on my devoted head, obliges me to take a house at the seaside, and let this until the Exhibition is over'.[27] Yet Dickens was normally not averse to popularity. It was the Exhibition itself that he was avoiding. At a time when all were speaking of it, and praising it, Dickens' conscience made him feel an outcast: in another letter a few weeks later he described revealingly how 'I am living in a gipsy tent here, until Tuesday next, or so. You will find me usually before 2 – boiling a kettle suspended by a cord from three sticks, and living chiefly on stolen fowls and broken victuals'.[28]

Dickens' feelings with regard to the Exhibition were echoed to an extent by William Makepeace Thackeray who, perhaps not coincidentally, was also on the Working Classes Committee. Thackeray appeared less deeply affected by the social implications of the Exhibition. He wrote the famous 'Ode' to the event (included at the beginning of Chapter 5) and was moved by the opening ceremony, describing it as 'a noble awful great love inspiring goose flesh bringing sight . . . no particular item is wonderful but the general effect the multitude the riches the peace the splendour the security the sunshine great to see – much grander than a coronation – the vastest & sublimest popular festival that the world has ever witnessed . . .'[29] Nevertheless, behind effusiveness lurked doubts. Rather than as a work of inspiration, Thackeray described writing the 'Ode' as a mechanical act, telling a friend that if he had heard she had

had an arm cut off 'I should have gone on with Queen of innumerable isles tidumtidytidumtidy and not stirred from the chair.'[30]

Thackeray appeared to sense – as did Dickens – that the Exhibition was the construction of a particular set of people, rather than being truly representative of the country. In *Punch*, he wrote 'Monsieur Gobemouche's Authentic Account of the Grand Exhibition' in mock-French as well as a poem, entitled 'The Crystal Palace', in mock-Irish dialect. While humorous, both were written from the viewpoint of outsiders unable to fully comprehend the Exhibition's motives. The pretensions of the rhetoric that surrounded the Exhibition were sent up: Gobemouche, mixing Soyer's Symposium with the Exhibition, announced 'Binks's Symposium':

It is rumoured that active arrangements are in progress for the opening, on an extensive scale, of a grand Baked Potato Can of all Nations, or Eel Pie and Kidney Pudding Symposium, under the immediate direction of Binks, the renowned *chef* of cosmopolitan cook-shopery. The Can has been fitted up, regardless of expense, from an original design furnished by the famous Rusti Khan, and dug up on the banks of the Thames, by one of the Coolies or Coalies of the neighbourhood.[31]

SPECIMENS FROM MR. PUNCH'S INDUSTRIAL EXHIBITION OF 1850
(TO BE IMPROVED IN 1851).

Punch's alternative exhibition. *Punch* was quick to point out the Exhibitions one-sided image of industrialisation and modern life. (*Punch*, Volume XVIII, 1850, p. 145)

Punch – as a good satirical magazine should – homed in on the hypocrisies and contradictions contained in the rhetoric surrounding the event. Along the lines of Dickens, it was also often biting in its attacks on the Exhibition's social message, depicting, for example, an alternative exhibition of Britain's neglected poor.

Criticism of the Exhibition for excluding radical working-class demands came from left-wing observers. Radical journals, like the *Friend of the People*, for example, attacked the 'essentially aristocratic' nature of the opening ceremony, and wished it had been undertaken 'not in the presence of the richest, but of the worthiest of the nation, selected by popular election, to represent not a class, but *all*'. Letters were printed in the journal calling for the Exhibition to celebrate not free trade but 'those principles which could unite all nations in one common bond of brotherhood, each contributing to the welfare of all' – in other words international socialism.[32] *The Leader*, in an article entitled 'The Workman and the International Exhibition', welcomed the trade generated by the Exhibition and even, despite being republican, accepted the Exhibition's being 'Prince-patronized' on the basis that 'it is a matter of rejoicing to see a Prince so employed'. On the other hand, it commented:

> Underneath the magic brilliance which dazzles the bewildered visitor in the Great Exhibition, how few distinguish the grim misery which lies hidden there! Who passes from the work to the workman, and asks – What of all that glory does he share? What of all that joy will light up his home? What of hope his dim old age? Does the fair lady who admires that exquisite piece of cutlery, whose polish rivals her mirror, remember that he who gave it its lustre spit blood? As the delicate beauty gazes upon the infinite variety of steel pens, does she suspect that women, who had left neglected and crying children at home, sat in the last stage of pregnancy over the piercing press, which imparted elasticity to the springing nib?

It now called for workers to converge on the Crystal Palace:

> Let the child be there who is dragged out of 'beds which are never cold' at five o'clock in the morning, by the little nightworkers, who have returned home and are waiting for their turn to sleep; let the young factory man be there as he is to be found at home, without knowledge or emulation; the young factory woman without self respect; manhood and womanhood without content or hope; old age, trembling at its decay of power, and at the workhouse destiny before it. Let models be exhibited of their narrow streets, yards, gutters, cesspools, cheerless houses, bare cupboards, and, if possible, the drama enacted at the factory counter and in the truck-shop on the Saturday night, and then tell us . . . whether 'this be a green, flowery world with azure everlasting sky stretched over it, the work and government of a God'; or of a murky simmering Tophet of copperas fumes, cotton fuz, gin, riot, wrath and toil, created by a demon and governed by one?[33]

Other radical observers remarked on the self-serving nature of the Exhibition. Karl Marx commented perceptively that the Crystal Palace was a pantheon in which the bourgeoisie had erected gods in its own image and was now worshipping them.[34]

Yet it was not only those concerned with social issues who rejected the modernist, pro-industrial message of the Exhibition, but also conservatives. Thomas Carlyle, for example, was contemptuous of industrial, urban society. He rejected what seemed to him the chaos of the masses, a characteristic that he found reflected in the Exhibition, referring to it variously as an 'inane tornado', a 'Sanhedrin of windy fools', a 'congregation of empty windy mortals', a 'big Glass Soapbubble', where 'palaver, noise, nonsense and confusion, in all its forms, have been the order of the day'. Like Dickens, he escaped from London: he went to the north and Scotland.[35]

Protectionists formed another group that, because of its views, was able to see through the Exhibition's claim to represent the world objectively. *John Bull*, the Tory protectionist newspaper, continued to oppose the Exhibition's free trade and industrial slant. 'As a mere show place,' it admitted:

> there can be no question that the Exhibition has done more than any other show ever got up, to gratify the eye and to amuse and, to a certain extent, instruct the mind. And as for the paying-box, the Commissioners' eyes must glisten with delight when they open their till, gorged as it is with golden guineas. But then comes the question, have we not paid too dear for this whistle? Somewhere about one hundred thousand pounds have been extracted from the pockets of an impoverished population as a tax upon sight-seeing. It admits of a doubt whether this money might not have been expended in a manner more profitable for the individuals who spent it, and for the nation at large.

In terms that showed its recognition of the Exhibition's distorted sense of objectivity, and that echoed astoundingly Marx's words, it continued: 'A great national vanity fair, with its thousands to gaze at it, will hardly be found in the long run a sufficient compensation for the waste of money, of private and public time, and for the extensive injury to trade, which are the only tangible results, at present, of the "Great Exhibition of all Nations".'[36] While for the Exhibition's supporters, the glass of the Crystal Palace symbolised clarity and objectivity, for its detractors it meant distortion and vanity – a point that was also made in verse:

> The palace of Crystal's the thing to be seen!
> The project of Albert – (Right well He doth mean.)
> 'Twill dazzle the natives so gullibly green . . .[37]

Finally, another realm in which the modernist message of the Exhibition had an impact was that of aesthetics. In many people's eyes, industrialisation had produced an aesthetic crisis in that articles were now being produced with little direct input from designers. In consequence, and because new techniques and new wealth enabled producers to recreate willy-nilly the ornamental styles of the past, chaos reigned. Over-ornamentation, eclecticism and crudity of design were the result. The Exhibition suggested two solutions. The first was that embodied in Paxton's Crystal Palace. This proposed that instead of trying to recreate past styles, or looking for new ornamentation, industrially produced buildings should speak for themselves. The second was that of Cole. He, and those around him at the Society of Arts and *Journal of Design*, felt that the gap between art and industry could be bridged once more by educating designers about principles of ornamentation in the past. This did not mean, as Pevsner and many others have thought, simply regurgitating past styles. Rather, Cole *et al* believed that in the past ornament had been suitable to the materials used and the nature of the artefact. As Richard Redgrave stated in his report on design at the Exhibition for the Royal Commission, 'the primary consideration of construction is so necessary to pure design, that it almost follows that, whenever style and ornament are debased, construction will be found to have been first disregarded; and that those styles which are considered the purest, and the best periods of those styles, are just those wherein constructive utility has been rightly understood and most thoroughly attended to'.[38] If designers could be made aware of this, they could then begin to find a new style applicable to industrial production. Exhibitions, meanwhile, could be used to promote such produce in the consumer's mind. Both solutions were modernist, in that both of them sought essentially to promote industrialisation rather than hinder it.

Probably the most notorious opposition to both solutions came from John Ruskin, who, simultaneously to the running of the Exhibition, was working on his guide to architectural principles, *The Stones of Venice*. Like others, Ruskin perceived the impact of industrialisation on design as a crisis. For him, the ideal situation was that of medieval Italian masters, who were directly responsible for the aesthetic quality of their work and who invested their work with their personal emotions and characteristics. In architecture, ornament was that 'which proceeds from an individual mind, working through instruments which assist, but do not supersede, the muscular action of the human hand, upon the materials which most tenderly receive, and most securely retain, the impressions of human labour'.[39] Artefacts like this *meant* something to their producers and their owners. As far as Ruskin was concerned, the Crystal Palace was the produce of machinery and bore no such personal or emotional value. The images used by Ruskin when talking about the building smacked of emptiness, blankness, a void.

Ruskin saw the Crystal Palace as meaningless and was contemptuous of assertions by Paxton and other engineer-architects that this was the new aesthetic style of an industrial age. 'For three hundred years,' he stated:

> the art of architecture has been the subject of the most curious investigation; its principles have been discussed with all earnestness and acuteness; its models in all countries and of all ages have been examined with scrupulous care, and imitated with unsparing expenditure. And of all this refinement of enquiry – this lofty search after the ideal, – this subtlety of investigation and sumptuousness of practice, – the great result, the admirable and long-expected conclusion is, that in the centre of the nineteenth century, we suppose ourselves to have invented a new style of architecture, when we have magnified a conservatory![40]

Essentially, it was the divorce of production from design and the whole system of political economy which supported it that Ruskin mourned. His objections to the de-humanisation of production would later lead to the wider political and economic critique of *Unto This Last* and the more socialistic outlook of William Morris.

Ruskin also disagreed fundamentally with the Exhibition's educational message. Where Cole felt education could solve the design problem, Ruskin doubted whether the principles of ornament could be learnt at all. Dickens said of Cole that he was 'a professed pugilist; always in training, always with a system to force down the general throat like a bolus . . . he had it in charge from high authority to bring about the great public-office millennium, when Commissioners should reign upon earth'.[41] Ruskin felt similarly. For him, Cole's educational schemes 'corrupted the system of art-teaching all over England into a state of abortion and falsehood from which it will take twenty years to recover'.[42] In fact, Cole and Ruskin had much in common when it came to the view that ornament ought to be suitable to construction and that simplicity of ornament was to be preferred. Still, Ruskin felt the awareness of such principles ought to come about organically, rather than by Cole's more didactic method, which he saw as hindering, rather than helping. Pessimistically, he pronounced that:

> The peculiar character of the evil which is being wrought by this age is its utter irreparableness. Its newly formed schools of art, its extending galleries, and well-ordered museums will assuredly bear some fruit in time, and give once more to the popular mind the power to discern what is great, and the disposition to protect what is precious. But it will be too late. We shall wander through our palaces of crystal, gazing sadly on copies of pictures torn by cannon-shot, and on casts of sculpture dashed to pieces long ago. We shall gradually learn to distinguish originality and sincerity from the decrepitudes of imitation and palsies of repetition; but it will be only in hopelessness to recognise the truth, that architecture and painting can be 'restored' when the dead can be raised – and not till then.[43]

II

The fact that the Exhibition had a modernist message was also clear in the reactions of foreign observers. Particularly in continental Europe, but also in the United States, industrialisation had re-configured politics and society to the extent that important interests had developed both for and against modernisation. The Exhibition's message – and it was a broad one fusing support for industrialisation with notions of social and national unity – was consumed greedily by both opponents and supporters, and used as ammunition within the context of their own domestic battles. On the one hand, this meant that the Exhibition and British life were subjected to intense scrutiny: *The Times* self-consciously reminded readers that 'our country and its institutions are at this moment undergoing a minute and intelligent criticism from numbers of observant foreigners'.[44] On the other, it led to contrasts being drawn between life in Britain and circumstances at home. The foreign reaction to the Exhibition resulted, therefore, in closer harmonisation between British modernisers and their foreign counterparts. But it also contributed to a growing sense of national identity and differences between nations.

In the United States early responses to the Exhibition were generally indifferent, easily degenerating into the hostile. The *laissez-faire* tradition of manufacturers, the decentralised nature of industry, the practical difficulties and costs involved of transport, and the generally inward-looking political scene all contributed to the late formation of committees to arrange for goods to be sent over and the low official priority given to the Exhibition. There were signs that some manufacturers were curious about the foreign market. There were also signs of a latent alliance with Republicans, who sensed an opportunity to prove the worth of the American way of life abroad: in November 1850, the *New York Herald* stated that:

> we are very anxious to know what success the mechanics of the United States will meet at this Fair. We are very well convinced, however, that they will take their due share of the premiums; and more, that the specimens of American industry which will be exhibited there, will not only give the people of England, but those of the whole of Europe, a juster appreciation, and a more perfect knowledge of what this republic is than could be attained in any other way.
>
> We are so happily constituted that the more we are tested the more we triumph. The human mind in the United States being as free and untrammelled [sic] as it possibly can be, takes everything within its grasp and knows no limits but those prescribed by nature and her laws.[45]

Such self-confidence was tinged with political comment on Britain. This not only echoed past Anglo-American conflicts but also recognised the features of the particular modernist message being sent by the Exhibition, which jarred with the democratic, egalitarian ethos in the United States: 'Can it be possible that [England] overwhelmed as she is with a national debt of a magnitude almost beyond compilation, with a government of the most expensive description, with a nest of non-producers in the shape of aristocrats, eating away its vitality, with corruption pervading every fibre and muscle of the body politic, can compete with a young, vigorous, athletic, powerful republic like the United States? We should think not.'[46]

By early 1851, however, it became obvious that the obstacles to a successful American exhibition in London were considerable. Sensing perhaps that they had overestimated public support for the event, patriotically hoping to forestall humiliation, but also implicitly recognising the Exhibition's message of the unity of the aristocracy with the masses, some of the press became more derisive. For example, the *New York Herald* editorial now stated that: 'we think the World's Fair will be a humbug. That clever fellow, Prince Albert, determined to make himself popular with the whole shop-keeping and lodging house-keeping interest of London, and he designed the grand show that was to enrich them and levy a tax on all the civilized nations of the earth. . . . Our only hope that the World's Fair will prove anything but a perfectly complete failure is in the movements of the socialists[47] who are to visit London.'[48]

However, such overt Republican opposition to the Exhibition hid a wider support for it from manufacturing interests and among the American public. The number of exhibitors was disappointing – around 500 – but then on the other hand, it was not that small, given the practical obstacles involved. Moreover, other newspapers maintained an interest, even though it was based on a desire, 'to "strut their stuff" before the old world and especially England'.[49] There was much initial acrimony between the British and American press: *Punch*, for example, acidly noted the contrast between the large eagle hanging above the American section and the lack of exhibits beneath, then hammered home the jibe and returned American social criticism by suggesting 'why not have sent some choice specimens of slaves? We have the Greek Captive in dead stone – why not the Virginian slave in living ebony?'[50] The American *Whig Review* regarded the Exhibition as 'the First Olympiad of Cant', an 'intolerable hoax

Punch on America. (*Punch*, Volume XVIII, 1850, p. 190)

. . . seized on by every ruler in Europe in danger of not ruling,' and 'flunkeyism . . . and unfathomable nonsense'.[51] However, once the value of America's simple but useful exhibits began to be recognised, the Republican opposition subsided into support and glowing pride for domestic manufacturers.

This shift can be traced in the reports of Horace Greeley for the *New York Herald*; he followed American exhibitors to London and acted as United States Commissioner. Published in a volume in 1852, these offer a fascinating, entertaining and deep insight into Anglo-American relations in the 1850s. Greeley began his reports with an apology to any readers expecting accounts of high society in Europe. He then launched into descriptions of his disastrous journey across the Atlantic – concluding that 'utter indifference to life and all its belongings is one of the characteristics of a genuine case of sea-sickness' – and began with a social critique based on tours of London workhouses. By the opening of the Exhibition, however, Greeley was already showing signs of weakness in the face of what was shown: the Crystal Palace he praised as 'better than any one thing it contains, it is really a fairy wonder, and is a work of inestimable value as a suggestion for future architecture', prophetically announcing 'depend on it, stone and timber will have to stand back for iron and glass hereafter, to an extent not yet conceivable'. The sight of the aristocracy leading the ceremony was grudgingly accepted with the comments that 'if it were a new thing to see a Queen, Court and aristocracy engaged in doing marked honour to Industry, they certainly performed gracefully the parts allotted them . . . And while I must regard [Queen Victoria's] vocation as one rather behind the intelligence of this age and likely to go out of fashion at no distant day, yet I am sure that change will not come through *her* fault.' Later, he was forced to admit that 'I do not wholly like these cold and stately English, yet I think I am not blind to their many sterling qualities', and that 'personally, the English do not attract nor shine; but collectively they are a race to make their mark on the destinies of mankind'. English women were even accorded the dubious praise that they 'studiously avoid peculiarities of dress or manner and repress idiosyncrasies of character', and conform 'to the orthodox standard of womanhood'.[52] By the time Greeley published his book, however, he had to note in relation to the Exhibition that 'more recently, the tide has completely turned, until the danger now imminent is that of extravagant if not groundless exultation'.

Though at first criticised, the American exhibition revealed its value in a sequence of high-profile events during the summer. A.C. Hobbs, who had been sent from New York to look after Day & Newell's locks, unpicked some of the most respected British locks. One of these, by Chubb's, had been used at the Bank of England for years. Hobbs picked this twice in under half an hour. Another, by Bramah, carried a prize of £200 for anyone who could unpick it. This Hobbs did in 51 hours. The Day and Newell locks, however, proved themselves to be unpickable. The Bank of England, in response to all this, ordered a complete set of Day & Newell locks. McCormick's reaper, meanwhile, which British observers initially thought weak and which even Greeley described as 'a cross between an Astley's chariot, a treadmill, and a flying machine', proved itself highly robust in trials in Essex. At another trial at Hounslow, American farm equipment proved itself more than worthy. Colt's revolvers were also recognised as exhibits of strong potential. Possibly the most signal victory, however, was unconnected with the Exhibition: on 28 August the United States yacht *America* soundly beat Britain's *Titania*, built by Robert Stephenson, in a race for the Hundred Guinea Cup – afterwards known as the America's Cup.[53] After years of trying, the United States had now proved itself a sea-going nation to be reckoned with, something that came as a severe shock in Britain with its long history of naval supremacy.

All this forced a reappraisal by the British press. *The Times* now conceded that 'Great Britain has received more useful ideas and more ingenious inventions from the United States, through the Exhibition, than from all other sources'.[54] *Punch*, always willing to turn the guns on home targets, announced 'Timber for Sale – A great quantity of Planks, Sticks, Masts and Spars, to be had cheap – Inquire at the Royal Yacht Club House, Cowes'.[55] There was still some disappointment at the number of

Council Medals awarded to America at the Exhibition – a result of the Royal Commission's rather narrow definition of good design. Nevertheless, American ingenuity had been visibly demonstrated. The *Official Catalogue* recorded the American exhibits as showing a model of industrial design unlike that of Britain or France, but worthy in its own right,[56] and America received *per capita* more awards than Britain.[57]

With national success and the generous response of British newspapers, Republican opponents of the Exhibition, instead of opposing its modernist message, now exuded delight. American exhibitors had proven themselves and were not seen to be simply emulating the British example. Republicanism would afterwards turn its back once more on the modernist agenda propounded by the European exhibition. Nevertheless, the new unity that had been forged between American manufacturers and Republicans would turn out to be long-lived. The Exhibition had provided the first major forum where such an alliance could be rehearsed. It also helped transfer British modernist ideas across to America: with victory, American observers were less critical of the Royal Commission's programme and partook of ideas that would later become influential on the other side of the Atlantic.

This process was encapsulated in the dinner given by George Peabody – the American who had financed the costs of so many of his countrymen – in honour of American exhibitors. Held on 27 October at the London Coffee House, where in the previous century, Franklin and Strahan had met and discussed Anglo-American amity, those present included the United States Ambassador, the British Ambassador to Washington, the former Secretary of the Treasury, the Junior Governor of the Bank of England and many other diplomatic and political personalities and dignitaries. A 'loving cup' was passed around. The American Ambassador welcomed the Exhibition as 'showing the world the encouraging prospect, that the time has come when labour, dignified labour, must be respected; that the time has come, when there must be a just appreciation of those, who are the creators of wealth; and that it is to the efforts of the labourer, that every country must be mainly indebted for its glory and its power'. Lord Granville, meanwhile, hoped that it would produce 'feelings, never to be effaced, of respect and regard for one another; to induce the feeling that we all belong to the same blood, all speak the same language, and, though differing in some minor details, still that we both fully and equally prize and value the love of liberty and the progress of the human kind'.[58] This meeting revealed vividly the Victorian liberal torch being handed across the Atlantic to a new generation of reformers and modernisers.

Such an extension of the liberal modernist agenda to other countries had been part of Albert's plan and also fitted in with the government's free trade policy. However, it was primarily in continental Europe that Albert had hoped to influence affairs and it was here, perhaps, that the Exhibition was most provocative. In France, the economic and social situation was particularly fragmented. Industrialisation had produced a small number of manufacturers and merchants who were interested in foreign markets, and supported commercial liberalisation. In general, though, French production was based on smaller manufacturers more intent on protecting the home market. Both groups looked to the government to provide support. The modernist agenda in France was therefore split with an emphasis on the protection of home industry. Modernisers were faced, however, by a vast agricultural and artisan population – mostly outside urban centres like Paris, wine-growing areas and ports –

which was also heavily protectionist. To stay in power any French government which did not want control by the masses (and, potentially, a return to 1789) and wished to increase state power, needed to harness the forces of industry and the influential bourgeois class. The Exhibition – with the artistic education agenda of the Royal Commission – offered Louis Napoleon the opportunity of showing himself favourable to commercial liberalisation, but also of being seen to do something for national industry without giving major concessions. There was also the possibility of proving to French manufacturers that they could compete abroad and relaxing the grip of protectionism on smaller producers. Napoleon did not come out in support of free trade overnight. Nevertheless, he saw eventual commercial liberalisation as the only hope for France. He needed the support of the free traders. Ultimately, however, his position hinged on the smaller manufacturers.[59] Napoleon flung himself and the government whole-heartedly into the project. He sent over not just the jury of the French exhibition of 1849 but also 296 reporters from smaller businesses. He had enormous sums voted by the Assembly for the French effort and supported the project in official newspapers.[60]

There were many forces ranged against Napoleon – royalists, revolutionaries, agriculture and many artisans. The debate about commercial liberalisation was therefore highly charged and it coloured much of the French reportage regarding the Exhibition. Perhaps Louis's most significant opponent was the conservative Thiers, who supported industrialisation and even welcomed the Exhibition, but took the view that protectionism was the only way forward. Thiers was vying with Napoleon for the hearts and minds of smaller manufacturers. After visiting London, he returned to Paris to give a speech on 27 June to the Assembly in which he argued that French manufacturers were superior and ought not to embroil themselves in the international market. However, Michel Chevalier, the highly influential economist – and later Minister of Commerce under Napoleon – saw the future in the Exhibition. He hoped that France's industry would see its own strengths there and open up to the international market, in particular Britain.[61] Louis Blanqui, a liberal who opposed Napoleon's quasi-protectionism as much as the Republic's increasing autocracy, sent home glowing reports of British life and institutions, praising the Royal Commission and the government for having introduced such a liberal measure, and comparing their attitude with the suspicious protectionism of the French. For him, the Exhibition demonstrated the laws of progress, which France presently was attempting to deny.[62] Free traders, like Joseph Bard, presented British institutions in such glowing terms that their reports were probably counterproductive. Bard's accounts for French readers maintained that 'there is no nation in the world which offers the same cohesion, energy and unity as that of Great Britain', an assertion which bore little resemblance to reality, but which rested on the image given out by the Exhibition.[63] The political economy question shaped a reportage which, even when it was not political, was dominated by the contrasts between industrialised Britain and artisan, agricultural France.[64]

Just as the Royal Commission was hoodwinking the British public into its way of seeing things, the Exhibition allowed Napoleon a propaganda success over protectionist opponents. The triumph of France was predictably recognised in Britain by all experts connected with the Royal Commission and many others, and was reflected in the number of medals received. As Napoleon had foreseen, manufacturers went wild with joy. Whereas there had been initially much scepticism among them regarding the Exhibition, towards the end of the summer in 1851 there overwhelming enthusiasm – as demonstrated by the Parisian reception for Lord Granville and the Royal Commissioners.[65] Napoleon's government now exploited this to the full, organising an official prize-giving for French exhibitors on the Champs Elysées with members of the French Commission and the diplomatic corps present, giving each exhibitor a Legion of Honour cross, and later publishing an official French report on the Exhibition documenting French triumph.[66]

The Exhibition, then, was helpful in bringing together the forces of modernisation in France. This was a coalition that had much in common with the British modernist agenda – and it is interesting to note that the Exhibition was the stepping-stone to further Anglo-French cooperation: the contacts made, both in terms of personnel and politics, paved the way for a state visit of Albert and Victoria the following year, the Crimean War alliance, and the commercial treaty of 1860, which ushered in a period of commercial liberalisation in Europe. However, French manufacturers were also being confirmed in their belief in their own path towards industrialisation. The Exhibition had both integrated *and* separated Britain and France.

The situation with regard to the German states was similar, if complicated by their politically fragmented character. Generally speaking, industrialisation had affected the northern German states more than the southern ones, meaning that there was an interest in commercial liberalisation in Prussia and the coastal states of Hamburg and Hanover, while in the south, led by Austria, protectionism dominated in a society still based largely on agriculture and small-scale production. However, industrialisation had touched the southern German states, and the governments there were keen to expand their export potential in order to raise badly needed revenues. A contest had been going on for several decades between protectionism and commercial liberalisation in the states – one which was intensified by Austro-Prussian rivalry after 1848. Gradually, Prussia's policy of slow liberalisation with guarded protection of industry began to gain support among manufacturers and nationalists across the Germany.

Albert knew the impact the Exhibition would have in a region where commercial policy and industrialisation were such hot issues. Since the turn of the century, Britain had been seen as the source of new industrial technology. There was also a long history in Germany of state promotion of industry via exhibitions, and many of the states had encouraged artisans, manufacturers and academics to write reports on them – a system which was now extended to London.[67] From the start, then, the Exhibition was bound to be subjected to close scrutiny. Yet the Great Exhibition – and Britain itself – also represented an advert for industrialisation, free trade, and national unity at a time when all these things were loaded with political significance in the German states. The impact of this could be seen in the countless official and unofficial reports on the event, as well as the intensive newspaper coverage. Altogether, the Great Exhibition was the occasion for an enormous information-gathering exercise by Germans.

German nationalists – as far as they dared speak after the clampdown on nationalism after 1849 – were all too aware of the deficiencies of the *Zollverein's* showing. Lothar Bucher, a supporter of Prussian-led unification in exile in London for his activities during 1848 and later adviser to Bismarck, was sensitive to German weaknesses in his articles for the *Nationalzeitung* newspaper, reporting that 'there is no Germany in Hyde Park. Germany is once again an illegal expression. The honourable colours of the German Empire are now only fit for pipe-fodder, and the workers sent to set up the exhibits were chosen from subjects loyal to the separate states. . . . It's not just the fact that we have to extract from it the collection of peoples known as Austria. The way the other parts of Germany are presented is also so complex that neither I, nor any other mortal, can unravel its meaning in 12 weeks.'[68] South German nationalists in favour of unification including Austria were equally aware of this fact: the reporter for the *Augsburger Allgemeine Zeitung*, which carried a series during the Exhibition entitled 'London Letters', asked 'whether in the "Exhibition of All *Nations*" the *Zollverein* should be the body representing us?'[69]

In the south, there was heavy criticism, even fear, of the industrial model presented by Britain and its social consequences. The *Augsburger Allgemeine Zeitung* told its readers: 'One speaks so often of the imbalance between capital and labour. This Exhibition, where industrial production of taste and excess is carried to monstrous proportions, is as good a demonstration as any of this imbalance. The factory owner, the crowd of gawping rich folk, sun themselves here in the light of industrial power, which is itself simply a reflection of the global power of capital.'[70] Many of the artisan reports from Württemberg, for example, entered in on diatribes against industrialisation based on aesthetic grounds, claiming that craftsmanship and solidity was far better than cheapness of production. This type of reportage often descended into national stereotyping – remarkably similar to that in American and French reports – where the British were seen as stiff, lacking grace and anti-social.[71]

In industrial circles, however, particularly in the north but also – importantly – in the south German states, the Exhibition was seen as highly valuable and a great success.[72] The south German states of Württemberg and Bavaria achieved an unexpectedly high quota of medals, despite their artisan production. Government officials and leading industrialists, receiving praise at home, were encouraged towards further industrialisation and exploitation of the international market.[73] Prussian industrial circles, meanwhile, were also boosted and the official *Zollverein* report on the Exhibition in Berlin was optimistic for the chances of future German industrialisation.[74]

There were good reasons for this. At the same time as the Exhibition, the Prussian government was locked in a battle with Austria, which wished to substitute its own protectionist commercial leadership for the relatively liberal, Prussian-led *Zollverein*. It was already clear that if Prussia could encourage industry and interest in foreign markets in the southern German states, they would be less likely to go with Austria. The Exhibition allowed Prussia to take the lead in representing the German states abroad. The Exhibition's modernist programme supported Prussia's cause. It made Prussia seem the more progressive state in the eyes of industrial interests throughout Germany. Liberal nationalists – like Bucher – would eventually identify Prussia as the state most likely to bring national unity and moderate liberalism. The Exhibition forged closer links between civil servants and industrialists in different German states, creating a stronger network of people committed to further industrialisation. As it did in France, the Exhibition also knitted together British and German modernisers, while many of the particular strengths of German producers *vis-à-vis* British ones became obvious. For many larger-scale producers, success bred confidence. And for the crucial small-scale producers of southern Germany, the Exhibition demonstrated that foreign markets were nothing to be feared. Despite the fact that objections to the British industrial model remained, and that British pre-eminence served to convince many of the need for continued protection, overall the Exhibition tipped the balance in favour of modernisation and the growing power of Prussia.

Glory to the God of heaven!
Peace on earth! Tow'rds men good will!
Now shall honours due be given
To the best of human skill;
Always will we deal with others
As we would they dealt with us,
And rejoice, as men and brothers,
To befriend each other thus!

Nobly hast thou fruited, Labour!
Brightly hast though flowered, Art!
Well has England hail'd as neighbour
Every nation to her heart!
Yes, – for all on earth are brothers
High and low, and far and near,
And the more we see of others
All the more we hold them dear! . . .

For it is a glorious teaching,
Albert, thou hast taught mankind, –
Greatly to perfection reaching,
And enlarging heart and mind;
Stirring us, and stirring others
Thus to do the best we can
And with all the zeal of brothers
Help the Family of Man!

Martin Tupper, *Hymn of the Crystal Palace*, EX.1851.101., NAL

7

AFTERMATH, RESULTS AND CONCLUSIONS

I

When the Exhibition closed on 15 October 1851, there was no certainty about what should be done with the building or with the profit that the Royal Commission had made – an enormous £186,000. The popularity of the Crystal Palace had led to protests about its impending removal and a vote in Parliament granting a stay of execution until May 1852. A Royal Commission of Inquiry composed of Lord Seymour, William Cubitt, and Dr Lindley (head of Kew Botanical Gardens) was convened in December 1851 to recommend a solution. Between October 1851 and April 1852, however, the situation was in a state of flux. One certainty was the head of steam that had now been built up among the public and in those circles which had been involved in the Exhibition in support of the principles it had embodied – in particular that of industrial education. This was demonstrated by the countless petitions sent to the Royal Commission from around the country calling for some kind of technical institution. It was also evident from the donation of various collections from the Exhibition, which were meant to serve as the embryo of some more permanent museum. The other certain outcome of the event was the Royal Commission's pot of gold, which suddenly put it in a position of importance.

In August 1851, Albert had insisted on spending 'any surplus, which may accrue, towards the establishment of future Exhibitions or objects strictly in connexion with the present Exhibition'. 'The purchase of the Crystal Palace,' he continued, 'for the purpose of establishing a Winter Garden, or a Museum of Antiquities, or a public promenade, ride, lounging place &c &c, has, in my opinion, no connexion whatever with the objects of the Exhibition.' Instead, Albert pointed out the land available in Kensington, opposite the Exhibition building: 'I would buy that ground and place on it four institutions, corresponding to the four great sections of the Exhibition: – Raw Material, Machinery, Manufactures and Plastic Art'. Such institutions, Albert proposed, would promote 'the industrial pursuits of all nations'.[1]

Albert's plans revealed the influence of German ideas about central institutions of education and their value to industry. However, they were far more ambitious and idealistic than anything attempted in the German states. What he proposed was a cosmopolitan industrial university. The international aspect was gradually whittled down as it was discussed at the Royal Commission and as the government became increasingly involved. Nevertheless, the South Kensington development was essentially accepted by the Royal Commission; purchases of land began in December 1851 and in January 1852 the Royal Commission received a new charter. This allowed it to own land, subject to occasional directions from the Treasury, which continued the quasi-official tradition of the Exhibition. By December 1852 other estates had been bought, after Disraeli, the new conservative Chancellor of the Exchequer, who had been converted to the Exhibition's cause (and in return won Albert and Victoria's sympathies towards him), arranged a government grant of £150,000 to match to the Royal Commission's outlay.

Meanwhile, public pressure, the lectures on the Exhibition at the Royal Society of Arts, and then the Royal Commission's own Second Report in 1852, propelled the government to make some move towards supporting industrial education. Under the influence of Granville, promoted soon after the Exhibition from Vice-President of the Royal Commission to the post of Foreign Secretary, Cole had been appointed head of a new Department of Practical Art at the Board of Trade, which would head the schools of design, supply drawing masters to primary and grammar schools, and had offices and a Central School of Art in Marlborough House. In 1852 this was beefed up under the new Conservative administration of Derby (formerly Lord Stanley) – which now saw the potential advantages of the project in terms of national strength, public profile and royal sympathy. It became a Department of Science and Art, absorbing the Museum of Practical Geology, School of Mines, Geological Survey, and the Museum of Irish Industry. The science side was headed by Playfair. The Department's collections at Marlborough House included the donations from the Crystal Palace.

In 1856, the division between art and science was recognised as an artificial one and the two departments were united, with Playfair as Cole's deputy. The industrial impetus for centrally administered education gradually grew. Later, the Department transferred from the Board of Trade to the Board of Education, and became 'effectively the main government agency for secondary education throughout the country'.[2] In the 1880s it formed the nucleus of the state's efforts to promote higher education in technology and design.

Initially, Henry Cole had been rather sceptical about Albert's grand plan, preferring a self-supporting establishment that would grow organically out of public support and would be based on the gradual amalgamation of London intellectual societies already begun by the Society of Arts. He also at first supported the idea of using the Crystal Palace to house a new industrial educational institution, either in Hyde Park or, failing this, in Battersea.[3] The Society of Arts, in the immediate aftermath of the Exhibition, considered moving out of the Adelphi and into the Crystal Palace, where it might form the nucleus of a collection in intellectual institutions. Albert, however, felt that all this undermined the South Kensington project: the Prince's Secretary, Phipps, told Cole that his plan 'appears to "pull all the plums" out of the plan promulgated by the Prince . . . and to attach them permanently to the Crystal Palace, and also to the Society of Arts, the original connection of which with the Great Exhibition has been the foundation of almost all its difficulties'.[4] Relations between the Society and its President were still cool after earlier difficulties.

Cole now wisely concentrated on his duties at the Department of Science and Art, and worked with Albert. In 1856, the Department of Science and Art moved to South Kensington and its collections were housed in a new South Kensington Museum, opened by Queen Victoria in 1857. Continuing the tradition of the Crystal Palace – though certainly not its aesthetic ambitions – the museum was housed in a temporary corrugated iron structure which became known as 'the Brompton Boilers'. This was the embryo of today's Victoria and Albert Museum which replaced it in 1899.

The Society of Arts, meanwhile, had been rejuvenated by the Exhibition's success. Using the connections it had made abroad and the selling point of its role as originator of the project, it was able to expand its membership and secure its financial situation. Despite some bitterness that the Exhibition's profits had not found their way into its coffers and a sense that the members of the Executive Committee had looked after themselves rather than the Society, it prospered. Today it continues its activities for the arts, science and industry.

As Albert's grand scheme began to compete for government attention and resources

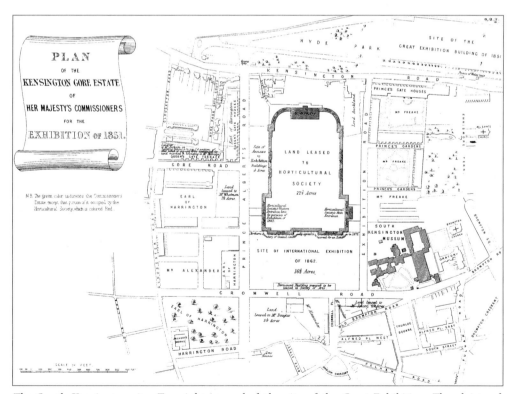

The South Kensington site. Top right is marked the site of the Great Exhibition. The cloistered gardens at the centre would eventually become home to the Imperial College and other institutions. The Natural History Museum was built on the site of the 1862 exhibition. The South Kensington Museum would become the Victoria and Albert.

MR. JOHN BULL IN HIS WINTER GARDEN

John Bull now sitting rather comfortably in Paxton's proposed Winter Garden. (*Punch*, Volume XXI, 1851. p. 79)

with the Crimean War, Cole's more gradualist views once more gained influence with the Royal Commission. The crunch came with the government's decision in 1858 to leave the National Gallery in Trafalgar Square instead of moving it to South Kensington to become, as Albert had hoped, the jewel in the Kensington crown. This was a bitter pill for the Royal Commission and Cole was now able to persuade it to mortgage part of its estate, pay back the government and run as a self-supporting body. Gradually, as Cole had foreseen, societies and institutions now began to be pulled towards South Kensington; these included the Horticultural Society, which leased a large area of the land for gardens and arcades, the Royal Academy of Music and the natural history collections of the overcrowded British Museum, which formed a Natural History Museum. The Royal Commission also permitted the 1862 International Exhibition to take place on the land where the Natural History Museum would later be erected. In 1907, the Royal College of Science and the Royal School of Mines in South Kensington were amalgamated to form Imperial College. By the turn of the century, the estates of the Royal Commission of 1851 had made it a wealthy organisation. It still exists, housed within the precincts of Imperial College and devoting its energies to the principles of the Exhibition of 1851 through scholarships and other activities.

The South Kensington complex – or 'Albertopolis' – today includes Imperial College, the Royal College of Music, the Victoria and Albert Museum, the Natural History Museum and the Albert Hall. It owes its existence to Albert's insistence that the surplus from the Great Exhibition of 1851 be used to provide space for industrial education. Its rather haphazard make-up, however, reflects the failure of the state to provide Albert with the means for a unified, rational institution. Instead, the organic growth and development of institutions there demonstrates more the influence of Henry Cole.

The decision of the Royal Commission to part company with the Crystal Palace meant that when the Commission of Inquiry met in December 1851 the choice was either between the state stepping in and buying the building, or some sort of self-supporting, popular proposal being put together for its future. Charles Wentworth Dilke, former Executive Committee member, suggested moving the British Museum, together with its reading room, to the Crystal Palace. Cole suggested relocating the Crystal Palace to Battersea and opening there a patent museum and a centre for other related societies. Paxton wanted a Winter Garden, which would allow promenades and the display of sculpture and other educational exhibits. The advantages of a modular structure were explored in terms of slicing the building up and taking part to Kew to build a new conservatory there.[5] Meanwhile, the press was full of other suggestions, including one in the *Builder* for the material to be used to construct a 1,000 ft high 'Prospect Tower' in which art and manufactures from round the country could be displayed.[6]

Public support for the building continued and several concerts and 'promenades' took place there early in 1852 supported by Fox and Henderson, who were able to make money from tickets while the whole question dragged on. A vast fete on 3 April 1852 in support of keeping the building where it stood attracted similar numbers of visitors to those who had attended the opening of the Exhibition and brought the surrounding area to a standstill. During the fete, petitions were signed by well over 100,000 people.[7] Still, though the new Conservative government supported Albert's Kensington plan, it found it difficult to accept a breach of faith with influential residents near Hyde Park. Derby was averse to any government support for entertainment, as opposed to education. The British

PERFORMANCE OF OUR FRIEND SIBBY, IN THE LOBBY OF THE HOUSE OF COMMONS, AFTER THE DECISION TO PULL DOWN THE CRYSTAL PALACE.

Sibthorpe's reaction to parliament's vote.

Museum and Kew options were too expensive. Ultimately, Albert himself communicated to Derby his own view that the building should go. On 29 April 1852, Parliament decided to pull the Crystal Palace down.[8]

The building was immediately bought by a consortium made up of Samuel Laing, the Chairman of the London, Brighton and South Coast Railway, Francis Fuller, John Scott Russell, and others, and over the next two years was taken down in Hyde Park and reconstructed in Sydenham in south-east London. The consortium's bid reflected the pulling-power not only of the building, but also of the educational message popularised by the Exhibition. Many of the same people who had been involved with the Great Exhibition now worked once more to reconstruct it, and also improve upon it, at Sydenham. Fox and Henderson were again contractors. Paxton extended and improved his building and was Director of the Winter Garden, Park and Conservatory. Owen Jones was Director of Decorations, while Digby Wyatt was Director of Works. The Fine Arts Courts were reconstructed and extended by Wyatt. The Crystal Fountain was given its old position at the centre.

The first pillar was raised on 5 August 1852. On 10 June 1854, the building was opened by Queen Victoria in the presence of 40,000 spectators. Lord Derby gave the Crystal Palace Company a charter 'to preserve the high moral and educational tone which they had shown in giving practical effect to their magnificent scheme'.[9]

At first, the Crystal Palace represented a commercial rival to Albert's Kensington plan. Albert and Victoria often visited Sydenham – there was, after all, much glory attached to the building, and Victoria especially remained sentimental about it. However, there was a danger that it might rob the Royal Commission's actions in South Kensington of any claim to be the real inheritor of the Exhibition tradition. This was all the more likely as so many people involved in the original event worked at Sydenham, and in the early years while thousands of people flocked to Sydenham, Albert's less glamorous Kensington project was doing slow battle with governments. At one point, even Henry Cole considered jumping the Kensington ship after numerous head-hunting offers from the Sydenham project. However, gradually the entertainment aspects of Sydenham gained ground over education as the venture was forced to make money. The Crystal Palace became a popular new attraction in its own right, famous, among other things, for its gardens, sculpture, many royal and official visits – including one by Emperor Napoleon in 1855 – its Handel Festival (echoing that first *Messiah* rendition on 1 May 1851), musical festivals and as a venue for many other large-scale events. Later these were joined by attractions such as speedway racing, firework displays and concerts. The example of Paxton's 'People's Palace' was copied, most famously at the Alexandra Palace, in north London, but also elsewhere round the country.

Eventually, around the turn of the century, the Crystal Palace euphoria began to wane. This was partly to do with changing notions of recreation, which no longer revolved round education, and partly the result of a wider reduction in support for Victorian values like free trade and cosmopolitanism, which the Exhibition had propounded, and which had given the building symbolic value.

The building caught fire and burnt to the ground in 1936. The exact cause of the blaze remains unknown. Originally the Crystal Palace had been accepted over other building designs on the basis that a commitment to vigilance against fire would be kept up. By 1936, this commitment, and the resources it demanded, were no longer there.

A photograph from the *Illustrated London News* showing the Crystal Palace as it was re-erected at Sydenham. Since the fire of 1936 the undeveloped site – with its broken architecture and monuments – has remained an eerie testament to the grandeur of the Exhibition.

Behind this neglect lay the decreasing interest of the public in the Palace. Today, overlooking London, the grounds of the Crystal Palace survive, strewn with bits of masonry and sculpture.

II

One of the biggest problems in assessing the results of the Exhibition is preserving objectivity. The event was the result of a modernising alliance and served for decades as a talisman of the alliance's unity. Those connected with the Exhibition, and its supporters, were unlikely to see the event as anything but successful in promoting their various causes – industrial development, aesthetic improvement, British exports and so on. The modernist agenda has changed in the long-term, placing some aspects of the Exhibition in doubt: the more nationalistic industrial agenda at the turn of the century gave rise to an 'Exhibition fatigue,'[10] a departure from cosmopolitanism and a cynicism about the benefits to trade. The generational shift marked in the anti-Victorian literature of Pevsner began a long process of investigation of the aesthetic agenda of the Exhibition. In general, however, the continued dominance of modernisation as a force in life and politics down to the present day has prevented the *real* significance of the Exhibition coming to light.

The Great Exhibition was an advert for industrialisation and the values that went with it. A good chunk of the alliance that had promoted and supported it came from industrial circles. The fact that much of the Exhibition was about promoting technological and design education meant it was also an advert for a new stage in industrial development. Yet the Exhibition highlighted the value of art and science to industry partly because segments of the older intellectual bourgeoisie and aristocratic circles feared for their own positions in the face of industrialisation. And because it upheld values of ownership, moderate political change and opposed social revolution, the Exhibition gained even wider support among those traditional classes, as well as in society generally. The Exhibition was therefore an advert not just for industrialisation, but for an industrial programme that included the ruling élite rather than opposed them.

The Great Exhibition is only intelligible within the context of the severe battles of industrial interests to enter the political establishment in Britain and the atmosphere of polarisation that existed in Europe at mid-century. The existence of an effective parliament in Britain meant that new industrial and commercial interests were able to assert their voice politically to a far greater degree than on the continent. Nevertheless, the struggle over political reform, and particularly over free trade, drove deep wedges into British society. This, plus the revolutionary events of 1848, made the political élite in Britain eager to support the Exhibition and the compromise over industrialisation that lay at its heart. Though there were other ways in which the élite was converted, the Great Exhibition was perhaps the most obvious, demonstrative proof of the political establishment's support for industry and the masses – at least that part of it committed to social stability.

Possibly the most obvious beneficiary of this compromise between the ruling élite and industry was the monarchy. For decades the monarchy in Britain had been in decline, deeply undermined by the scandalous years of George IV, and more and more distant from industrialising society. The Great Exhibition provided Albert with an opportunity to reinvigorate the monarchy by extending its court ceremonial to industrial affairs and demonstrating solidarity with the people. Though continental monarchs ruling by divine right cast horrified looks across the Channel, Albert and Victoria succeeded remarkably easily in turning the tide of popular opinion. Most people turned out not to want social revolution in the Marxist sense and were quite happy to tolerate a monarchy that put itself at the service of industry and the labouring classes. The longevity of industrialisation has meant such populist gestures by monarchs have become a matter of course, in fact have needed to be greatly extended. The Great Exhibition was the most significant first step in this direction.

Albert benefited personally from all this. Prior to the Exhibition, he had been viewed suspiciously. As little more than spouse of the Queen in a male-dominated society, he was seen as somehow ineffectual and disposable. Though the Exhibition had many originators rather than one, Albert recognised in it an opportunity to create a new position for himself based on demonstrations of support for industry and the working classes, and was happy to put himself at its head. This was a bargain that worked both ways – the Exhibition's promoters found the stamp of monarchy useful for their own reasons. Albert was enormously successful: the subsequent emotional attachment to the Prince – bordering on a cult after his death reaching an intensity not known again until Princess Diana's time – owed much to the image of him as a modern prince in contrast to previous and continental models. In large part, this was the result of the Great

Exhibition. It is no accident that the memorial to Albert in Hyde Park is weighed down with images and figures echoing the rhetoric surrounding the Exhibition. The memorial stands next to the original site of the Crystal Palace – the concrete foundations of which, it is said, still lie under the turf – and overlooks the South Kensington estate.

The Great Exhibition was therefore enormously important in forging a new social unity that accepted industrialisation. For those elements of the working classes committed to ownership and social stability, it was evidence that the ruling élite had their interests at heart and were committed to moderate reform. This way of thinking was encouraged through the system of local committees and the apparently democratic way in which exhibits were selected. Only a few were aware that there was an element of whitewash in all this. Until the turn of the century, such rather philanthropic exercises as the Great Exhibition served to maintain peace among the working classes. Certainly, in the early years after 1848, the event helped reunite the discordant forces in British society.

The Great Exhibition was also possibly crucial to the general acceptance in Britain of the doctrine of free trade and to a healing of the wounds left in British political life by the anti-Corn Law question. At the beginning of the Exhibition, the protectionist lobby appeared to be reviving, with large rallies being held and press attacks on free trade growing. As the Liberal government looked weak, it seemed only a matter of time before protectionism and landed aristocratic interests reasserted themselves. However, though the Royal Commission had studiously refrained from overtly connecting the Exhibition with commercial liberalism in order to draw Conservatives and protectionists across to its camp, it was fairly obvious that the event promoted free trade. As the *Manchester Guardian* put it, 'the acts of the government and the Royal Commission have not shown the faintest recognition of this connection; but no mind of ordinary thoughtfulness can have failed to perceive it; and we may be sure that if there had not been a universal faith in the permanency of free trade, the Exhibition would either never have been opened, or would never have achieved the brilliant success that it has obtained'.[11] As this success now became obvious, as the monarchy bowed its head to industry, and as the masses flooded into the Crystal Palace, the forces of protectionism fell apart remarkably quickly.

The leader of the Conservatives, Lord Derby, who had already astutely linked himself to the Royal Commission, now told protectionists 'I do not doubt that while this great Exhibition shall show to foreign countries the marvels of our industry, it will show to us also the marvels of the industry of our foreign competitors – no dishonourable rivalry, no hostile feeling, no angry competition will be excited; but mutual emulation of each other's peaceful prowess, mutual desire to prompt harmonious intercourse, and that friendly communication which is kept up by commerce.'[12] Soon Disraeli himself was forced to concede that 'the time has gone by when the injuries which the great producing interests endure can be alleviated or removed by a recurrence to the laws which, previously to 1846 protected them from such calamities. The spirit of the age tends to free intercourse and no statesman can disregard with impunity the genius of the epoch in which he lives'.[13] Though feelings of international fraternity could not prevent the onset of the Crimean War in 1853–6, the influence of cosmopolitanism in British political life was given new vitality by the Exhibition, and even Conservative leaders were compelled to bow to the force of industry. Perhaps one immediate result of the Exhibition was that it allowed the Russell government to hold on to power until early in 1852, when the threat from protection had passed. However, the Conservative Party administration that followed now posed no threat to the position of free trade and industrialisation in Britain.

There is some difficulty in attributing all of this to the Exhibition: the years after 1851 were characterised by an economic boom that also did much to calm social unrest and convince the population of the truths of free trade. Yet the fact that Conservatives turned around their views so quickly suggests that the propaganda victory of the Great Exhibition had a lot to do with it. There is similarly no concrete evidence to suggest that the period of international commercial liberalisation that began with the Anglo-French treaty of commerce in 1860 was a direct result of the Exhibition. Nevertheless, the messages broadcast by the Exhibition, and in particular the personal contacts which were made in London between like-minded people from different countries, did much to support it.

The Exhibition was also crucial to the development of British liberalism. The movement that had promoted it was made up of many different forces. In order to bind this movement together, a rhetoric was developed that combined the ideas of all its members. This was a rhetoric that proposed the value of education, the benefits of industry, the need for moderate political change, free trade, and so on. British liberalism before the Great Exhibition had developed in the realms of the political theories of Jeremy Bentham or James Mill, and in political economic terms in the battles for free trade. But these discussions had been largely autonomous. The Great Exhibition movement combined political liberals and commercial liberals together. Via the principle of property, it also included moderate conservatives and even aristocratic forces. The moderate liberal consensus embodied in the Exhibition movement became a political force that dominated British politics for several decades after 1851. This domination was established soon after the event ended with the appointment of Lord Granville as Foreign Secretary in December 1851; he replaced Palmerston, whose independence of mind had shocked Albert and Victoria. (This affair in itself demonstrated the royal pair's increased influence as a result of the Exhibition.)

With so many Royal Commissioners in it, this new administration looked remarkably like an 'Exhibition government'. After the Conservative interlude in 1852, Lord Aberdeen's government looked even more like a rerun of the Royal Commission. Gradually, over the coming years, Gladstone, Aberdeen's Chancellor of the Exchequer, came to dominate British politics. He, more than anyone, embodied the consensual liberal message first broadcast at the Great Exhibition.

One of the most important features of the Exhibition movement was that it did serve to integrate many different forces supporting modernisation – not just in Britain but internationally. The results of the unity this created and the exchanges of information arising from it are difficult to assess. Because the Exhibition produced an image of the world that accorded largely with their own views, however, it certainly strengthened the conviction of all these various modernising groups and served to magnify their efforts. It helped serve as proof in the battle against anti-industrial interests. It either swept under the carpet the thorny issues of indigenous rights in the southern hemisphere and working-class poverty, or optimistically suggested further modernisation as the answer. This promotion of modernisation happened in different ways in different countries: in some, the government was involved in the Exhibition, and used it to strengthen its campaign to industrialise the home economy; in others it was the small-scale entrepreneur who took succour from the Exhibition's message. Through its system of prizes and the publicity given to certain manufacturers, the Exhibition cemented economic ties both within and across national borders. It was also the case that international contact at the Exhibition encouraged some that further modernisation was necessary for reasons of national rivalry – a way of thinking which in Britain would lead to the National Efficiency movement. The sum total of all this was a strengthening of the argument for modernisation internationally.

The Exhibition was a powerful stimulus to further industrialisation. It helped raise modernising forces in the echelons of power. It helped celebrate values that underpinned industrialisation – mechanisation, technological advance, improvements of design. It promoted education and gave it a boost in a very real sense through the foundation of museums and collections of design material across Europe modelled on, or even using, its objects, and the initiatives of the Royal Commission and the government after the Exhibition. In addition, the 1850s were a period when industrialists in Europe and North America began to look outwards to foreign markets. The Great Exhibition created market awareness at an international level and this served as the basis of future industrial development and expansion. It was particularly useful to colonialists in making their goods known on the British market, but also allowed European industrialists to identify commercial gaps to be filled. Despite the difficulties of research, many examples have been found of technology transfer taking place through the Great Exhibition.[14] But as experts are now beginning to realise, this was perhaps less important in spreading industrialisation than the development of 'social overhead capital' – in other words the educational standards, technical training and development facilities capable of utilising technology transfer.[15]

As industrialisation progressed, modernising forces internationally felt the need to recreate the events of 1851. The Great Exhibition resulted in a tradition of exhibitions that continued on a periodic basis down to the Expos of the present day. The 1851-inspired events included those in Paris (1855), London (1862), Paris (1867), Vienna (1873), Philadelphia (1876), Paris (1878), Sydney (1879), Brussels (1888), Chicago (1893), Paris (1900) and many others. The exhibition movement developed: increasing national rivalry marked the character of the events. High technology and economic growth meant the development of separate, specialised exhibitions, and the freedom for international ones to take their rhetorical flavour to often outlandish proportions. Meanwhile, in Britain, an indigenous exhibition tradition still exists which is more closely linked to that of 1851 and passes through the Festival of Britain celebrations of 1951 to those for the Millennium.

One area that was heavily affected by the Great Exhibition was exhibition architecture. Within the international tradition, many elements derive directly or indirectly from 1851. Paxton's Crystal Palace was, for example, emulated closely by the exhibition buildings at Dublin (1852), New York (1853) and Munich (1854). The need for an architectural *coup de théâtre*, or a piece of symbolism, accidentally achieved by the arch over Paxton's transept, has made itself felt in the reappearance of arches, or, more frequently, domes, in one exhibition building after another. In 1855, Napoleon III decided against a temporary building for the Paris exhibition, and the 1862 London exhibition chose an enormous, brick edifice (albeit with glass roof and *two* domes).

These contrived the theme of monumentality. Still, the recurring *desiderata* of cheapness, flexibility of use and ease of construction, have also led to echoes in the tent-like structures of the Munich Olympics or the Greenwich Millennium Dome. The Crystal Palace, as a celebration of the use of new building materials like iron, led to developments like the Eiffel Tower (built for the Paris exhibition of 1889) or the giant ferris wheel at Chicago (1893). The celebration of technology and industrial design, though somewhat unintended in Paxton's building, prepared the way for later constructs like the Atomium, built for the Brussels exhibition of 1958.[16]

Outside the sphere of exhibitions, the Crystal Palace did not immediately revolutionise architecture in the way many contemporary observers expected. Traditional materials, lack of space, continued aesthetic notions about public buildings prevented Paxton's example being used to a great extent anywhere but in the functional realms of stations and conservatories, the latter an area of construction which enjoyed a boom in late Victorian Britain, partly popularised by the Crystal Palace. The modular glass and metal method of building was, as Greeley proposed, taken up on the other side of the Atlantic – building vertically rather than horizontally. Though new building materials and other engineering stars made skyscrapers possible, they carry an architectural torch which passed through Paxton's hands.

It is difficult to assess whether or not the Great Exhibition actually succeeded in changing aesthetic standards of industrial production as Cole and the Society of Arts intended. At one level, it seems the plethora of over-decorated artefacts at the Exhibition simply encouraged public enthusiasm for artistic design, rather than shaping it. Cole, however, had wanted to raise awareness about design and its importance to industry. In this sense, he can perhaps be credited with some success. The debate about this would result eventually in the work of William Morris and the art nouveau school. Yet Cole's idea of transferring to a new industrial setting past principles of design failed. William Morris owed more to John Ruskin's backward-looking artisan ideology, than he did to Cole's attempt to unite industry and art; Morris was not interested in solving the aesthetic problems caused by mass production so much as returning to pre-industrial modes of fabrication. The art nouveau school, meanwhile, looked to an entirely new set of principles. Those had nothing to do with notions of applying classical design principles to a new setting. They instead looked to an aesthetic standard set by industrial goods alone. However, the public's preference for goods that are cheap or prove social status has meant its taste has remained largely autonomous.

The main significance of the Great Exhibition was that it helped harness the forces of industrialisation and, by making them acceptable, promoted them in Britain and the world. There were many different groups involved in the event, and the aims of the Exhibition were various and often contradictory. In total, however, they represented a push for modernisation that helped overcome obstacles which still existed at mid-century. This process continues down to the present. The type of rhetoric created for the first time in support of the Exhibition is still used to support technological progress, industrialisation and globalisation today. The Great Exhibition was a dramatic contribution to the creation of the modern, industrialised society in which we live.

NOTES

RA	Royal Archives, Windsor Castle
RC1851	Archive of the Royal Commission for the Exhibition of 1851
RA–RC1851	Windsor Archives, on permanent loan to the Royal Commission for the Exhibition of 1851, from the Royal Archives, Windsor Castle
RSA	Royal Society of Arts
NAL	National Art Library

Introduction

1. See, for example, the literature cited in Pohl, 1989.
2. Fay, 1951; Ffrench, 1950; Luckhurst, *The Story of Exhibitions*, 1951; Pevsner, 1951.
3. Jenkins, 1994, pp. 48–9.
4. For example Brandt, 1904.
5. For example the anti-German account in Hobhouse, 1937.
6. Hobhouse, 1983; Martin, 1876.
7. Hudson, 1954; Luckhurst, *The Exhibition of 1851*, 1951.
8. Pevsner, 1951.
9. Altick, 1978; Maré, 1972.
10. This point is made by Kroker, 1975, p. 119.
11. *Lectures on the Results of the Great Exhibition*, 1853.
12. Pevsner, 1951.
13. *Art Journal Illustrated Catalogue of the Industry of All Nations*, 1851.
14. Pevsner, 1951, p. 36.
15. Ibid., p. 114.
16. Ibid., p. 139.
17. 14 June 1998, *The Sunday Times Bookshop*, p. 5.
18. Quoted in Jervis, 1983, p. 7.
19. Burton, 1972, p. 93.
20. Jervis, 1983, p. 8.
21. A point made forcefully in the introduction to Marsden, 1990.
22. Corfe, 1979, p. 8.
23. Greenhalgh, 1988, p. 17 and p. 225.
24. Open University, 1986, p. 5.
25. Davis, 1986, p. 7.
26. Open University, 1986, and Searle, 1998.
27. See for example Hilton, 1988; Parry, 1994.
28. Haltern, 1971.

1. The Roots of the Exhibition

1. Brübach, 1994.
2. Luckhurst, *The Story*, 1951, p. 12.
3. Schwankl, 1996, p. 18.
4. Hudson, 1954, pp. 3–18.
5. Kalb, 1994, chapter 2.
6. Hudson, 1954, p. 11.
7. Luckhurst, *The Story*, 1951, pp. 14–16.
8. Schwankl, 1996, p. 16.
9. Luckhurst, *The Story*, 1951, p. 16.
10. Schwankl, 1996, p. 17.
11. Luckhurst, *The Story*, 1951, chapter 8.
12. Cleve, 1996, pp. 22–9.
13. Schwankl,1996, p. 20.
14. Haltern, 1971, p. 82; Kalb, 1994, chapter 2; Schwankl, 1996, p. 21.
15. Beckmann, 1991, p. 114.
16. Ibid., Preface.
17. Cleve, 1996, p. 288.
18. Haltern, 1971, pp. 30–4.
19. Luckhurst, *The Story*, 1951, chapter 4.
20. Derry, 1960, pp. 583–9.
21. Ibid., p. 285.
22. Luckhurst, *The Story*, 1951, chapter 5.
23. Emmerson, 1977, p. 7.

24. Haltern, 1971, p. 35.
25. Luckhurst, *The Story*, 1951, p. 82.
26. Ibid., p. 82.
27. Cleve, 1996, pp. 29–35.
28. Derry, 1960, p. 298.
29. Haltern, 1971, p. 35.
30. Hudson, 1954, p. 176.
31. 21 May 1845, Minutes, Committee of Miscellaneous Matters, RSA.
32. 28 May 1845, Minutes, Committee of Miscellaneous Matters, RSA.
33. *Official . . . Catalogue*, 1851, Volume I.
34. See p. 23.
35. While I agree here with Utz Haltern that Albert had little care for personal self-aggrandisement, on the other hand I disagree with him that this argument about the origins is tangential: it reveals much about the way Albert fitted into the project and how his image was being used to 'sell' it. See Haltern, 1971, pp. 44–5.
36. 4 June 1845, Minutes, Committee of Miscellaneous Matters, RSA.
37. 30 June 1845, Minutes, Committee of Miscellaneous Matters, RSA.
38. [undated] Handwritten Report, John Scott Russell Papers, Volume I, RSA.
39. Emmerson, 1977, p. 47.
40. [undated] Handwritten Report, John Scott Russell Papers, Volume I, RSA.
41. Ibid.
42. Emmerson, 1977, p. 31.
43. Jervis, 1983, chapter 6.
44. Luckhurst, *The Story*, 1951, p. 94.
45. See pp. 28, 37, 39, 206.
46. [undated] Handwritten Report, John Scott Russell Papers, Volume I, RSA.
47. Luckhurst, *The Story*, 1951, p. 94.
48. 24 February 1848, December 1846–October 1849, Minutes of Council, Volume I, RSA; Cole, 1884, p. 121.
49. Cole, 1884, p. 121.
50. 10 May 1848, December 1846–October 1849, Minutes of Council, Volume I, RSA; Cole, 1884, p. 108.
51. 10 May 1848, 14 June 1848, 16 November 1848, 29 November 1848, 24 January 1849, 14 February 1849, December 1846–October 1849, Minutes of Council, Volume I, RSA.
52. 14 February 1849, 23 February 1849, December 1846–October 1849, Minutes of Council, Volume I, RSA.
53. Cole, 1884, p. 122.
54. 'A Few Extracts from the Diary of Francis Fuller, in May, 1886, Having Reference to the Origin of the Great Exhibition of all Nations Held in London in 1851', John Scott Russell Papers, Volume I, RSA.
55. 'A Few Extracts . . .', John Scott Russell Papers, Volume I, RSA.
56. Cole, 1884, pp. 123–5.
57. 26 June 1848, December 1846–October 1849, Minutes of Council, Volume I, RSA.
58. Haltern, 1971, p. 44.
59. 30 June 1849, Minutes of a Meeting at Buckingham Palace, John Scott Russell Papers, Volume I, RSA.
60. Cole, 1884, p. 126.
61. 30 June 1849, Minutes of a Meeting at Buckingham Palace, John Scott Russell Papers, Volume I, RSA.
62. 14 July 1849, Minutes of a Meeting at Osborne House, John Scott Russell Papers, Volume I, RSA.
63. Ibid.
64. 16 July 1849, Cole to Phipps, RA F24.
65. 17 July 1849, Phipps to Cole, RA F24.
66. 18 July 1849, Cole to Phipps, RA F24.
67. 7 August 1849, December 1846–October 1849, Minutes of Council, Volume I, RSA.
68. 1 August 1849, Minutes of a Private and Confidential Meeting at Osborne House, John Scott Russell Papers, Volume I, RSA.
69. Cole, 1884, p. 147.
70. 23 August 1849, December 1846–October 1849, Minutes of Council, Volume I, RSA.
71. 1 August 1849, Minutes of a Private and Confidential Meeting at Osborne House, John Scott Russell Papers, Volume I, RSA.

2. The Royal Commission

1. Digby Wyatt, *A Report*, 1849.
2. 12 July 1849, Letters, Volume I, RA–RC1851.
3. Emmerson, 1977, p. 37.
4. 27 August–2 October 1849, Henry Cole Diaries, AA.55.CC, NAL; [undated], Handwritten Report of Commissioners to the Manufacturing Towns, John Scott Russell Papers, Volume I, RSA.; 12 September 1849, Labouchere to Prince Albert, Letters, Volume I, RA–RC1851.
5. 10 August 1849, Palmerston to Cowley

et al, John Scott Russell Papers, Volume II, RSA.

6. 20 September 1849, Normanby to Phipps, RA F24.

7. [undated] Handwritten Report, and October 1849, Report made to HRH the Prince Albert, President of the Society of Arts, &c of Preliminary Inquiries into the Willingness of Manufacturers and Others to Support Periodical Exhibitions of the Works of Industry of all Nations, John Scott Russell Papers, Volume II, RSA.

8. 12 September 1849, Phipps to Prince Albert, RA F24.

9. 14 September 1849, Prince Albert to Cole, quoted in Cole, 1884, p. 129.

10. 9 October 1849, Cole to Phipps, Cole Correspondence, 55.BB, NAL.

11. Reports . . . of Preliminary Inquiries.

12. Handwritten Report . . . of Preliminary Inquiries.

13. 20 September 1849, Normanby to Phipps, Letters, Volume I, RA–RC1851.

14. Reports . . . of Preliminary Inquiries.

15. 'The Queen's name should never, even provisionally, be pledged to anything, unless by Her Majesty's sanction directly expressed.' 8 October 1849, Phipps to Cole, quoted in Cole, 1884, p. 131.

16. 27 November 1849, Grey to Cole, Letters, Volume I, RA–RC1851

17. 20 September 1849, Normanby to Phipps, Letters, Volume I, RA–RC1851.

18. Port, 1976, p. 20.

19. 10 September 1849, Prince Albert to Stockmar, quoted in Jagow, 1938, p. 153.

20. As Cole recounted, 'it was fully understood that reporters would be present'. Cole, 1884, p. 134.

21. 12 September 1849, Phipps to Prince Albert, RA F24.

22. 12 September 1849, Phipps to Cole, RA F24.

23. Report of a Meeting Held at the Mansion House, London, October 17, 1849, in Support of the Great Exhibition of the Works of Industry of all Nations, John Scott Russell Papers, Volume II, RSA.

24. Cole, 1884, pp. 134–44; Haltern, 1971, pp. 49–50.

25. 18 October 1849, *The Times*.

26. Rhodes, 1983, p. 192.

27. See pp. 14–26.

28. 3 July 1849, Cole to Phipps and 16 July 1849, Phipps to Cole, Letters, Volume I, RA–RC1851.

29. 24 October 1849, Diary of Henry Cole, AA.55.CC, NAL.

30. Cole, 1884, p. 149.

31. 15 November 1849, Prince Albert to Richmond, Letters, Volume I, Letters, RA–RC1851.

32. 7 December 1849, Diary of Henry Cole, AA.55.CC, NAL.

33. 11 December 1849, Diary of Henry Cole, AA.55.CC, NAL.

34. 13 January 1850, Diary of Henry Cole, AA.55.CC, NAL.

35. 18 December 1849, Richmond to Lord John Russell, Letters, Volume I, RA–RC1851.

36. 30 November 1849, Prince Albert to Labouchere, Letters, Volume I, RA–RC1851.

37. 27 November 1849, Cole to Grey, Letters, Volume I, RA–RC1851.

38. [undated], *The Times*, Letters, 1849–50, Volume II, RA–RC1851.

39. Haltern, 1971, p. 53.

3. 'An Ordeal of Doubt, Discussion and Even Opposition'

1. 25 October 1850, Prince Albert at the York Banquet, Letters, 1850–1, Volume V, RA–RC1851.

2. 'Appendices to the First and Second Meetings of the Commissioners', enclosed in 18 January 1850, *Minutes of the Proceedings of Her Majesty's Commissioners for the Exhibition of 1851 11th January 1850 to 24th April 1852* (London, Clowes, 1852), RC1851

3. 24 November 1849, Hume to the Editor of the *Daily News*, Letters, 1849, Volume I, RA–RC1851.

4. 24 November 1849, Digby Wyatt to Hume, Letters, 1849, Volume I, RA–RC1851.

5. 26 November 1849, Minute of Conversation between Mr Hume and Mr Scott Russell, Letters, 1849, Volume I, RA–RC1851.

6. 19 December 1849, Special Council Meeting, Minutes of Council, October 1849 to December 1850, Volume II, RSA.

7. 19 December 1849, Cole to Phipps, Letters, 1849, Volume I, RA–RC1851.
8. 20 December 1849, *The Times*.
9. 27 December 1849, Potter to Russell, Letters, 1849, Volume I, RA–RC1851.
10. 28 December 1849, Potter to Russell, Letters, 1849, Volume I, RA–RC1851.
11. 1 January 1850, Labouchere to Potter, and 4 January 1850, Potter to Labouchere, Letters, 1849, Volume I, RA–RC1851.
12. 29 December 1849, *Patent Journal*, Letters, 1849–50, Volume II, RA–RC1851.
13. 9 and 10 January 1850, Northcote to Grey, Letters, 1849–50, Volume II, RA–RC1851.
14. 10 January 1850, Northcote to Grey, Letters, 1849–50, Volume II, RA–RC1851.
15. See p. 30.
16. 13 January 1850, Labouchere to Grey, Letters, 1849–50, Volume II, RA–RC1851.
17. 13 January 1850, Grey to Labouchere, Letters, 1849–50, Volume II, RA–RC1851.
18. 15 March 1850, Grey to Fuller, Great Exhibition GCP/51a, RSA.
19. See 15 October 1851, Munday to Prince Albert, The Exhibition of 1851, 1851–53, RA F25.
20. 'Report of the Commissioners for the Exhibition of 1851, to the Right Hon. Spencer Horatio Walpole, &c &c', *Official . . . Catalogue*, 1851, Volume IV.
21. 20 January 1850, Northcote to Grey, Letters, 1849–50, Volume II, RA–RC1851.
22. 2 February 1850, Northcote to Grey, Letters, 1849–50, Volume II, RA–RC1851.
23. 4 February 1850, Peel to Prince Albert, Letters, 1849–50, Volume II, RA–1851.
24. 26 January 1850, Northcote to Grey, Letters, 1849–50, Volume II, RA–RC1851.
25. 14 February 1850, Minutes, RC1851.
26. 8 February 1850, Northcote to Grey, Letters, 1849–50, Volume II, RA–RC1851.
27. 13 January 1850, Grey to Labouchere, RA F24.
28. Appendix A, 31 January 1850, Minutes, RC1851.
29. 31 January 1850, Minutes, RC1851.
30. Appendix A, 14 March 1850, Minutes, RC1851.
31. 22 February 1850, *The Times*.
32. Appendix B, 7 February 1850, Minutes, RC1851.
33. 28 February 1850, Minutes, RC1851.
34. 13 March 1850, Francis Smedley to Northcote, 14 March 1850, Minutes, RC1851.
35. 7 February 1850, Minutes, RC1851.
36. 13 February 1850, Minutes of a Meeting at Buckingham Palace, John Scott Russell Papers, Volume III, RSA.
37. Appendix A, 18 April 1851, Minutes, RC1851.
38. Haltern, 1971, p. 65.
39. 28 February 1850, Minutes, RC1851.
40. 21 February 1850, Minutes, RC1851.
41. [undated], Printed Notice of Competition Rules, John Scott Russell Papers, Volume II, RSA.
42. Appendix E, 28 February 1850, Minutes, RC1851.
43. Appendix G, 7 March 1850, Minutes, RC1851.
44. 7 February 1850. and 21 February 1850, Minutes, RC1851.
45. Haltern, 1971, p. 99.
46. 21 March 1850, Printed Report of Grand Banquet to HRH Prince Albert at the Mansion House, London in Honour of the Exhibition of 1851, John Scott Russell Papers, Volume II, RSA.
47. Golby, 1986, p. 1.
48. Cullen, 1975, chapter 6.
49. Martin, 1876, p. 244.
50. 21 June 1850, Minutes, RC1851.
51. 14 March 1850, Minutes, RC1851.
52. 11 May 1850, Granville to Grey, PP Vic Box C Great Exhibition to 1855, RA.
53. Cole, 1884, p. 188.
54. 22 February 1850, *The Times*.
55. 19 and 23 March 1850, unattributed newspaper reports, Letters, Volume III, RA–RC1851.
56. 20 March 1850, Granville to Grey, Letters, Volume III, RA–RC1851.
57. 29 March 1850, *John Bull*.
58. 4 May 1850, *John Bull*.
59. See 28 March 1850, Cole to Grey,

Letters, Volume III, RA, RC1851 and 11 April 1850, Minutes, RC1851.

60. 16 May 1850, Peel to Prince Albert, Letters, Volume III, RA–RC1851.

61. These reports contained in Letters, Volumes III and IV, RA–RC1851.

62. 15 April 1850, Lacy to Digby Wyatt, in 18 April 1850, Minutes, RC1851.

63. 11 May 1850, Playfair to Granville, Letters, Volume III, RA–RC1851.

64. 15 June 1850, Diary of Henry Cole, AA.55.CC., NAL.

65. Beaver, 1986, p. 21; Rhodes James, 1983, pp. 88–9.

66. 18 June 1850, *The Times*.

67. 23 June 1850, *The Times*.

68. Cole, 1884, p. 163.

69. 25 June 1850, *Athenaeum*.

70. 27 June 1850, *The Times*.

71. 28 June 1850, Printed Excerpt of Proceedings in the House of Commons, Letters, Volume IV, RA–RC1851.

72. 2 July 1850, Lord John Russell to Queen Victoria, Letters, Volume IV, RA–RC1851.

73. 29 June 1850, *John Bull*.

74. 29 June 1850. and 1 July 1850, Minutes, RC1851.

75. 3 July 1850, *Globe*.

76. 4 July 1850, Northcote to Grey, Letters, Volume IV, RA–RC1851.

77. Jagow, 1938, pp. 161–2.

78. 27 July 1850, Northcote to Grey, Letters, Volume IV, RA–RC1851.

79. 3 and 4 July 1850, Diary of Henry Cole, AA.55.CC., NAL.

80. 30 June 1850, Lord John Russell to Prince Albert Letters, Volume IV, RA–RC1851.

81. 2 July 1850, Prince Albert to Lord John Russell, Letters, Volume IV, RA–RC1851.

82. 28 June 1850, Resolution Passed Unanimously at a Meeting of the Deputations from the Principal Towns, Letters, Volume IV, RA–RC1851.

83. 6 July 1850, *Manchester Guardian*.

84. 5 July 1850, Russell to Prince Albert, RA F24.

85. See 26 October 1850, *The Times*.

86. 6 July 1850, Minutes, RC1851.

87. 28 May 1850, Playfair to Grey, Letters, Volume III, RA–RC1851.

88. 29 May 1850, Grey to Playfair, Letters, Volume III, RA–RC1851.

89. 7 June 1850, Diary of Henry Cole, AA.55.CC., NAL.

90. Luckhurst, *The Story*, 1951, pp. 108–9.

91. Appendix D, 6 July 1850, Minutes, RC1851.

92. Luckhurst, *The Story*, 1951, p. 108.

93. 16 July 1850, Minutes, RC1851.

94. 15 July 1850, Granville to Prince Albert, Letters, Volume IV, RA–RC1851.

95. 12 July 1850, Peto to Grey, Letters, Volume IV, RA–RC1851.

96. 12 July 1850, Diary of Henry Cole, AA.55.CC., NAL.

97. 16 July 1850, Minutes, RC1851.

98. On the issue of the arched transept see Cole, 1884, p. 171; Fox, 1904, pp. 1–8; Haltern, 1973, p. 73; Luckhurst, 1951, pp. 110–11; 'A Temple Made of Glass', Maré, 1972.

99. 27 September 1850, *The Times*.

100. This is one of the most serious defects of Haltern, 1973.

101. Compare Appendix E, 28 February 1850 with Appendix C, 11 April 1850, Minutes, RC1851.

102. 15 July 1850, Minutes, RC1851; 23 November 1850, Turner to John Scott Russell, Great Exhibition GCP/51a, RSA.

103. Beaver, 1986, p. 16.

104. See p. 35.

105. 'The Private History of the Palace of Glass,' *Household Words*, 18 January 1851, XXXXIII.

106. *Punch*, XIX, 1850, p. 81.

107. See 'A Temple Made of Glass' Maré, 1972.

108. Derry, 1960, p. 592.

109. See pp. 194–5.

110. Pevsner, 1951, p. 139.

111. Handwritten Address for the Exhibition of Medieval Art, Great Exhibition, GCP/51a, RSA.

112. 27 July 1850, *John Bull*.

113. 4 January 1851, *Builder*.

114. 25 January 1851, *Builder*.

115. The discussions are recorded in 1 February 1851, *Builder*.

116. 15 February 1851, *Builder*.

117. 13 January 1851, *Builder*.

4. *Setting up Shop*

1. Burton, 1972, p. 142.

2. 28 October 1850, *The Times*.

3. Ibid.

4. [undated] *Spectator*, Letters, Volume V, RA–RC1851.

5. 29 October 1850, Letters, Volume V, RA–RC1851.

6. Martin, 1876, p. 334.

7. Appendix XXIV, 'Report of Mr Alexander Redgrave on the visits of the Working Classes, First Report of the Commissioners for the Exhibition of 1851', *Official . . . Catalogue*, 1851, Volume IV.

8. 25 November 1850, Digby Wyatt, Circular, Great Exhibition. Miscellaneous Papers, RSA.

9. Appendix C, 2 May 1851, Minutes, RC1851; 10 December 1850, *Morning Chronicle*.

10. 15 August 1850, Minutes, RC1851.

11. 17 May 1850, John Scott Russell to Grey, PP Vic Box C Great Exhibition to 1855, RA.

12. 6 July 1850, Minutes, RC1851.

13. 'Conditions of Tender for the Privilege of Supplying Refreshments in the Building', John Scott Russell Papers, Royal Commission, Volume II, RSA.

14. *Punch*, 1851, Volume XX, p. 111.

15. 27 January 1851, Granville to Grey, PP Vic Box C Great Exhibition to 1855, RA.

16. 'First Report of The Commissioners for the Exhibition of 1857 to the Right Hon. Spencer Horatio Walpole', in *Official . . . Catalogue*, 1851, Volume IV, p. 1.

17. See, for example, the Royal Commission's invitation to the Society of Arts, 18 December 1850, Minutes of Council, December 1850–May 1852, Volume III, RSA.

18. See, for example, 16 November 1850, *Morning Chronicle*.

19. 5 January 1851, Grey to Granville, PP Vic Box C Great Exhibition to 1855, RA.

20. 27 January 1851, Granville to Grey, PP Vic Box C Great Exhibition to 1855, RA.

21. 'First Report . . .', p. xxxvii.

22. 23 January 1851, Paxton to Russell, Letters, 1850–1, Volume V, RA–RC1851.

23. 23 January 1851, *The Times*.

24. 23 January 1851, Grey to Paxton, RA F24.

25. 24 January 1851, Granville to Grey, RA F24.

26. 20 March 1850, Memorandum Dilke, John Scott Russell Papers, Volume II, RSA.

27. 31 October 1850, Minutes, RC1851.

28. Preface, *Official . . . Catalogue*, 1851, Volume I.

29. 2 January 1851, Cole to Grey, Letters, 1850–1, Volume V, RA–RC1851.

30. 3 January 1851, Grey to Cole, Letters, 1850–1, Volume V, RA–RC1851.

31. 6 November 1850, Playfair to Grey, Letters, 1850–1, Volume V, RA–RC1851.

32. 3 February 1851, Minutes, RC1851.

33. 13 and 16 January 1851, Playfair to Grey, Letters, 1850–1, Volume V, RA–RC1851.

34. *Official . . . Catalogue*, Volume I, pp. 109–11.

35. 27 September 1849, Diary Notes, John Scott Russell Papers, Exhibition – Earliest Proceedings, Volume II, RSA.

36. See on this 22 October 1850, Lloyd Memorandum on Jewellery, Letters, 1850–1, Volume V, RA–RC1851 and see p. 138.

37. 14 November 1850, Minutes, RC1851.

38. 23 August 1850, Reid to Grey, PP Vic Box C Great Exhibition to 1855, RA.

39. J. Forbes Royle, Papers referring to the Proposed Contributions from India for the Industrial Exhibition of 1851, EX.1851.291, NAL.

40. 22 June 1850, Extract of a Communication from the Imperial Commissioner to H.E. Her Majesty's Plenipotentiary, Letters, 1850–1, Volume V, RA–RC1851.

41. 19 October 1850, Bowring to Grey, Letters, 1850–1, Volume V, RC1851; 7 January 1851, Reid to Grey, PP Vic Box C Great Exhibition to 1855, RA.

42. 13 December 1850, Granville to Grey, Letters, 1850–1, Volume V, RA–RC1851.

43. 9 December 1850, Reid to Grey, Letters, 1850–1, Volume V, RA–RC1851.

44. 3 August 1850, Henry Cole, 'Notes on the Dublin Exhibition, July 1850 . . .', PP Vic Box C Great Exhibition to 1855, RA.

45. 'First Report . . .', p. xxxiv.

46. See Appendix XII, 'First Report . . .'

47. 14 November 1850, Minutes, RC1851.

48. 27 May 1850, Reid to Grey, Letters, 1850, Volume III, RA–RC1851.

49. Appendix A, 14 November 1850, Minutes, RC1851.

50. 22 November 1850, Bowring to Grey, Letters, 1850–1, Volume V, RA–RC1851.
51. 6 January 1851, Bowring to Grey, Letters, 1850–1, Volume V, RA–RC1851.
52. 'First Report . . .', p. xxxiv.
53. 5 March 1851, Minutes, RC1851.
54. Haltern, 1971, p. 206.
55. 27 November 1849, Bacon to Russell, John Scott Russell Papers, 1851, Earliest Proceedings, Volume II, RSA.
56. Dalzell, 1960, pp. 14–24.
57. Appendix XII, 'First Report . . .'
58. Schwankl, 1996, p. 267.
59. 28 April 1850, Ferdinand to Prince Albert, M49, RA.
60. Appendix B, 14 November 1850, Minutes, RC1851.
61. 15 March 1851, Granville to Grey, Letters, 1850–1, Volume V, RA–RC1851.
62. At the first meeting of the Commission it was decided to ask foreign governments to nominate representatives. 11 January 1850, Minutes, RC1851.
63. Haltern, 1971, p. 145.
64. 26 March 1851, Minutes of Council, December 1850–May 1852, Volume III, RSA.
65. 17 March 1851, Bunsen to Russell, John Scott Russell Papers, Royal Commission, Volume II, RSA.
66. Jagow, 1938, part 3.
67. 2 April 1851, Bloomfield to Palmerston and 5 April 1851, Magenis to Palmerston, RA F24.
68. 2 April 1851, Bloomfield to Palmerston, RA F24.
69. 3 April 1851, Temple to Palmerston, RA F24.
70. 8 April 1851, Frederick William IV to Albert, RA F24.
71. 14 April 1851, Albert to Frederick William IV, RA F24.
72. 10 April 1851, Normanby to Palmerston, RA F24.
73. 'First Report . . .', p. xxxiv.
74. 24 April 1851, Granville to Palmerston, RA F24.
75. 24 April 1851, Prince Albert to Lord John Russell, RA F24.
76. 24 April 1851, Granville to Palmerston, RA F24.
77. 25 April 1851, Russell to Prince Albert, RA F24.
78. 24 April 1851, Palmerston to Lord John Russell, RA F24.
79. 26 April 1851, Prince Albert to Lord John Russell, RA F24.
80. 26 April 1851, Palmerston to Prince Albert, RA F24.
81. Rhodes James, 1985, p. 202. Rhodes James gives a first published account of this exchange. However, his version of events is surprisingly harsh in its judgment of Lord Palmerston who, after all, had good constitutional reasons for objecting to Albert's intentions.
82. 12 November 1850, Mayne to H. Waddington, Work 6/126, PRO.
83. 'First Report . . .', Appendix XXIV.
84. Appendix B, 21 January 1851, Minutes, RC1851.
85. 19 November 1850, Granville to Grey, Letters, 1850–1, Volume V, RA–RC1851.
86. 'First Report . . .', Appendix XXIV.
87. Appendix B, 2 May 1851, Minutes, RC1851.
88. 17 April 1851, *Daily News*.
89. 17 April 1851, *The Times*.
90. *Punch*, Volume XX, 1851, p. 174.
91. 17 April 1851, Bazley, to Prince Albert, RA F24.
92. 19 April 1851, Russell to Prince Albert, RA F24.
93. 20 April 1851, Prince Albert to Lord John Russell, RA F24.

5. The Great Exhibition Experience

1. 27 April 1851, Diary of Henry Cole, AA.55.CC., NAL.
2. 19 April 1851, Lord John Russell to Prince Albert, RA F24.
3. 28 April 1851, Minutes, RC1851.
4. See Hobsbawm and Ranger, 1983.
5. Haltern, 1971, p. 162.
6. Binney, Thomas, *The Royal Exchange and the Palace of Industry* (Religious Tract Society, 1851), EX.1851.156, NAL.
7. Fay, 1951, p. 26.
8. 18 April 1851, *Morning Chronicle*.
9. 3 May 1851, *Manchester Guardian*.
10. 22 April 1851, Prince Albert to the Archbishop of Canterbury, PP Vic Box C Great Exhibition to 1855, RA.

11. Rhodes James, 1983, p. 205.
12. 28 April 1851, Minutes, RC1851.
13. *The Crystal Palace Sydenham. To Be Sold by Auction . . . .*, EX069, RSA.
14. For details of the ceremony see 'Programme of the State Opening of the Exhibition of the Works of Industry . . .', John Scott Russell Papers, Royal Commission, Volume II, RSA; 'Programme of the Musical Performances . . .', John Scott Russell Papers, Royal Commission Volume III, RSA; 1 May 1851, *Globe*; 2 May 1851, *Daily News*.
15. *Punch*, Volume XX, 1851, p. 190.
16. 2 May 1851, *Daily News*.
17. Golby, 1986, pp. 2–3.
18. 2 May 1851, *Daily News*.
19. 1 May 1851, Diary of Henry Cole, AA.55.CC., NAL.
20. Martin, 1876, p. 367.
21. 2 May 1851, *Daily News*.
22. Quoted in Martin, 1876, p. 367.
23. 3 May 1851, *John Bull*.
24. Ibid.
25. 1 May 1851, Duchess of Kent to Queen Victoria, RA F24.
26. 3 May 1851, Lady Lyttelton to Queen Victoria, RA F24.
27. 3 May 1851, *John Bull*.
28. 1 May 1851, Russell to Queen Victoria, RA F24.
29. *Punch*, Volume XX, p. 188.
30. 2 May 1851, *Morning Chronicle*.
31. *Punch*, Volume XX, 1851, p. 190.
32. 5 May 1851, Leopold to Queen Victoria, RA F24.
33. 2 May 1851, *The Times*.
34. 2 May 1851, *Daily News*.
35. 2 May 1851, *Morning Chronicle*.
36. See 2 May 1851, Russell to Prince Albert, RA F24.
37. *Punch*, Volume XX, 1851, p. 190.
38. 8 May 1851, Queen Victoria to Lady Lyttelton, RA F24.
39. Many accounts give the length as 1,848 ft. This figure results from measuring from the centre of the end pillars.
40. *Fireside Facts*, 1851, chapter 18.
41. Cleve, 1996, pp. 94–9.
42. 'Miscellaneous Objects of Interest Placed in the Main Avenues,' *Official . . . Catalogue*, 1851, Volume II.
43. Hunt, 1851, p. 9.
44. Ibid., p. 10.
45. 26 October 1850, *Morning Chronicle*.
46. *Official . . . Catalogue*, 1851, Volume I, p. 120.
47. Ibid., Volume I, p. 120.
48. Ibid., Volume I, p. 402.
49. 'Class 7', *Official . . . Catalogue*, 1851, Volume I.
50. Hunt, 1851, p. 54.
51. 'Class 10', *Official . . . Catalogue*, 1851, Volume I.
52. See p. 65.
53. 'Class 3', *Official . . . Catalogue*, 1851, Volume I.
54. 'Class 23', *Official . . . Catalogue*, 1851, Volume II.
55. See pp. 218–15.
56. Jervis, 1983.
57. 'Class 19', *Official . . . Catalogue*, 1851, Volume II.
58. Hunt, 1851, p78.
59. 'France', *Official . . . Catalogue*, 1851, Volume III.
60. Ibid.
61. 'Austria', *Official . . . Catalogue*, 1851, Volume III.
62. Fay, 1951, p. 44.
63. 'United States', *Official . . . Catalogue*, 1851, Volume III.
64. Greeley, 1851, p. 29.
65. Appendix XIV, *Official . . . Catalogue*, 1851, Volume IV.
66. 'Information for the use of Foreign Exhibitors . . . July 1850', John Scott Russell Papers, Volume III, RSA.
67. Rhodes James, 1983, p. 201.
68. Norrish, 1950–1, pp. 547–8.
69. 'Skeleton Report on Research into the 1851 Exhibition', [1951?], RSA.
70. 'Channel Islands,' *Official . . . Catalogue*, 1851, Volume II.
71. 'United States,' *Official . . . Catalogue*, 1851, Volume III.
72. 28 April 1851, Minutes, RC1851.
73. 12 May 1851, Minutes, RC1851.
74. Appendix XIX, 'First Report . . .', *Official . . . Catalogue*, 1851, Volume IV.
75. [undated], 'Exhibition of 1851. Instructions from the Council of Chairmen to the Juries', Great Exhibition of 1851. Miscellaneous Papers, RSA.
76. Appendix XIX, 'First Report . . .', *Official . . . Catalogue*, 1851, Volume IV.

77. [undated], 'Exhibition of 1851.
    Instructions from the Council of
    Chairmen to the Juries', Great Exhibition
    of 1851 Miscellaneous Papers, RSA.
78. 5 July 1851, Minutes, RC1851.
79. Appendix LVI, *Official . . . Catalogue*,
    Volume IV, 1851.
80. Briggs, 1988, p. 73.
81. Ibid.
82. Appendix XXVIIa, *Official . . . Catalogue*,
    Volume IV, 1851.
83. 30 January 1851, *Morning Chronicle*.
84. Press reviews contained at end of *Official
    . . . Catalogue*, 1851, Volume IV.
85. 'Preface', *Journal of Design*, VI (September
    1851–February 1852).
86. Martin, 1876, p. 372.
87. [undated] *Morning Chronicle*, Doc.86,
    Letters, Volume V, RA–RC1851.
88. 26 March 1851, Minutes of Council,
    Volume III, December 1850–May 1852,
    RSA.
89. 10 April 1851, *Morning Chronicle*.
90. Jagow, 1938, p. 177
91. *Journal of Design*, V, 28 (1851), p. 114.
92. 28 June 1851, *Builder*.
93. Cole, 1884, pp. 200–1; Fitzmaurice,
    1906, p. 42.
94. Cole, 1884, p. 182.
95. 13 and 19 October 1851, Queen
    Victoria's Diary, printed in Fay, 1951.
96. Jagow, 1938, p. 180.
97. Bergengrün, 1908, p. 163
98. *Punch*, 1851, Volume XX, p. 240.
99. Appendix XVI, *Official . . . Catalogue*,
    Volume IV, 1851.
100. Ibid.
101. See p. 205.
102. Appendix XVIII, *Official . . . Catalogue*,
    Volume IV, 1851.
103. *Fireside Facts*, 1851, chapter 18.
104. Appendix XXIX, *Official . . . Catalogue*,
    Volume IV, 1851.
105. Burton, 1972, p. 144.
106. Appendix XXIV, *Official . . . Catalogue*,
    Volume IV, 1851; Maré, 1972, p. 4.
107. Appendix XXIV, *Official . . . Catalogue*,
    Volume IV, 1851.
108. Maré, 1972.
109. Appendix XXIV, *Official . . . Catalogue*,
    Volume IV, 1851.
110. Morris, 1938, p. 104.
111. Brown, 1993; Morris, 1938; Volant and

112. 7 October 1851, Grey to Prince Albert,
    RA F25.
113. *Lectures on the Results . . .*, 1851, p. 436.
114. Schumacher, 1968, p. 170.
115. Ibid., chapter 5.
116. See p. 112.
117. Cole, 1884, p. 194.
118. See, for example, Bard, 1851; Delepine,
    1851.
119. *Fireside Facts*, 1851, Preface.
120. Titles from Dilke, Collected Music,
    EX.1851.101, NAL.
121. See the collection in EX.1851.107, NAL.
122. See *Homes and Antiques*, April 1995, p. ii;
    October 1996, p. iv; and May 1997, p. iv.
123. 'Reasons for Converting the Crystal
    Palace into a Winter Garden', John Scott
    Russell Papers, Volume III, RSA.
124. 14 July 1851, Reid to Grey, PP Vic Box C
    Great Exhibition to 1855, RA.
125. *Shall we keep the Crystal Palace and have
    Riding and Walking in all Weathers* (John
    Murray, 1851).
126. 10 August 1851, Memorandum by the
    Prince on the Appropriation of the
    Surplus, RA F25.
127. 18 July 1851, Fay, 1951.
128. 19 August 1851, Minutes, RC1851.
129. Maré, 1972.
130. 'Programme of the Proceedings on the
    Presentation of the Juries' Reports and
    the Closing of the Exhibition', John Scott
    Russell Papers, Volume III, RSA.

6. Reactions to the Exhibition

1. *Fireside Facts*, p. 7.
2. 18 June 1851, *Manchester Guardian*.
3. 2 May 1851, *Morning Chronicle*.
4. Louis Alexis Chamerovzow, *The
   International Exhibition of 1851 being a
   few Observations upon the General
   Advantages which May be Expected to Arise
   from It* (T.C. Newby, London, 1851).
5. Anon., *Projects and Prospects of the Day*
   (Effingham Wilson, Royal Exchange,
   London, 1850).
6. Binney, 1851.
7. 2 May 1851, *The Times*.
8. Freeden, 1978, p. 7.
9. Introduction, *Official . . . Catalogue*,
   Volume I, 1851.

Warren, 1859.

10. *Punch*, Volume XX, 1851, p. 288.
11. Both contained in EX.1851.147., NAL.
12. *Punch*, Volume XX, 1851, p. 188.
13. *Lectures . . . ,* 1851.
14. *Lectures . . . ,* 1851, p. 441.
15. Haltern, 1973, p. 155.
16. Kennedy, 1988, p. 190 and p. 220.
17. 3 May 1851, *Household Words.*
18. 18 January 1851, *Household Words.*
19. Maré, 1972.
20. 26 April 1851, *Household Words.*
21. 5 July 1851, *Household Words.*
22. 28 December 1850, *Household Words.*
23. Ibid.
24. Storey, 1988, p. 57.
25. 31 May 1851, *Household Words.*
26. Storey, 1988, p. xii.
27. 7 May 1851, Dickens to Richard Owen, quoted in Storey, 1988, p. 357.
28. 20 May 1851, Dickens to Spencer Lyttelton, quoted in Storey, 1988, p. 395.
29. Ray, 1945, p. 768.
30. Ibid., p. 766.
31. *Punch*, Volume XX (1851), 198.
32. Hoffenberg, 1996, pp. 31–41.
33. [undated], *The Leader,* John Scott Russell Papers, Volume II, RSA.
34. Haltern, 1973, p. 281.
35. Hoffenberg, 1996, pp. 15–25.
36. 31 May 1851, *John Bull.*
37. 14 December 1850, *John Bull.*
38. Redgrave, *Report . . . ,* 1852, p. 3.
39. Quoted in Wihl, 1983, p. 187.
40. Quoted in Golby, 1987, pp. 174–5.
41. Bonython, 1982, p. 7.
42. Ibid., p. 7.
43. Golby, 1987, p. 177.
44. 19 May 1851, *The Times.*
45. Quoted in Dalzell, 1960, pp. 26–7.
46. Ibid., p. 26.
47. See p. 113.
48. Dalzell, 1960, p. 28.
49. Ibid., p. 35.
50. *Punch*, Volume XX, 1851, p. 209.
51. Dalzell, 1960, p. 30.
52. Taken from Greeley, 1851.
53. Emmerson, 1977, p. 47.
54. Dalzell, 1960, p. 44.
55. Ibid.
56. *Official . . . Catalogue,* Volume III, 1851.
57. Appendix XLI, *Official . . . Catalogue,* Volume IV, 1851.
58. Taken from *An Account . . . ,* 1851.
59. See Price, 1981.
60. Haltern, 1971, p. 132.
61. Ibid., p. 108.
62. Blanqui, *Lettres . . . ,* 1851.
63. Bard, *Une Semaine . . . ,* 1851.
64. See, for example, Delepine, 1851.
65. See p. 168.
66. Haltern, 1971, p. 247; Luckhurst, *The Story . . . ,* 1951, p. 114.
67. See Beckmann, 1991; Davis, 1995.
68. Bucher, 1851, p. 44.
69. 6 June 1851, *Augsburger Allgemeine Zeitung.*
70. 18 May 1851, *Augsburger Allgemeine Zeitung.*
71. 18 June 1851, *Augsburger Allgemeine Zeitung.*
72. See Henderson, 1975, pp. 106–11.
73. See, for example, Vischer, 1875.
74. Henderson, 1975, p. 110.

7. Aftermath, Results and Conclusions

1. 10 August 1851, Memorandum by the Prince on the Appropriation of the Surplus, RA F25.
2. Open University, *Arts Foundation Course . . . ,* 1986, p. 22.
3. 30 January 1852, Minutes of the Crystal Palace Commission of Inquiry, Work 6/126, PRO. Also 30 September 1851, Cole to Phipps, RA F25.
4. 2 October 1851, Phipps to Cole, RA F25.
5. See Minutes of the Crystal Palace Commission of Inquiry, Work 6/126, PRO.
6. Maré, 1972.
7. 4 April 1852, *Observer.*
8. 12 March 1852, Derby to Prince Albert and 13 March 1852, Prince Albert to Derby, RA F25.
9. Anon., *The Crystal Palace Sydenham,* 1911, p. 12.
10. Brandt, 1904, p. 88.
11. 18 June 1851, *Manchester Guardian.*
12. Ibid.
13. 'Speech to the Electors of Buckinghamshire,' 2 June 1852, printed in *Edinburgh Review*, XCVI (October 1852), p. 530.
14. Kroker, 1975, p. 122.
15. Kalb, 1994, p. 73.
16. Friebe, 1983, pp. 9–10; Hodeir, 1983.

BIBLIOGRAPHY

All places of publication London unless otherwise states.

I) PUBLISHED PRIMARY SOURCES

Albert, Prince, *The Principal Speeches and Addresses of His Royal Highness the Prince Consort. With an Introduction, Giving Some Outlines of His Character*, John Murray, 1862

Alexander, William, *Plan and Description of the Original Electro-Magnetic Telegraph with Prefatory Note to the Royal Commissioners of the Exhibition of the Works of Industry of All Nations*, Longman, 1851

An Account of the Proceedings at the Dinner Given by Mr George Peabody to the Americans Connected with the Great Exhibition at the London Coffee House, Ludgate Hill, on the 27th October 1851, William Pickering, 1851

Arnold, Howard Payson, *The Great Exhibition: with Continental Sketches, Practical and Humorous*, New York, Hurd & Houghton, 1868

Art Journal Illustrated Catalogue of all Nations, 1851. The Great Exhibition, New York, Gramercy Books, 1995.

Aveling, Revd Thomas, *Great Sights: A Discourse . . . on the Sabbath Evening Preceding the Opening of the Great Exhibition*, Snow, 1851

Babbage, Charles, *The Exposition of 1851; Or, Views of the Industry, The Science, and the Government of England*, John Murray, 1851

Bard, Joseph, *Une Semaine à Londres*, Paris, Borrani, 1851

Benson, A.C. (ed.), *The Letters of Queen Victoria*, John Murray, 1907

Berlyn, Peter and Fowler, Charles, *The Crystal Palace: Its Architectural History and Constructive Marvels*, James Gilbert, 1851

Binney, Revd Thomas, *The Royal Exchange and the Palace of Industry; or, the Possible Future of Europe and the World in Three Parts*, The Religious Tract Society, 1851

Blanqui, M., *Lettres sur L'Exposition Universelle de Londres Precedées d'un Préambule et Suivies du Rapport Presenté a l'Institut National de France*, Paris, Capelle, 1851

Bucher, Lothar, *Kulturhistorische Skizzen aus der Industrieausstellung aller Völker*, Frankfurt am Main, C.B. Lizius Verlag, 1851

Burnet, Richard, *Letters sent to the Devonport Telegraph regarding the Great Exhibition 1851*, [unnamed publisher], [1851?]

Clarke, H.G., *London in All Its Glory*, Clarke, 1851

Cole, Henry, *Fifty Years of Public Work*, George Bell & Sons, 2 vols, 1884

The Crystal Palace Sydenham To Be Sold by Auction . . . on Tuesday 28th day of November, 1911 at the Estate Room, 20 Hanover Square, London . . . by Howard Frank, of Messrs. Knight, Frank and Rutley, 1911

Delepine, *Guide du Visiteur à Londres, avec Plan de la Metropole. Recueil complet de tous les documens, materiaux, informations, relatifs à la Capitale de la Grande Bretagne. Indispensable à tout voyageur où etranger*, Edition Français, James Gilbert, 1851

Edwards, Sutherland, *An Authentic Account of the Chinese Commission*, H. Vizetelly, [1851?]

Ellis, Hercules, *The Rhyme Book*, Longman, Brown, Green & Longman, 1851

Fireside Facts from the Great Exhibition from the Editor of 'Pleasant Pages', Houlston & Stoneman, 1851

Fox, Francis, *River, Road, and Rail. Some Engineering Reminiscences*, John Murray, 1904

Greeley, Horace, *Glances at Europe: in a Series of Letters from Great Britain, France, Italy, Switzerland, &c. during the Summer of 1851 Including Notices of the Great Exhibition, or World's Fair*, New York, Dewitt & Davenport, 1851

Hunt, R., *Hunt's Hand-Book to the Official Catalogues: An Explanatory Guide to the Natural Productions and Manufactures of the Great Exhibition of the Industry of all Nations, 1851*, Spicer Brothers, [1851?]

——, *Synopsis of the Great Exhibition of 1851*, Spicer Brothers, and W. Clowes & Sons, 1851

Jagow, Kurt (ed.), *Letters of the Prince Consort 1831–1861*, John Murray, 1938

Lectures on the Results of the Great Exhibition of 1851. Delivered before the Society of Arts, Manufactures, and Commerce at the suggestion of Prince Albert, Series 1, 2 vols, and Series 2, 1853

Loftie, W.J., *Kensington. Picturesque and Historical*, Field & Tuer, 1888

Maguire, John Francis, *The Industrial Movement in Ireland, as Illustrated by the National Exhibition of 1852*, Cork, John O'Brien, 1853

Mayhew, H. and Cruikshank, G., *1851: or the Adventures of Mr and Mrs Sandboys and Family, who came up to London to 'Enjoy Themselves', and to see the Great Exhibition*, David Bogue, 1851

Pearson, Stephen, *Pearson's Philosophical and Historical Pleasantries for 1851, Relating to the Most Eminent Characters of the Day*, John K. Chapman & Company for Stephen Pearson, 1851

The Philosopher's Mite to the Great Exhibition of 1851, Houlston and Stoneman, 1851

Redding, Cyrus, *Stranger in London; or Visitor's Companion to the Metropolis and its Environs, with an Historical and Descriptive Sketch of the Great Exhibition*, Henry G. Bohn, 1851

Redgrave, R., *Report of Design: Prepared as a Supplement to the Report of the Jury of Class XXX of the Exhibition of 1851*, William Clowes, 1852

Richardson, Revd John, *The Real Exhibitors Exhibited; or An Inquiry into the Condition of Those Industrial Classes who Have really Represented England at the Great Exhibition*, Wertheim & Macintosh, 1851

Rodenberg, Julius, *Tag und Nacht in London. Ein Skizzenbuch zur Weltausstellung*, Berlin, Oswald Seehagen, 1862

Royal Commission of 1851, *Official Descriptive and Illustrated Catalogue of the Great Exhibition of 1851*, Spicer Brothers, 4 vols, 1851

The Royal Road to Reading, through the Great Exhibition; in which those who were too young to visit the exhibition, may learn to read about it, by the Editor of 'Pleasant Pages', Houlston & Stoneman, [1851?]

Ruskin, John, *The Opening of the Crystal Palace Considered in some of its Relations to the Prospects of Art*, Smith, Elder & Co., 1854

——, *Unto This Last*, Sunnyside, George Allen, 1895

Stockmar, Ernst Freiherr von, *Denkwurdigkeiten aus den Papiern des F.L.F. von Stockmar*, Braunschweig, Vieweg, 1872

Volant, F. and Warren, J.R. (eds), *Memoirs of Alexis Soyer; with Unpublished Receipts and Odds and Ends of Gastronomy*, W. Kent & Co., 1859

Wieck, F.G., *Die Wunder des Glaspalastes. Ein Festgeschenk fur die Jugend. Nebst einem Vorwort von Dr. Carl Vogel*, Leipzig, F.F. Weber, 1851

Wyatt, M.D., *A Report of the French Exposition of the Products of Industry Prepared by the Direction of, and Submitted to the President and Council of the Royal Society of Arts*, Chapman & Hall, 1849.

Wyld, James, *Wyld's Map of London and Visitor's Guide to the Great Exhibition 1851*, Charing Cross East, 1851

II) SECONDARY SOURCES

Ackroyd, Peter, *Dickens*, Minerva, 1991

Adelman, Paul, *Gladstone, Disraeli and Later Victorian Politics*, Longman, 1970

Aldcroft, Derek H., *The Development of British Industry and Foreign Competition, 1875–1914*, George Allen & Unwin, 1968

Allan, D.G.C., *The Houses of the Royal Society of Arts. A History and a Guide*, RSA, 1974

Allwood, John, *The Great Exhibitions*, Studio Vista, 1977

Altick, Richard D, *Victorian People and Ideas*, Dent, 1973

——, *The Shows of London*, The Belknap Press of Harvard University Press, 1978

Bailey, Frank, 'The Economics of British Foreign Policy, 1815–1850', *Journal of Modern History*, 12, (1940), 449–64

Bairoch, Paul, *The Industrial Economies: The Development of Economic and Social Politics*, Cambridge European Economic History, Volume 8, Cambridge, Cambridge University Press, 1989

Barker, Theodore, 'Workshop of the World', *History Today*, 44, 6, (1994), 30–6

Barnett, Correlli, *The Collapse of British Power*, Methuen, 1972

Beaver, Patrick, *The Crystal Palace. A Portrait of Victorian Enterprise*, Chichester, Phillimore, 1986

Beckett, Derrick, *Telford's Britain*, Newton Abbot, David & Charles, 1987

Beckmann, Uwe, *Gewerbeausstellungen in Westeuropa vor 1851*, Frankfurt am Main, Peter Lang, 1991

Behagg, Clive, *Politics and Production in the Early Nineteenth Century*, Routledge, 1990

Bell, Quentin, *The Schools of Design*, Routledge, 1968

Benedict, Burton, 'International Exhibitions and National Identity', *Anthropology Today*, 7, 3 (1991), 5–9

Bennett, J.A., *Science at the Great Exhibition*, Cambridge, Whipple Museum of the History of Science, 1983

Bentley, Michael, *Politics without Democracy, 1815–1914*, Fontana, 1984

Bergengrün, Alexander, *Staatsminister August Freiherr von der Heydt*, Leipzig, Hirzel, 1908

Biagini, Eugenio, *Liberty, Retrenchment and Reform. Popular Liberalism in the Age of Gladstone*, Cambridge, Cambridge University Press, 1992

Black, Eugene C., *British Politics in the Nineteenth Century*, Macmillan, 1970

Blaug, Mark (ed.), *Dissenters*, Aldershot, Elgar, 1992

Boerner, Claus H., 'Messen und Ausstellungen. Impulsgeber und Indikatoren für die Wirtschaft einer Region', *Wirtschaft und Standort*, 10, (1978), 7–9

Bonython, Elizabeth, *King Cole. A Picture Portrait of Sir Henry Cole, KCB 1808–1882*, Victoria and Albert Museum, 1982

Bordaz, Robert, *Le Livre des Expositions Universelles, 1851–1989*, Paris, Union Centrale des Arts Décoratifs, 1989

Brandt, Otto, 'Zur Geschichte und Würdigung der Weltausstellungen', *Zeitschrift für Sozialwissenschaft*, 7 (1904), 81–96

Briggs, Asa, 'Thomas Attwood and the Economic Background of the Birmingham Political Union', *Cambridge Historical Journal*, 9, 2, (1948), 190–217

——, *Victorian Things*, B.T. Batsford, 1988

Brown, Anna, *Entertaining the Beau Monde: Lady Blessington at Gore House, 1836–1849*, Diss. Birkbeck College, 1993

Brübach, Nils, *Die Reichsmessen von Frankfurt am Main, Leipzig und Brauschweig (14–18. Jahrhundert)*, Stuttgart, Franz Steiner, 1994

Burton, Elizabeth, *The Early Victorians at Home 1837–1861*, Longman, 1972

Calkins, W.N., 'A Victorian Free Trade Lobby', *Economic History Review*, 13, (1960–1), 90–104

Carpenter, Kenneth, 'European Industrial Exhibitions before 1851 and Their Publications', *Technology and Culture*, 13, 3, (1972), 465–7

Clapham, J.H., *An Economic History of Modern Britain*, Cambridge, Cambridge University Press, 1926

Clarke, John, *British Diplomacy and Foreign Policy 1782–1865*, Unwin Hyman, 1989

Cleve, Ingeborg, *Geschmack, Kunst und Konsum. Kulturpolitik als Wirtschaftspolitik in Frankreich und Württemberg (1805–1845)*, Göttingen, Vandenhoek und Ruprecht, 1996

Corfe, Tom, *The Great Exhibition*, Cambridge, Cambridge University Press, 1997

Costin, W.C., *Great Britain and China, 1833–60*, Oxford, Clarendon, 1937

Court, W.H.B., *A Concise Economic History of Britain*, Cambridge, Cambridge University Press, 1954

Crouzet, François, 'Trade and Empire: The British Experience', in Ratcliffe, 1975

——, *Britain Ascendant: Comparative Studies in Franco-British Economic History*, Cambridge, Cambridge University Press, 1990

Cullen, M.J., *The Statistical Movement in Early Victorian Britain*, New York, Harvester, 1975

Dalzell, Robert F., *American Participation in the Great Exhibition of 1851*, Amherst, Massachusetts,

Amherst College Press, 1960

Darby, Philip, *Three Faces of Imperialism*, Yale University Press, 1987

Daunton, M.J., '"Gentlemanly Capitalism" and British Industry, 1820–1914', *Past and Present*, 122, 5, (1989), 119–58

Davis, John R., *Württemberg at the London Exhibitions. A Study in the Dissemination of Knowledge and the Role of the State in Industrialisation*, Kingston University European Research Centre, 1995

——, *Britain and the German Zollverein, 1848–66*, Basingstoke, Macmillan, 1997

Davis, Lance E. and Huttenback, Robert A., (eds), *Mammon and the Pursuit of Empire. The Political Economy of British Imperialism*, Cambridge, Cambridge University Press, 1986

Dawson, W.H., *Richard Cobden and Foreign Policy*, Allen & Unwin, 1926

Derry, T.K. and Williams, Trevor I., *A Short History of Technology. From the Earliest Times to AD1900*, Oxford, Clarendon, 1960

Döring, Wilhelm, 'Ziele und Entwicklungen im Ausstellungswesen', *Der Markenartikel*, 16, (1954), 287–92

Eccleshall, Robert, *British Liberalism. Liberal Thought from the 1640s to the 1980s*, Longman, 1986

Emmerson, George S., *John Scott Russell. A Great Victorian Engineer and Naval Architect*, John Murray, 1977

Engelhardt, Ulrich, *Handwerker in der Industrialisierung. Lage, Kultur und Politik vom späten 18. bis ins frühe 20. Jahrhundert*, Stuttgart, Klett-Cotta, 1984

Evans, Eric J., *Sir Robert Peel. Statemanship, Power and Party*, Routledge, 1991

Farnsworth, Susan H., *The Evolution of British Imperial Policy During the Mid-Nineteenth Century*, Garland, 1992

Fay, C.R., *Palace of Industry, 1851. A Study of the Great Exhibition and its Fruits*, Cambridge, Cambridge University Press, 1951

Feuchtwanger, E.J., *Gladstone*, Macmillan, 1989

Fielden, 'Mid-Victorian Radical Cobden After Repeal', *Modern History Review*, 6, 2, (1994), 17–20

Ffrench, Yvonne, *The Great Exhibition of 1851*, Harvill, 1950

Findling, John E., *Historical Dictionary of World's Fairs and Expositions, 1851–1988*, Greenwood Press, 1990

——, *Chicago's Great World Fairs*, Manchester and New York, Manchester University Press, 1994

Fitzmaurice, Lord Edmond, *The Life of Granville George Leveson Gower: Second Earl Granville K.G. 1815–1891*, 2 vols, Longman, 1906

Fraser, Derek, *Urban Politics in Victorian England*, Leicester, 1976

Freeden, Michael, *The New Liberalism. An Ideology of Social Reform*, Oxford, Clarendon, 1978

Friebe, Wolfgang, *Architektur der Weltausstellungen 1851 bis 1970*, Stuttgart, Kohlhammer, 1983

Friemert, Chup, *Die Gläserne Arche. Kristallpalast London 1851 und 1854*, Munich, Prestel-Verlag, 1984

Gallagher, John and Robinson, Ronald, 'The Imperialism of Free Trade', *Economic History Review*, 6, 1, (1953), 1–15

Gash, Norman, *Sir Robert Peel*, Longman, 1986

Geary, Frank, 'Accounting for Entrepreneurship in Late Victorian Britain', *Economic History Review*, 43, 2, (1990), 283–7

Gelernter, David, 1939, *The Lost World of the Fair*, New York, Free Press, 1995

Gibbs-Smith, C.H., *The Great Exhibition of 1851*, HMSO, 1981

Gluckman, Dale Carolyn and Takeda, Sharon Sadako, 'When Art Became Fashion: The Making of an International Exhibition', *Curator*, 36, 4, (1993), 272–85

Golby, J.M. (ed.), *Culture and Society in Britain 1850–1890*, Oxford, The Open University, 1986

Greenhalgh, Paul, *Ephemeral Vistas. The Expositions Universelles, Great Exhibition and World Fairs 1851–1939*, Manchester, Manchester University Press, 1988

Greenleaf, W.H., *The British Political Tradition. The Rise of Collectivism*, Methuen, 1983

Haltern, Utz, *Die Londoner Weltausstellung von 1851. Ein Beitrag zur Geschichte der bürgerlich-industriellen Gesellschaft im 19. Jahrhundert*, Münster, Verlag Aschendorf, 1971

——, 'Die "Welt als Schaustellung". Zur Funktion und Bedeutung der internationalen Industrieausstellung im 19. und 20. Jahrhundert', *Vierteljahrschrift für Sozial- und*

Wirtschaftsgeschichte, 60, (1973), 1–40

Hamerow, Theodore S., *The Birth of a New Europe. State and Society in the Nineteenth Century*, University of North Carolina Press, 1983

Harding, R.E., *The Piano-Forte. Its History Traced to the Great Exhibition of 1851*, Old Woking, Surrey, Gresham Books, 1978

Harris, Jose, *Private Lives. Public Spirit. A Social History of Britain 1870–1914*, Oxford, Oxford University Press, 1993

Hawkins, Angus, B., 'A Forgotten Crisis: Gladstone and the Politics of Finance during the 1850s', *Victorian Studies*, 26, (1982–3), 287–320

Headrick, Daniel R., *The Tentacles of Progress. Technology Transfer in the Age of Imperialism, 1850–1940*, Oxford, Oxford University Press, 1988

Heller, Peter B., *Technology Transfer and Human Values. Concepts, Applications, Cases*, New York, University Press of America, 1985

Henderson, W.O., *Britain and Industrial Europe 1750–1870*, Leicester, Leicester University Press, 1972

——, *The Rise of German Industrial Power, 1834–1914*, Temple Smith, 1975

Hilton, Boyd, *Corn, Cash, Commerce. The Economic Politicies of the Tory Governments 1815–1830*, Oxford, Oxford University Press, 1977

——, *The Age of Atonement. The Influence of Evangelicalism on Social and Economic Thought 1795–1865*, Oxford, Clarendon, 1988

Hobhouse, Christopher, *1851 and the Crystal Palace. Being an Account of the Great Exhibition and its Contents*, John Murray, 1937

Hobhouse, Hermione, *Prince Albert: His Life and Work*, Hamish Hamilton/*The Observer*, 1983

Hobsbawm, E.J., *Industry and Empire. An Economic History of Britain since 1750*, Weidenfeld & Nicolson, 1968

——, *The Age of Capital 1848–75*, Weidenfeld & Nicolson, 1975

——, and Range, Terence, (eds), *The Invention of Tradition*, Cambridge, Cambridge University Press, 1983

Hodeir, C., 'L'Expo des Expos', *Histoire*, 60, (1983), 96–100

Hoffenberg, Peter, 'Equipoise and Its Discontents' (paper delivered at a conference at the Leeds Centre for Victorian Studies), July 1996

Howe, Anthony, *The Cotton Masters 1830–1860*, Oxford, Clarendon, 1984

Hudson, Derek and Luckhurst, Kenneth, *The Royal Society of Arts 1754–1954*, John Murray, 1954

Gilmore Holt, Elizabeth, *The Art of all Nations 1850–73. The Emerging Role of Exhibitions and Critics*, Princeton, New Jersey, Princeton University Press, 1981

Huynen, Johannes Marie Hubert, 'Trends in Trade Fairs', Diss. Utrecht University, 1973

Jenkins, T.A., *The Liberal Ascendancy, 1830–1886*, Basingstoke, Macmillan, 1994

Jeremy, David J., *Business and Religion in Britain*, Aldershot, Gower, 1988

—— (ed.), *International Technology Transfer. Europe, Japan and the USA, 1700–1914*, Aldershot, Elgar, 1991

—— (ed.), *Technology Transfer and Business Enterprise*, Aldershot, Elgar, 1994

Jervis, Simon, *High Victorian Design*, Boydell, 1983

Jones, Charles A., *International Business in the Nineteenth Century. The Rise and Fall of a Cosmopolitan Bourgeoisie*, Brighton, Wheatsheaf, 1987

Kalb, Christine, *Weltausstellungen im Wandel der Zeit und ihre infrastrukturellen Auswirkungen auf Stadt und Region*, Frankfurt am Main, Peter Lang, 1994

Kennedy, Paul, *The Rise and Fall of the Great Powers*, Fontana, 1988

Kenwood, A.G. and Lougheed, A.L., *The Growth of the International Economy 1820–1980. An Introductory Text*, Allen & Unwin, 1983

Kindleberger, Charles P., *Economic Response. Comparative Studies in Trade, Finance, and Growth*, Harvard University Press, 1978

King, Edmund, 'The Great Exhibition at Hyde Park and Its Publications', *Royal Society of Arts Journal*, 144, (1996), 58–62

Kitson Clark, G., *The Making of Victorian England*, Methuen, 1962

Kroker, Evelyn, *Die Weltausstellungen im 19. Jahrhundert. Industrieller Leistungsnachweis,*

Konkurrenzverhalten und Kommunikationsfunktion unter Berücksichtigung der Montanindustrie des Ruhrgebietes zwischen 1851 und 1880, Studien zur Naturwissenschaft, Technik und Wirtschaft im Neunzehnten Jahrhundert, Volume 4, Göttingen, Vandenhoek und Ruprecht, 1975

Kunze, Helmut, 'Die großen Ausstellungen 1798 bis 1967', *Der Aufbau*, 22, (1967), 230–5

Luckhurst, Kenneth W., *The Story of Exhibitions*, Studio, 1951

——, *The Exhibition of 1851. Three Cantor Lectures delivered in 1951*, Royal Society of Arts, 1951

Maag, Georg, *Kunst und Industrie im Zeitalter der ersten Weltausstellung. Synchronische Analyse einer Epochenscwelle*, Munich, Wilhelm Fink Verlag, 1986

McCord, Norman, *The Anti-Corn Law League 1838–1846*, Unwin, 1968

——, *British History 1815–1906*, Oxford, Oxford University Press, 1991

Malchow, H.L., *Gentleman Capitalists. The Social and Political World of the Victorian Businessman*, Basingstoke, Macmillan, 1991

Maré, Eric de, *London 1851. The Year of the Great Exhibition*, The Folio Society, 1972

Marquardt, Ernst, *Geschichte Württembergs*, Stuttgart, J.B. Metzlersche Verlagsbuchhandlung, 1961

Marsden, Gordon, *Victorian Values. Personalities and Perspectives in Nineteenth Century Society*, Longman, 1990

Martin, Theodore, *The Life of the Prince Consort*, 2 vols, Smith, Elder & Co., 1876

Mathias, Peter and Davis, John A., *Innovation and Technology in Europe. From the Eighteenth Century to the Present Day*, Oxford, Blackwell, 1991

Mitchell, B.R., *European Historical Statistics 1750–1970*, Macmillan, 1975

Möller, Holger, *Das deutsche Messe- und Ausstellungswesen. Standortstruktur und räumliche Entwicklung seit dem 19. Jahrhundert*, Forschungen zur deutschen Landeskunde, 231, Stuttgart, Zentralausschuß für deutsche Landeskunde, 1989

Morley, John, *The Life of Richard Cobden*, Fisher Unwin, 1903

Morris, Helen, *Portrait of a Chef. The Life of Alexis Soyer, Sometime Chef to the Reform Club*, Cambridge, Cambridge University Press, 1938

Norrish, R.G.W., 'Lyon Playfair and his Work for the Great Exhibition of 1851', *Royal Society of Arts Journal*, 99, (1950–1), 547–8

O'Brien, Patrick K., and Keyder, Caglar, *Economic Growth in Britain and France 1780–1914*, Allen & Unwin, 1978

—— and Pigman, G.A., 'Free Trade, British Hegemony and the International Economic Order in the Nineteenth Century', *Review of International Studies*, 18, (1992), 89–113

—— and Quinault, Roland, (eds), *The Industrial Revolution and British Society*, Cambridge, Cambridge University Press, 1993

O'Day, Alan, *Government and Institutions in the Post-1832 United Kingdom*, Lewiston/Queenstown/Lampeter, The Edwin Mellen Press, Studies in British History Volume 34, 1995

Open University, *Arts Foundation Course 102, Unit 16, The Great Exhibition*, Milton Keynes, Open University Press, 1986

Parry, Jonathan, *The Rise and Fall of Liberal Government in Victorian Britain*, Yale University Press, 1993

Peiter, H.D., 'Institutions and Attitudes: The Consolidation of the Business Community in Bourgeois France, 1880–1914', *Journal of Social History*, 9, (1976), 510–25

Pelling, Henry, *Popular Politics and Society in Late Victorian Britain*, Macmillan, 1968

Pevsner, Nikolaus, *Wyatt, Matthew Digby. The First Cambridge Slade Professor of Fine Art*, Cambridge, Cambridge University Press, 1950

——, *High Victorian Design. A Study of the Exhibits of 1851*, Architectural Press, 1951

Pilbeam, Pamela, *The 1830 Revolution in France*, Basingstoke, Macmillan, 1991

Platt, D.C.M., 'British Portfolio Investment Overseas before 1870: Some Doubts', *Economic History Review*, 32, 1, (1980), 1–16

Plum, Werner, *World Exhibitions in the Nineteenth Century: Pageants of Social and Cultural Change*, Bonn-Bad Godesberg, Friedrich-Ebert-Stiftung, 1977

Pohl, Heinz-Alfred, 'Die Weltausstellungen im 19. Jahrhundert und die Nichtbeteiligung Deutschlands in den Jahren 1878 und 1889', *Mitteilungen des Instituts für Österreichische Geschichtsforschung*, 97, 3–4, (1989), 381–424

Port, M.H. (ed.), *The Houses of Parliament*, Yale University Press, 1976

Porter, Bernard, *Britain, Europe and the World 1850–1986*, Allen & Unwin, 1987

——, *Britannia's Burden. The Political Evolution of Modern Britain 1851–1990*, Arnold, 1994

Price, Roger, *An Economic History of Modern France 1730–1914*, Macmillan, 1981

Ramm, Agatha, 'The Great Exhibition' (unpublished paper given at Bedford College), 1951

Ratcliffe, Barrie (ed.), *Great Britain and Her World, 1750–1914*, Manchester, Manchester University Press, 1975

Ray, G.R., *The Letters and Private Papers of William Makepeace Thackeray*, 4 vols, Oxford, Oxford University Press, 1945

Rhodes James, Robert, *Albert, Prince Consort. A Biography*, Hamish Hamilton, 1983

Rieger, Bernhard, 'British and German Concepts of the Future: Comparing Reactions to the World Fair in Paris in 1900' (paper to the Neale Colloquium) 1998

Rosenberg, Nathan and Vincenti, Walter G., *The Britannia Bridge: The Generation and Diffusion of Technological Knowledge*, The MIT Press, 1978

—— and Frischtak, Claudio, *International Technology Transfer: Concepts, Measures, and Comparisons*, New York, Praeger, 1985

Sabel, Charles and Zeitlin, Jonathan, 'Historical Alternatives to Mass Production: Politics, Markets and Technology in Nineteenth Century Industrialisation', *Past and Present*, 106–9, (1985), 133–76

Schmidt, Willi, 'Die frühen Weltausstellungen und ihre Bedeutung für die Entwicklung der Technik', *Technikgeschichte*, 34, 2, (1967), 164–78

Schumacher, Martin, *Auslandsreisen deutscher Unternehmer 1750–1851*, Cologne, Rheinisch-Westfälisches Wirtschaftsarchiv, 1968

Schwankl, Herbert R., *Das Württembergische Ausstellungswesen, Beiträge zur südwestdeutschen Wirtschafts- und Sozialgeschichte*, volume 8, Stuttgart, Scripta Mercaturae Verlag, 1996

Searle, G.R., *The Quest for National Efficiency. A Study in British Politics and Political Thought, 1899–1914*, Oxford, Blackwell, 1971

——, *Entrepreneurial Politics in Mid-Victorian Britain*, Oxford, Oxford University Press, 1993

——, *Morality and the Market in Victorian Britain*, Oxford, Clarendon, 1998

Selle, Gert, *Die Geschichte des Design in Deutschland von 1870 bis heute. Entwicklung der industriellen Produktkultur*, Cologne, DuMont Buchverlag, 1978

Semmel, Bernard, *The Rise of Free Trade Imperialism*, Cambridge, Cambridge University Press, 1970

Shepherd, Thomas, *London in the Nineteenth Century*, Bracken Books, 1983

Sixta, Gerhard, 'Die Weltausstellungen – Ausdruck gegenwärtiger Gestaltungsprinzipien', *Der Aufbau*, 22, (1967), 242–4

Smith, Micheal Steven, *Tariff Reform in France, 1860–1900*, Croom Helm, 1980

Speltz, Alexander, *The History of Ornament. Antiquity to Modern Times*, Studio Editions, 1989

Stansky, Peter, *The Victorian Revolution. Government and Society in Victoria's Britain*, New York, Franklin Watt, 1973

Stearn, William T., *The Natural History Museum at South Kensington. A History of the British Museum (Natural History) 1753–1980*, Heinemann, 1981

Storey, Graham, Tillotson, Kathleen and Burgis, Nina, (eds), *The Letters of Charles Dickens*, Oxford, Clarendon Press, 1988

Stiles, Andrina, *Religion, Society and Reform, 1800–1914*, Hodder & Stoughton, 1995

Tant, A.P., *British Government: The Triumph of Elitism. A Study of the British Political Tradition and its Major Challenges*, Aldershot, Dartmouth, 1993

Turner, G.L.E., 'Science at the Great Exhibition', *Annals of Science*, 40, 4, (1983), 403–4

Vischer, L., *Die industrielle Entwicklung im Königreich Württemberg und das Wirken seiner Centralstelle für Gewerbe und Handel in ihren ersten 25. Jahren. Nach Erhebungen aus den Akten und unter Benützung von Aufzeichnungen des Herrn Präsidenten Dr. v. Steinbeis . . .*, Carl Grüninger, Stuttgart, 1875

Wihl, Gary, '"Neither a Palace Nor of Crystal": Ruskin and the Architecture of the Great Exhibition', *Architectura*, 13, 2, (1983), 187–202

Wolfzettel, Friedrich, 'Georg Maag: Kunst und Industrie im Zeitalter der ersten Weltausstellung', *Poetica Zeitschrift für Sprach- und Literaturwissenschaft*, 19, 1–2, (1987), 134–8

INDEX